D. H. Lawrence, Desire, and Narrative

EARL G. INGERSOLL

University Press of Florida
Gainesville/Tallahassee/Tampa/Boca Raton
Pensacola/Orlando/Miami/Jacksonville/Ft. Myers

06 05 04 03 02 01 6 5 4 3 2 1

Library of Congress Cataloging-in-Publication Data
Ingersoll, Earl G., 1938–
D. H. Lawrence—desire and narrative / Earl G. Ingersoll.
p. cm.
Includes bibliographical references and index.
ISBN 0-8130-1850-1 (alk. paper)
1. Lawrence, D. H. (David Herbert), 1885–1930—Criticism and interpretation.
2. Psychoanalysis and literature—England—History—20th century.
3. Lacan, Jacques, 1901—Contributions in criticism. 4. Desire in literature.
5. Narration (Rhetoric). I. Title.
PR6023.A93 Z631938 2001
823'.912—dc21 00-048824

The University Press of Florida is the scholarly publishing agency for the State University System of Florida, comprising Florida A&M University, Florida Atlantic University, Florida Gulf Coast University, Florida International University, Florida State University, University of Central Florida, University of Florida, University of North Florida, University of South Florida, and University of West Florida.

University Press of Florida
15 Northwest 15th Street
Gainesville, FL 32611–2079
http://www.upf.com

D. H. LAWRENCE, DESIRE, AND NARRATIVE

Florida A&M University, Tallahassee
Florida Atlantic University, Boca Raton
Florida Gulf Coast University, Ft. Myers
Florida International University, Miami
Florida State University, Tallahassee
University of Central Florida, Orlando
University of Florida, Gainesville
University of North Florida, Jacksonville
University of South Florida, Tampa
University of West Florida, Pensacola

To my wife, Mary,

who helped me stay the course

Contents

Preface

My project over the past decade has been to begin a reading of D. H. Lawrence's longer fiction in the context of the writings of Jacques Lacan. In particular I have been drawn to Lacan's writing as it has been read by theorists such as Shoshana Felman, Peter Brooks, and Jane Gallop, who have contributed to what might be called a New Psychoanalytic Criticism. Begun in the late 1970s , this *nouvelle critique* has attempted to establish new reading practices by replacing older efforts at applying psychoanalytic insights *to* literary texts with a refreshingly new practice of reading psychoanalytic writings *with* literary texts. Lawrence's fiction has by and large not been submitted to this *nouvelle critique.*

The chapters that follow explore the triad of D. H. Lawrence, Desire, and Narrative. "Lawrence" is represented by six novels, read intertextually with the psychoanalytic writings of Lacan as they have been read by a community of critics and theorists whose reading practices, if not their allegiances, bear witness to an understanding of Lacanian insights. The approaches in individual chapters shift with the aspect of narration that serves as the focus of that particular novel. Chapter 1 attempts to set up a framework of Lacan's readers whose writing might legitimately be termed a New Psychoanalytic Criticism. In addition, this first chapter examines Lawrence's first novel, *The White Peacock,* as a representation of the fundamental tropes of metaphor and metonymy. Chapter 2 grapples with what is now almost a century of Freudian-biographical criticism of Lawrence's first major novel, *Sons and Lovers,* in an attempt both to deliteralize the simplistic Oedipal structure and to demythologize the biographical Lawrence. Chapter 3 returns to the tropes of metonymy and metaphor to explore the limits of their usefulness in confronting the problem of *The Rainbow*'s ending within the context of Peter Brooks's Freudian-Lacanian narratology. Chapter 4 investigates the phenomenon of the gaze in *Women in Love,* as our understanding of looking has been shaped by theorizing about the gaze stimulated by Lacan's writing. Chapter 5 represents a postmodern gesture by focusing upon the posthumously published novel *Mr Noon,* whose slightness as a literary text decenters the project's concentration upon Lawrence's major novels. Finally, chapter 6 explores the presence of Lacan's Phallus in Lawrence's last novel, *Lady Chatterley's Lover.* Just as we are beginning to read Lawrence's textual production post–*Women in Love* as postmodern,[1] with *Lady Chatterley's Lover* as a nostalgic revisiting of earlier themes, so too this final chapter revisits the gender of tropes and the gaze from earlier chapters as a small gesture toward closure.

A project of this scope could not have been completed without incurring numerous debts that require acknowledgment. I want to begin by thanking the many Lawrence scholars who have offered support to this project, especially Jim Cowan, Keith Cushman, Betsy Fox, Lou Greiff, Virginia Hyde, Judith Ruderman, Carol Siegel, Michael Squires, and Jack Stewart. In addition, I would like to thank the two unidentified readers of the manuscript whose helpful advice contributed measurably to the success of this project.

I must also acknowledge the permission to cite from Lawrence's writing granted by Laurence Pollinger, Ltd., as representatives of the Estate of Frieda Lawrence Ravagli. Unless otherwise noted, citations are from the Cambridge University Press editions of Lawrence's novels and denoted as follows: *WP* (*The White Peacock*), *SL* (*Sons and Lovers*), *R* (*The Rainbow*), *WL* (*Women in Love*), *MN* (*Mr Noon*), and *LCL* (*Lady Chatterley's Lover*).

I would like to thank several journals in which earlier versions of material appeared: *The Midwest Quarterly* for "Gender and Language in *Sons and Lovers*" 37.4 (1996): 35–43; *Modern Language Review* for "D. H. Lawrence's *Mr Noon* as a Postmodern Text" 85.2 (April 1990): 304–9; *Studies in the Novel* for "Staging the Gaze in D. H. Lawrence's *Women in*

Love" 26.3 (fall 1994): 268–80; *Studies in Psychoanalytic Theory* for "*Lady Chatterley's Lover*: 'The Bastard Offspring of This Signifying Concatenation'" 1.1 (spring 1992): 57–68.

Finally, I would like to thank the staff of the University Press of Florida for making this project a reality, especially acquisitions editor Susan Fernandez for efficiently moving the project through the review process and project editor Jacqueline Kinghorn Brown for her help in producing the book.

1

READING LAWRENCE'S TEXTS WITH LACAN'S READERS

A Tale of Two Reputations

An instructive point of departure for this extended investigation of D. H. Lawrence's fiction is a comparison of Lawrence's reputation with the reputation of his Irish contemporary James Joyce. Joyce scholarship, now more extensive than the scholarship for any other writer except Shakespeare, runs the gamut from the "old" historical readings and New Critical exegesis, which dominated criticism two generations ago, to contemporary interests in postcolonial studies, culture studies, and queer theory.[1] Across that gamut, Joyce studies based in psychoanalysis range from traditional "applications" of Sigmund Freud or Carl Jung to newer varieties.[2] Post-structuralists from the beginning have embraced Joyce enthusiastically. Jacques Lacan read a paper at the Joyce Symposium in 1975, which he later published as *Joyce le symptome,* and Joyce was his focus during one year of his famous seminars. In 1984 Jacques Derrida delivered a two-hour paper at an international conference of the James Joyce Society and later published it as "Ulysses Gramophone," along with "Two Words for Joyce." Also in 1984 Derek Attridge and Daniel Ferrer edited *Post-Structuralist Joyce: Essays from the French.* Perhaps even more important to Joyce's dominant stature in the later twentieth century, Julia Kristeva, probably the feminist most instrumental in transforming Lacanian psychoanalysis into feminist theory, wrote on Joyce, as did other feminist theorists such as Hélène Cixous.[3]

We have only to attempt to imagine Derrida addressing a D. H. Lawrence conference or Cixous embracing a Lawrence text in her *écriture féminine* or an editor aspiring to gather essays for a *Post-Structuralist Lawrence* to begin to gauge the manner in which the larger movements of later twentieth-century theory have swept past "Lawrence." As a result, Lawrence studies have generally been mired in more traditional approaches. Studies of "Lawrence," if we may use that term to denote the sum total of his textual production, have frequently concentrated on "Lawrence" the man— as though anyone were ultimately knowable. One evidence of that scholarly preoccupation—one might even go so far as to say *obsession*—with Lawrence's life has been the plethora of biographies. Rigor mortis had barely set in before John Middleton Murry foisted his pop-Freudian *Son of Woman* on thirties readers hungry for details of Lawrence's "scandalous" life. After Murry, Lawrence's early champions Anaïs Nin and F. R. Leavis wrote defensively on Lawrence, and in the second half of the century Harry T. Moore, Daniel Schneider, and Jeffrey Meyers joined what has become the Lawrence biography industry. Recently the hefty three-volume Cambridge so-called definitive biography has been joined by celebrity biographies of Lawrence by Brenda Maddox and Janet Byrne, whose focus has been the Lawrences' marriage and in Byrne's case the life of Frieda Lawrence. In contrast, the 1959 Richard Ellmann biography of Joyce, which he revised in 1982, has stood alone as a compendium of what is known of Joyce's life.[4]

The contrast between Lawrence and Joyce offers other fascinating differences. Joyce produced a short-story collection, a play, several collections of poetry, and three longer prose narratives. Lawrence, in contrast, was prolific. His letters alone run to eight volumes, and in addition to the collections of poems, four volumes of short fiction, more than a dozen novels, and a dozen plays, there are the essays and polemics that comprise "Lawrence." As a result, students of Lawrence begin by asking not *who* but *which* was Lawrence? That is, is "Lawrence" the misogynist who generated the essay "Cocksure Women and Hensure Men" or the incipient feminist of *The Rainbow*? Is "Lawrence" the homophobe who wrote that sodomists made him dream of black beetles or the married man who probably had an "affair" with the Cornish farmer William Henry Hocking? In contrast to Lawrence's textual production, Joyce's oeuvre followed the modernist paradigm in its arc from the realism-naturalism of *Dubliners,* through the symbolist method of *A Portrait* and most of *Ulysses,* to the postmodernist exploration of *Finnegans Wake* following an arabesque toward the textual exhaustion of fictional representation, so that when he finished the *Wake* Joyce had nowhere to go. Arguably Lawrence had achieved a similar status with *Women in Love,* halfway through his short career, but he continued to write for yet another decade.[5]

The insistence on biographical criticism, although obviously not universal, has taken its toll on Lawrence studies. As Hilary Simpson suggested in 1982 in her book *D. H. Lawrence and Feminism,* there has been "a state of near-stagnation in Lawrence criticism, in spite of the seemingly endless flow of academic and critical attention which his work continues to attract" (14). An excellent analogy is Lawrence's contemporary W. B. Yeats, whose work Leonard Orr has characterized as "trapped within the literary historical construct of 'modernism.'" Orr might well be speaking of Lawrence when he explains: "In effect, Yeats has been left as a modernist because he has been studied almost exclusively from within a modernist framework, using the critical techniques developed under modernist and premodernist aesthetics: New Criticism, biographical criticism (and Freudian psychoanalytic criticism), textual criticism, source studies and explications of allusions, and positivist literary historical analyses" (1).[6] Generally, the study of Lawrence has not entered what we might call post-structuralist or postmodernist criticism. Indeed, with rare exceptions—most recently Gerald Doherty and Linda Ruth Williams, whose work is examined below—there has been relatively little effort to bring Lawrence studies into contact with what is the focus of this study—the usefulness of a narratology grounded in "Lacan." This ground, it might be added, has provided a fertile space for Lacan's readers, from earlier post-structuralists such as Kristeva and Cixous to more recent theorists such as Jane Gallop, Shoshana Felman, Robert Con Davis, Barbara Johnson, and Peter Brooks, to mention just a few members of that community of readers who have moved psychoanalytic criticism away from traditional Freudian or Jungian analysis.

The Problem of a Title

The title of this project—*D. H. Lawrence, Desire, and Narrative*—offered a significant challenge. The title's triad represents an effort toward moving the project away from traditional, but especially *structuralist,* approaches. Fredric Jameson, in his discussion of the "Imaginary and Symbolic in Lacan," offers a valuable model when he asserts that it is "by introducing a third term [the Real] into the hitherto infinite regression of the duality" of the Imaginary and Symbolic orders that we "may put an end to the Imaginary opposition into which our previous discussion of Lacan's two orders has risked falling again and again" (383–84). The fundamental risk in any project that sets out to read literary texts intertextually with writings in psychoanalysis—in the present case, what an earlier critic might have framed as a "Lawrence and Lacan"—is always the impulse to apply psychoanalysis to literature. The strategy of introducing a third term—in this case, *narrative*—can begin to shift away from a troublesome binary.[7]

If there is one single element that marks psychoanalytic criticism, it is this troubled relationship between literature *and* psychoanalysis. As Peter Brooks suggests, "Shoshana Felman has pointed out more effectively than any other critic" how that *and* has led to the privileging of psychoanalysis over literature, its handmaid.[8] In her essay "To Open the Question," the introduction to her collection of essays *Literature and Psychoanalysis: The Question of Reading: Otherwise,* Felman argues that the appearance of coordination, or two entities yoked by this *and,* conceals a relationship of what is actually *subordination.* She continues, "While literature is considered as a body of *language*—to *be interpreted*—psychoanalysis is considered a body of *knowledge,* whose competence is called upon *to interpret.* Psychoanalysis, in other words, occupies the place of a *subject,* literature that of an *object;*[9] the relation of interpretation is structured as a relation of master to slave, according to the Hegelian definition" (5). Felman opts for a "dialogue" between literature and psychoanalysis, "as between two different bodies of language and between two different modes of knowledge" (6). Following through with the Hegelian master/slave binary, Felman indicates that the answer is more than a simple reversal of the mastery that would privilege literature over psychoanalysis; rather, her "intention is to disrupt altogether the position of mastery as such, to try to avoid *both* terms of the alternative, to deconstruct the very structure of the *opposition,* mastery/slavery" (7). Carrying forward her deconstruction of this binary on which psychoanalytic criticism has rested for most of the century, Felman proposes the supplanting of "application" with "implication," or the notion that literature is implicit in psychoanalysis, as psychoanalysis is implicit in literature. If we define *literature* as "the language which psychoanalysis uses in order to *speak of itself,*" literature is not "outside" psychoanalysis, and "there are no *natural* boundaries between" (9). Completing her post-structuralist analysis of the problematic relationship that shapes my project, Felman stresses the notion of the "other" within, or the difficulty in distinguishing "outside" from "inside," by asserting that just as psychoanalysis has been preoccupied with the unconscious of literature, "*literature, in its turn, is the unconscious of psychoanalysis*" (10).

To extend the framework of this post-structuralist psychoanalytic reading, we might turn to the insights of Mark Currie, who has been helpful in framing my project. Currie notes a shift to post-structural narratology in the 1980s in a move from the conception of reading as "discovery" of what is "in" the text to a notion of reading as "invention" (2). "Structure," Currie asserts, "became something that was projected onto the work by a reading rather than a property of a narrative discovered by the reading" (3). Narratives became less "buildings," or constructions, and more "narratological inventions construable in an almost infinite number of ways" (3). Where traditional critics have aspired to read narrative, as theologians have read Nature as the book of God's secret design, ignoring whatever failed to support a notion of its unifying structure, the post-structuralist critic has emphasized the instability of "meaning."[10]

We would also do well at this juncture to revisit a key passage in the texts of the theorist perhaps most frequently associated with post-structuralism—Jacques Derrida. Derrida's puzzling assertion, "Il n'y a pas dehors texte," has been popularly misconstrued by post-structuralists as well as their detractors to mean something like, "There is nothing outside the text," or "Everything *is* text." As Currie has very usefully suggested, Derrida is probably more likely asserting that the text does not have an "outside," as the structuralists would have us believe (45). In this post-structuralist context, the text is like a Möbius strip, where inside and outside are one and the same. It might be argued that post-structuralism is inextricably bound up with the very structuralism in which it is grounded, for it would be a structuralist trap to conceive of post-structuralism as an outside to structuralism. As Jerry Aline Flieger brilliantly suggests in a similar context of "post-ing," the persistent fascination (along with the frustration) of the post-structuralist/postmodernist gesture inheres in the necessity of seeing the *post* as something much more complicated than a simplistic "after."

The title also points toward the challenge of exploring elements of narration in Lawrence's texts without subscribing entirely to what Robert Con Davis in his collection *Lacan and Narration* has construed as a "Lacanian narratology." Quite simply, my project operates inside and outside of what Davis has construed as a Lacanian narratology. Like Felman, Davis follows Lacan by positing a textual Other, or an unconscious in the text. At the foundation of a Lacanian narratology, Davis asserts, is a focus on "how language in literary texts is constituted, buoyed up, permeated, and decentered by the unconscious" (848).[11] Both in his introduction to the collection of essays he edited and by example in his contribution to that volume, "Lacan, Poe, and Narrative Repression," Davis is intent upon examining the manner in which the unconscious "speaks" in a text within the lapses and gaps in the discourse, an admirable approach more useful to Poe and even Joyce texts than to Lawrence's.

Why Lacan?

Having mentioned Lacan more than once, it is no longer possible to postpone an interrogation of Lacan's position in my project of reading Lawrence's longer prose narrative. Lacan is useful to psychoanalytic readings of fiction because his conception of the human subject as inevitably "split" qualifies him as a post-structuralist or postmodern thinker. The contemporary theorist Norman Holland has offered a fascinating notion of a "postmodern psychoanalysis."[12] Holland argues for what he calls "Early Modern," "High Modern," and "Postmodern" movements in art, criticism, and psychoanalysis. He finds a shift to the "High Modern" in Freud's tendency toward "seeing drives and 'the unconscious' as 'in' the individual," as though they were the bones or organs of the human body. Freud's notion of the psyche was similar to the modernists' notion of the work of art as self-contained, as an end in itself. According to Holland, "Id, ego, and superego now became the important self-contained entities, ends in themselves, like a Mondrian painting or a story by Faulkner. . . . Psychoanalysis was a closed system. The human being was made up of clear boundaries within which everything had a place and was in its place. One could find the truth about oneself like finding a lost glove" (298–99).

One entry to Lacan's reading of Freud is his notion of a "return to

Freud" in order to free his forerunner from the misconceptions that have grown up around "Freud." Freud has been misread, for example, as authorizing a schema of the psyche neatly divided into ego, id, and superego. That misreading is limiting, in large part because it helps to mythologize the unconscious as the dark, primitive jungle of the psyche. As Meredith Skura aptly comments, "In fact the very identification of a so-called unconscious as a thing or a separate part of the mind existing unknown to us is misleading. It is the product of a falsely neat dichotomy between our rational, acceptable thinking (supposedly all conscious) and our irrational, primitive, and unrepressed thinking (supposedly all unconscious)" (2). Skura recalls that "Freud himself later discarded the dichotomy of conscious and unconscious as an identification of parts of the mind" (2).

In his "return to Freud," Lacan attempted to direct attention to the early Freud of such underread works as *Wit and its Relation to the Unconscious* and *The Psychopathology of Everyday Life*. Defying the logic of chronological evolution in Freud's thinking, Lacan focused upon other early works of Freud such as *The Interpretation of Dreams,* accepting Freud's original evaluation of this work as his most important contribution to psychoanalysis. Lacan preferred the unconscious of the earlier Freud to the id-ego-superego hierarchy of the later Freud, which has dominated American ego psychology. It was in the Freud of *The Interpretation of Dreams* that Lacan discovered the locus of his most significant and original contributions to psychoanalysis.

In rereading the Freud of *The Interpretation of Dreams,* Lacan discovered the two fundamental principles on which the dream work depends—condensation and displacement. In Lacan's analysis, these principles of condensation and displacement represent the fundamental psychic processes. More important perhaps to those who have an investment in literature, condensation and displacement for Lacan are also the basic tropes of metaphor and metonymy, respectively. It is important to note that Lacan is probably misreading Freud by equating condensation with metaphor. The eclectic Lacan borrowed from the work of his friend Roman Jakobson, the structural linguist, who, as we shall see, tropes Freud's fundamental psychic principles in a significantly different manner.

Lacan reads the trope of metonymy as an expression of Freud's displacement. Metonymy works through displacement of one signifier by another, *ship* displaced, for example, by *sail. Ship* is latent and unexplained by this sliding of one signifier over another, or a displacement to a contiguous and insignificant signifier. In this way, Lacan finds a means of representing unconscious "desire," which exists always as lack or absence, although it is signified on the conscious level as "demand." In contrast, the operation of condensation in metaphor is more profound, since it is not another signifier but a signified that is replaced or repressed. The metaphorical term is a distorted representation of the repressed signified, the "symptom," or "the return of the repressed." It is the repressed signified, or what is *not* consciously expressed, that empowers metaphor. Signification is made possible by the "crossing of the bar," or the return of the repressed, and therefore, distorted signified in metaphor.[13]

For Lacan the relationship between the conscious and the unconscious is, then, inevitably intertextual. In his now-famous statement, "l'inconscient est structuré comme un langage," the unconscious is a repressed "text," structured according to its own language and involved in a subtle interchange with its "manifest content," to use Freud's term. As Davis explains, "In this way, the so-called manifest content . . . is resubjected in interpretation to the same process of combination *and* selection, metonymy and metaphor, that produced the manifest content in the dream work initially" (852–53). In a psychoanalytic context both metaphor and metonymy are involved, then, in the subtle interchange between conscious and unconscious, which may be understood linguistically. Metaphor finds a signifier to represent the signified that has been repressed into the unconscious; metonymy finds a contiguous signifier to escape the significant signifier.[14]

As Freud's most brilliant reader, Lacan is a valuable starting point for the construction of a framework within which to read Lawrence. Lacan's notion of the "subject" departs from the more traditional psychoanalytic concept of a "self," which might be divided against itself but is theoretically capable of unity. Lacan's subject is eternally split and changing, and, as Ed Jewinski points out, much closer to Lawrence's notion of the allotropic and highly *un*stable ego of his famous pronouncement to Edward Garnett. Or as Hilary Simpson suggests in her brief consideration of connections between Lacan and Lawrence, Lacan seems to bring the Lawrentian phallus back into theoretical discourse. She notes, "Lacan's style endows the phallus with something of the *numen* that it has in

Lawrence's work." Writing about Lacan's definition of the phallus, Simpson continues: "Interestingly enough, Lawrence occasionally uses the symbol of the phallus in similar ways; as, for example, in his concept of it as the 'third term,' and his determination to include within its range of values characteristics usually defined as feminine" (133).

In his development of the key tropes of metaphor and metonymy, Lacan borrowed liberally from the work of his friend Roman Jakobson. On the basis of his study of sufferers from aphasia, the structural linguist Jakobson hypothesized two diametrically opposed forms of this speech disorder. One form, "similarity disorder," restricts the sufferer to associative, or metonymic, perceptions, while eliminating substitutive, or metaphoric, perceptions. The other, "contiguity disorder," restricts the sufferer to substitutive, or metaphoric, perceptions, and eliminates associative, or metonymic, perceptions. Of interest to those with an investment in literature, Jakobson expanded his notion of these tropes to encompass literary genres and modes. He linked metaphor with poetry, or "romanticism and symbolism," and metonymy with prose, or "realism," with its narrative emphasis upon contiguity and its "synecdochic details."[15]

Jakobson may also have helped Lacan in his return to Freud. Going on to see the binary oppositions of similarity and contiguity, or metaphor and metonymy, in surrealism and cubism, as well as in drama and film, respectively, Jakobson argues for the application of a similar analysis to the Freud of *Interpretation of Dreams:* "A competition between both devices, metonymic and metaphoric, is manifest in any symbolic process, be it intrapersonal or social. Thus in an inquiry into the structure of dreams, the decisive question is whether the symbols and temporal sequences used are based on contiguity (Freud's metonymic 'displacement' or synecdochic 'condensation') or on similarity (Freud's 'identification and symbolism')" (258).

It is crucially important here to acknowledge Lacan's departure from Jakobson, from whom he undoubtedly borrowed the tropes of metonymy and metaphor as representations of Freud's fundamental psychic principles. As is clear in the Jakobson passage cited above, Jakobson read Freud's "displacement" and "condensation" *together* as "metonymy" and turned to Freud's principle of "identification and symbolism" for the similarity inherent in "metaphor." Whether Lacan misread/misrecognized what he found in Jakobson or deliberately sought to stamp his own conception of the tropes upon his understanding of Freud is a moot point. Lacan's eminent American exegete Ellie Ragland-Sullivan is extremely chary in crediting Jakobson for insights based upon his study of sufferers from the symptoms of diametrically opposed forms of aphasia. What is useful to recall in the discussion below of these two foundational tropes—whether we go down the path of Jakobson's followers, such as David Lodge, or the path of Lacan's, such as Jane Gallop and Barbara Johnson—is the inherently structuralist starting point for both of these thinkers.

As metonymy has had a lesser role in contemporary psychoanalytic theory, metonymy also has had a less substantial place than has metaphor in literary criticism. For several reasons, Lacan follows Jakobson in connecting metonymy with realist fiction, or realism in general.[16] First, if in the strictest sense of the term metonymy is that trope in which an attribute or an associated feature stands for the thing represented—"thirty sail for thirty ships," to use Lacan's example—it has about it that sense of naturalness implicit in using a detail associated with or a part of the thing being represented (synecdoche being subsumed by metonymy). That association may seem so natural that we miss its agency as figuration. As metaphor represents substitution—the signifier *travel* substituting for experience, or movement in time—metonymy represents displacement from one signifier, *sail,* to another signifier, *ship,* the signifier *ship* remaining "latent," or "unexplained" (Wilden 241). Realism as a mode may be seen as "metonymic" since the realist offers details associated with that infinite storehouse of details called "reality." As David Lodge explains, "The metonymic text . . . seems to offer itself to our regard not as a metaphor but as a synecdoche, not as a model of reality, but as a representative *bit* of reality . . . [based upon] a relationship of contiguity rather than similarity, for [realist] writers create the illusion that their stories are or were part of real history, from which they have been cut out and of which they are representative" (109).

It is these implications of metonymy and metaphor for an understanding of literary genre that have been central to what might be termed a "structuralist narratology." As the passage just cited clearly indicates, Lodge's notions of narrative owe a sizeable debt to Jakobson's structuralist analysis. Lodge's application of Jakobson to prose narrative two decades ago has recently been continued by Gerald Doherty in his own structuralist readings of Lawrence's fiction.

Troping *The White Peacock*

As preparation for an exploration of the usefulness of metaphor and metonymy as thematic and structural principles in the major Lawrence novels, it might be helpful to examine the operation of these two figures in an early text such as *The White Peacock* in order to establish the limits of usefulness in Lodge's essentially structuralist approach. In his important contribution to this area of narratology, *The Modes of Modern Writing,* Lodge is intent on illustrating the impact of the principles of "metaphor" on poetry and the symbolist novel and "metonymy" on realist prose. Lodge was working on this area of narratology, we might remind ourselves, while structuralism was extremely influential. That influence is apparent in Lodge's high regard for the theorist Roland Barthes and the linguist Roman Jakobson, who were among the most important structuralists at the time. In illustrating the principles of metonymy and metaphor by examining each in a different genre, Lodge misses the opportunity to consider the potential of the two principles to operate in the same text. By following Jakobson the structuralist in this way, Lodge leaves his readers with the impression of an either-or polarity for metonymy and metaphor. That polarity needs to be deconstructed as a first step toward recognizing a greater complexity in the operation of these two principles on which Jakobson and Lodge have focused.

First, it is worth noting that *The White Peacock* underwent a number of drafts before it appeared in 1911. During those early years, Lawrence was writing both fiction and verse. In fact, it could be argued that he might well have established a reputation as a major modern poet if he had never ventured into fiction writing. As continues to be the case, readers have been unwilling to acknowledge that writers can legitimately produce both poetry and fiction.[17] Indeed, if Lawrence had restricted his literary production to poetry he might never have attracted quite so many attempts at "psychoanalyzing" him through his texts. Furthermore, one wonders if his reputation among feminists might not also be higher if he had not written the fiction, as well as the essays, by which he is so often characterized as an unregenerate sexist. As Linda Ruth Williams has so aptly phrased it: "Lawrence, perhaps more than any other writer, is feminism's *bête noire,* the monster it loves to hate" (*Sex* 16).

If, following Jakobson's lead, we associate realist prose with the metonymic, and poetry—especially symbolist poetry—with the metaphoric, it might be valuable to explore, however briefly, *The White Peacock* for expressions of metaphor and metonymy indicative of the young author's attraction to writing both poetry and fiction. It might legitimately be speculated that this first novel remained a divided effort in part because the text cannot reconcile conflicting impulses toward "poetry" or the metaphoric and "fiction" or the metonymic within the framework Lodge built on Jakobson's thinking.

Because the metonymic is the more appropriate to an exploration of this text as an expression of realist prose narrative, metonymy offers a more effective starting point. Before moving forward with Jakobson's linking of metonymy to realist prose narrative, it is extremely important to note that Jakobson led Lacan and many of Lacan's followers to accept the collapsing of the tropes of synecdoche and metonymy into the single figure of "metonymy."[18] Thus, "metonymy" is more precisely a signifier employed because of its association with another signifier, while "synecdoche" is more specifically the "part for the whole." Lodge offers a helpful example of both tropes in one context: "The hand that rocks the cradle" (75). The phrase illustrates synecdoche because *hand* signifies "care-giver" and metonymy because *cradle* has been associated with "child." Accordingly, realist narrative is metonymic for Jakobson because its structuring principle is the contiguous or syntagmatic. Obviously enough, readers of realist prose narrative expect the text to follow the pattern of chronological sequence. Realist narrative is also metonymic, as Lodge suggests, because it offers the text as a part for the whole, a sample representation of a reality existing outside the text, a reality by which the realist text is evaluated as having or not having fulfilled its responsibility to provide a part of that whole. Because metonymy has subsumed the function of synecdoche for many followers of Jakobson and Lacan, it is important not to let that suppression go unacknowledged, for it is synecdoche, or part for whole, in metonymy that empowers its agency in a text much more than the rather obvious Jakobsonian notion of contiguous relationship of elements in narrative. Indeed, it is this synecdochic element in metonymy, as the term is reconstructed from classical poetics by first Jakobson and then Lacan, that is especially useful in exploring the metonymic and the metaphoric in *The White Peacock*.

The more traditional notion of the metonymic as the associative or contiguous principle in a narrative text is represented weakly in *The*

White Peacock. The novel fails to convince its readers that it knows where it is going. Events take place, characters move into and out of focus, but the narrative lacks a sufficient sense of plottedness, of action following a logical pattern of development. A related problem is the choice of Cyril as first-person narrator, requiring him to be everywhere in the narrative, even a silent observer apparently of the love scene between his sister, Lettie, and his friend George Saxton. If the metonymic can be allowed to subsume the synecdochic as a part for the whole, the management of this love scene foregrounds the narrative's artifice as an unconvincing specimen of the "whole" of reality it is committed to represent. It is clear enough eventually that the narrative is bent upon constructing George Saxton as a tragic figure because he cannot survive the final loss of Lettie to Leslie Tempest. Along the way, there is the hint of the potential relationships of Cyril with both George and with George's sister, Emily, but overall the principle of contiguity in this text lacks the energy to persuade the reader that segments of the text are yoked together through some power of narrative association.

The part for the whole, or synecdochic, element of the metonymic principle is ultimately more interesting and more relevant to this text in focusing on the narrator's details as specimens of the real world that the text seeks to represent. A good example of this text's attention to details is provided in the early description of the Saxton kitchen. Cyril's description of the scene is justified by George's being so immersed in reading a book that he ignores his visitor. The narrator seems almost to have contrived this reading activity of George to offer the setting of the scene expected in the conventional novel. The description begins: "The kitchen was very big," then veers into the narrator's self-indulgent predilection for personification: "the table looked lonely, and the chairs mourned darkly for the lost companionship of the sofa." The "bare" and "sober" atmosphere is not entirely unrelieved, however: "The only gay things were the chintz coverings of the sofa and the arm-chair cushions, bright red in the bare sombre room" (*WP* 3). This fussiness with the details of interior decorating may indicate something of the sensibility that encourages Annie to twit the narrator, with whom she is paired uneventfully, by calling him "Sybil."

If this prettifying attention paid to synecdochic detail were restricted to the domestic scene, its impact upon the texture of this novel might be ignored. However, when Cyril moves out into the world of nature, the details are once again described with the same mawkish personification. Having recorded his running "over the little bright brook that came from the weedy, bottom pond," the narrator bounces sentimentally along to describe "the stepping-stones" in order perhaps to tell how "the water slid sleepily among them" before moving on to the butterflies that "trifled from flower to flower and led me up the hill." There, "[t]he bracken held out arms to me, and the bosom of the woods was full of sweetness, but I journeyed on spurred by the attacks of an army of flies which kept up a guerilla warfare round my head" (6).

The predilection of this narrative for personification is so pervasive that one might be inclined to (mis)take it for the text's move toward the pole of metaphor or the poetic. These pretty personifications are far from the metaphoric principle, however. If the metaphoric is associated with the poetic in the Jakobsonian/Lacanian scheme, these figures are what might be expected in versifying, greeting-card sentiments, and other stale imitations of poetry. They fail to achieve the metaphoric or poetic because they lack the element of genuine transformation inherent in the term *metaphor,* a carrying across. It is this element of the transformative, associated by Jakobson with metaphor in a linguistic and literary sense, that this text never fully accomplishes, even though it may make an occasional gesture in that direction.

The effort toward the transformative power of metaphor reveals itself in the narrator's attempt to find symbolic equivalents for his sense of the George Saxton and Lettie Beardsall figures operating in a dimension beyond that in which meaning can be easily represented within the framework of realist prose. Cyril frames the contrast between his sister, Lettie, and George within the context of painting and painters about which the couple disagree. George is a "romanticist," while Lettie focuses his attention upon a realist painting entitled "Hoeing" by George Clausen.[19] She praises Clausen as a "real realist" and explains that "he makes common things beautiful, he sees the mystery and magnificence that envelops us even when we work menially" (28). Comparing George with the man hoeing in the Clausen painting, Lettie proceeds to stun George with her analysis of his being. She represents George's being appropriately through metaphor: "You are blind; you are only half-born. You are gross with good-living and heavy sleeping. You are a piano which will only play a dozen common notes" (28). Anticipating her eventual development as the "white peacock" of the title, Lettie tells George, "I'd like to make you suffer," presumably to awaken him from the drowse of "blood-consciousness" of the Brangwen men in *The Rainbow.* If Cyril is lent the versifying function in this text as the constructor of something approaching purple patches of lush nature verse, Lettie has the function of the poet as maker of metaphors offering a taste of the transformative power of that trope. It is she who figures George in this scene as a flower bulb she would like to "force" into bloom, tellingly through the agency of her capacity to make him "suffer." She tells him: "You never grow up, like bulbs which spend all summer getting fat and fleshy but never wakening the germ of a flower. . . . You have to suffer before you blossom in this life." Lettie herself feels she has blossomed because of the sense of death that has touched her in the Beardsall home and adds that her mother conceived her in hatred of her father: "That was death in her veins for me before I was born" (28). Clumsy as this metaphorizing may seem, it does reveal the poetic or metaphoric impulse, at least in its potential, in this text.

The metaphor of George as an awakening bud irritated into bloom through Lettie's agency as a variety of *belle dame sans merci* recurs in a pastoral scene involving real farm work, in contrast to the masquerade of labor traditionally associated with the pastoral. The unevenly matched competition in farm laboring here of the farmer George Saxton and the local aristocrat Leslie Tempest, whom Lettie will marry, allows Lettie to celebrate George's physical being as Cyril cannot openly do without setting off alarms concerning homoerotic desire in that man-to-man relationship. Turning from Leslie's inept imitation of "a man with a scythe" from some other painting by Clausen that she may have seen, Lettie focuses attention upon George's physique: "Your arms tempt me to touch them. They are such a fine brown colour, and they look so hard." He offers her permission to submit to this "temptation." When George says, "You feel so fine"—meaning, "A person feels so fine"—the assertion seems to be Lettie's, or even Cyril's as omnipresent observer/narrator. This assertion about how "fine" George's flesh feels foregrounds itself even more, when George follows it up by reaching into his "open shirt-front, and gently rubbing the muscles of his side," expressing presumably what Lettie—and perhaps her male (br)other, Cyril—would like to do as well. The scene closes with her gazing at George, "full at his physical beauty, as if he were some great firm bud of life" (48).

Because the scene offers the earliest expression in Lawrence's fiction of the male subject as the object of the gaze, it deserves comment at least in passing. Cyril functions here in a strangely double, if not downright contradictory, role. He is present as narrator, yet essentially absent as character; he is telling the story yet silent in the scene, a watcher through his sister's eyes of George's display of male beauty. Indeed, because he draws the look of Lettie, and by extension the gaze of her brother, Cyril, who seems to be functioning as a film camera, George is performing the representation of masculinity for the reader, split here between a female and male looker. In a sense, George is making a spectacle of himself, overtly for Lettie's eyes, covertly for Cyril's, and by extension for the eyes of the reader—like his audience in the scene, a reader of either sex. The scene lays the foundation for the economy of desire established in the later bathing scene where the reader is more fully implicated in George's even more self-consciously constructed performance of "to-be-looked-at-ness," to borrow Laura Mulvey's term (19).

The Implications of Trope

This same metaphor of awakening the bud of his being into life recurs in George's reminding Lettie of how she stimulated his desire for transformation. By this point, Lettie has indicated she will marry Leslie Tempest, clearly the better prospect. George, however, will not let her go without confirming the agency of that stimulation. He reminds her: "You began it. You played with me, and showed me heaps of things . . . things will never be the same—you have awakened my life—I imagine things that I couldn't have done" (116). Lettie has teased the bud of his emotional/sensual/erotic potential into being, just as Cyril has functioned as the agent of George's intellectual/cultural growth. As will become clearer, this metaphor of buds awakening into life also enhances the representation of desire in the scene of Lettie's last farewell to George.

By the time Lettie and George have the opportunity for one last scene in which their relationship might change the courses of their now separate lives, both are married. Lettie registers the impossibility of their sharing each other's futures in another one of the text's literary allusions. She reminds George that he has failed her by playing Orpheus to her Eurydice, presumably by lacking faith that she would indeed "follow" him. She invites him into the woods, a sort of pagan Greek greenwood where she might play dryad to George's faun. Lettie, as Cyril's other, dominates the discourse, drawing George's attention to "how we are netted down—boughs with knots of green buds" (214), and "Look at the harvest of bluebells—ripened for us!" (215). Here, the emphasis is no longer on the potential of George to ripen into a larger life, but on the web of commitments the two have individually woven for themselves. This metaphor of entrapment, introduced at the outset in George's mercy killing of the cat, Mrs. Nickie Ben, whose hind legs had been broken in a trap, confirms the "tragic" denial that George will ever find the means of achieving greater possibilities for being. In the end George becomes the literalized "fat and fleshy" bulb Lettie earlier metaphorized him as, when it still appeared possible for him to undergo the transformation into another life. It is precisely this transformation that is at the center of the metaphorical.

This analysis of Jakobson's tropes of metonymy and metaphor as the principles of figuration on which realist prose narrative and romantic/symbolist poetry, respectively, are grounded has up to this point confined itself to the structuralist approach apparent in Lodge, Doherty, and others who have applied Jakobson to literary texts. One movement toward the post-structural instituted in the preceding reading of *The White Peacock* tropically has been the attempt to establish the presence of both principles of figuration within the same literary text. A fuller discussion of this movement toward post-structuralism inherent in the dynamic of metaphor and metonymy must be postponed to a later chapter focusing on *The Rainbow.* That movement might be conceived of as a deconstruction of the structuralist binary of metaphor and metonymy to show that the two poles are not discrete, but engaged in a complex interchange. Going one step further, we might attend to the post-structuralist's reminder that binaries end up privileging one over the other in the pair, as becomes apparent in the inclination to name this binary "metaphor and metonymy"—rather than "metonymy and metaphor"—in the same way we find ourselves locked into the linguistic habit of listing "men and women," "gods and goddesses," right down to "salt and pepper."[20]

It is impossible to investigate the function of metaphor and metonymy in this first novel of Lawrence without recalling that among some "followers" of Lacan these tropes have accumulated gender associations appropriate to this polarity of realist prose and symbolist poetry that Lacan found in Jakobson. I problematize the term *followers* because the group includes theorists such as the French feminist Luce Irigaray and the American feminist Jane Gallop, both of whom have been influenced by

Lacan, but who have had serious arguments with his seemingly phallocentric teachings. In her book *Reading Lacan,* Gallop follows Irigaray in engendering metonymy and metaphor because of gender associations she sees growing out of sex differences inherent in male and female genitalia. She writes: "Metaphor is patent; metonymy is latent. The latency, the hiddenness of metonymy, like that of female genitalia, lends it an appearance of naturalness or passivity so that realism . . . appears either as the lack of tropes, or as somehow mysterious, the 'dark continent' [Freud's term for female sexuality] of rhetoric" (128). In the context of Lacan's thinking, metonymy may seem "natural," "latent," scarcely figurative, because it is merely a displacement of one contiguous signifier by another, rather than the phenomenon of a signifier repressing its signified beneath the bar.

Irigaray helps Gallop to deconstruct the binaries of masculine/feminine and metaphor/metonymy. Irigaray argues for a correlation between the privileging of metaphor over metonymy in contemporary psychoanalytic theory and a "phallocentric neglect of femininity" (127). Gallop then focuses upon the evidence of Lacan's work, concluding: "The most extreme and explicit form of metaphor's privilege in Lacan's text inhabits its association with liberation, which contrasts with metonymy's link to servitude . . . metonymy's ellipsis can be considered 'oppressive' (*É,* 502; *S,* 153). Metaphor, on the other hand, is 'the crossing of the bar.' The word for 'crossing'—'franchissement'—has an older meaning of liberation from slavery, enfranchissement. The 'bar' is an obstacle; metaphor unblocks" (*Reading Lacan* 128). Thus, metaphor is a linguistic framework in which the signified repressed beneath the bar has found a means of representation above the bar in the "manifest content" of the text, or in the conscious.

Because Gallop's and Irigaray's insights ground my entire project, and not merely this introductory examination of *The White Peacock,* it would be best to pause here and explore more fully the post-structural movements inherent in this feminist analysis of Jakobson/Lacan's discovery of linguistic/generic/psychoanalytic correlations. Gallop's deconstruction of the metaphor/metonymy binary as privileging metaphor over metonymy because of the latter's "latency" or "hiddenness," like the female genitalia, helps us to see why metonymy has indeed been so marginalized as scarcely to be acknowledged as a trope in critical discourse. It is, of course, that "naturalness or passivity," its "mysterious" sense of absence, that connects so helpfully with Irigaray's notion of "metonymy's link to servitude." Metonymy represents what has seemed a mere displacement, whether understood as an associated detail or a part-for-the-whole, while metaphor represents liberation, or travel, in contrast to metonymy's confinement. Metaphor for Lacan is dynamic because as a signifier it both represses another signifier below the bar (or *barre,* to use Lacan's term) of the signifier/signified algorithm Lacan constructs at the same time that it allows that signifier to cross the bar. Accordingly, metaphor is associated with power and therefore masculine, while metonymy is associated with confinement and therefore feminine. Irigaray and Gallop are implicated in post-structuralist thinking, however, because they demonstrate how metaphor is privileged over metonymy and subtly interconnected. Furthermore, despite their grounding of metonymy and metaphor in female and male genitalia, their analysis of these tropes allows gender to unmoor itself from sex differences, since they would agree that femininity/metonymy and masculinity/metaphor are textual positions, quite different from traditional notions of maleness and femaleness as essences or entities. The latter, structuralist analysis of supposed male/female essences gives way through Irigaray and Gallop's theorizing to a post-structuralist (or postmodernist)[21] notion of gender as social (or textual) construction grounded in positionality.

If, following Gallop and Irigaray, it is possible to read gender difference in the associations of metonymy/realist prose, on the one hand, and metaphor/symbolist poetry, on the other, it might be useful to look at the problematic condition of this first novel by Lawrence as a representation of "gender trouble."[22] The problems most frequently noted by its readers include the personifications and expressions of the pathetic fallacy he would avoid in his later poetry as well as in his fiction, just as he would abandon the use of first-person narrative in his later fiction, except for a couple of short stories and *Mr Noon.* The intent here, of course, is not to add to the consensus view of this first novel's weaknesses, but to explore those weaknesses as "gender trouble," as I have begun to define that term.

Michael Black, in his introduction to *The White Peacock,* identifies the first of these problems as the weakening of plot structure. Essentially, this novel is organized as the major parts of two cycles of the seasons—spring to winter—and then a final segment placed some fifteen years later, when Cyril returns to the Nethermere, from which he feels he and the other major actors in the text have been exiled. As Black reminds us,

Lawrence was very attracted to the cycling of the seasons as the time framework for his novels. *Women in Love* and *Lady Chatterley's Lover*, for example, both begin in the early spring and end in winter. If the metonymic can be associated with not only the principle of contiguity, following Jakobson/Lacan, but also femininity, following Irigaray/Gallop, *The White Peacock* demonstrates weakness in this metonymic logic of moving the plot forward to a conclusion that leaves the novel's readers with a sense of completion. To the degree that this is George Saxton's story and the text seems anxious to dramatize George's inevitable decline into the pathetic figure with grotesque belly and sticklike limbs that Cyril sees in the closing pages, it requires the quasi-epilogue segment to mark this all-too-slow deterioration. This is also Cyril's story, however. As storyteller he lacks a firm grasp on the metonymic or feminine principle associated with the contiguous structure of realist prose. One segment of the plot can move painfully toward its inevitable closure with George's death, but where is the sense of closure for Cyril? We can say that Cyril is merely the narrator here and that this is George's story, or Lettie's. However, Cyril is more than a mere observer, and that becomes very clear when Emily shocks him and the novel's readers by introducing Cyril to her future husband. Suddenly, readers are forced to recognize that Cyril has lost his youth as well as the prospects of marriage that in the conventional novel might have offered a sense of closure, and commencement, to his story.

The weakness here of the metonymic principle is mirrored by difficulties in the metaphoric or transformative principle as well. George's imminent death at the end offers an apparent closure; it is only apparent, however, because the text has failed to make George a subject sufficiently appealing that readers identify with his failed aspiration for personal transformation. Perhaps George deceives himself that only through the agency of Lettie can he achieve the transformation without which he is doomed to rot as an "overfed bulb." There is perhaps a possible transformation in this limited ending of the novel with George's death. The potential transformative power of the ending, however, seems mired in the negativity of his decline, leaving most readers with little sense of the tragic in a George who drinks himself to death, despite Cyril's memory of his friend from the earlier swimming scene, which makes him "choke" at the sickening transformation of that body as George exposes it by taking off his pajama jacket.

Even more than these problems with the failed potential for transformation in its ending, this text demonstrates little mastery of the metaphoric. Of the main figures in the novel, only Lettie has a sense of transformative potential in movement, travel, or the crossing of the bar (to recall Lacan's notion of metaphor as a principle of signification). The notion of the metaphoric, as Jane Gallop associates it with the masculine, is an appropriate concern here because the power inherent in the transformative has traditionally been associated with the male. Thus, one of the few things about which Lettie can express envy of George is his mobility, in sharp contrast to her confinement, traditionally associated with the feminine and the female. When George tells her that he has decided against moving away from Nethermere, Lettie responds: "If I were a man, I would go out west and be free." His reply, "Well—you're not a man," is uttered with a "timid bitterness" Lettie herself cannot have missed. And when she indicates her desire a moment later—"I should like to be out west, to have a little lake of my own, and swim with my limbs quite free in the water"—he can only rob the metaphoric potential of her utterances of desire by literalizing them: "Do you swim well?" and "I would race you—in your little lake" (211). The scene adds another dimension to Lettie's figuring of George as the Orpheus who lost Eurydice by looking backward. If the metaphoric/masculine/liberatory obtains here, it is only to remind us that George seems never to have had the potential to be an Orphean poet; it is Lettie, of all the characters, who has that potential, which as a woman in a patriarchal context she has no opportunity to pursue. In this respect, George Saxton establishes the type of the male—later evident in Anton Skrebensky and Anthony Schofield—who demonstrates an unwillingness to share the impulse to travel of female figures such as Lettie Beardsall and Ursula Brangwen.

George is not alone, however, in his failure to grasp the transformative potential inherent in the metaphoric and in the metaphor of crossing the bar. Immediately after the encounter in which George dooms himself by failing to share Lettie's impulse to go west imaginatively toward personal transformation, Cyril offers the novel's most famous chapter, "A Poem of Friendship." The chapter has gained its fame as Lawrence's first expression of desire in the man-to-man relationship. The friendship of George and Cyril is celebrated in a pair of vignettes of the physical intimacy of the two working together—the cold, rainy scene of spreading manure and planting potatoes in May, followed by the June scene of haying and bathing together.

The first of the two scenes serves as a prelude to the other. It emphasizes the rhythm of menial labor, associated here by Cyril with the movement of George's body and the crying of the lapwings or peewits (which recur even more importantly in the famous scene of Paul Morel's baptism to passion with Clara Dawes). When it begins to rain, George and Cyril huddle together in a hedge in a gesture of intimacy that Cyril cherishes: "It was at these times we formed the almost passionate attachment which later years slowly wore away" (219). The scene ends with Cyril's discovery of a lark's nest on the ground. Hardly coincidentally, the nest has two fledglings to which Cyril responds with some of the reverential awe evident in Paul Morel's ability to immerse himself in gazing at what he finds in nature. Also not coincidentally, the nestlings are characterized as male. "I gently put down my fingers to touch them; they were warm; gratifying to find them warm, in the midst of so much cold and wet! I became curiously absorbed in them. . . . When one fledgling moved uneasily . . . I was quite excited; but he nestled down again, with his head close to his brother's. In my heart of hearts, I longed for someone to nestle against, someone who would come between me and the coldness and the wetness" (220). Cyril goes on to express envy as one who is forever "wandering" rather than nestling, as he has just nestled with George in the hedge and will nestle in George's arms for a brief moment in the nude scene to follow.

The latter scene seems equally contrived as an obvious vehicle for Cyril's concealed desire for George. Although the scene has some justification in the warm, end-of-June haying activity, its function seems only to serve as a vehicle for Cyril's desire to celebrate his friendship with George once again (in much the same way that Freddie Honeychurch's invitation to George Emerson in E. M. Forster's *A Room with a View* to join him in a "bathe" seems a contrivance to allow the two men to frolic together nude).[23] As many readers have noted, George Saxton is very much in command here: it is he who suggests the swim and takes over Cyril's drying of himself with a towel while Cyril immerses himself in gazing at his nude friend. Cyril attempts to persuade readers that George needs to embrace him in order to rub him dry with the towel; the contrivance of this awkward gesture hardly distracts Cyril as he goes limp in George's arms—"as if I were a child, or rather, a woman he loved," Cyril explains. Enjoying "the sweetness of the touch of our naked bodies one against the other," Cyril indicates that it "satisfied in some measure the vague, indecipherable yearning of my soul; and it was the same with him" (222). If we wonder how Cyril knows that George shared his "yearning," the narrator indicates in the next breath that they gazed at each other, "and our love was perfect for a moment, more perfect than any love I have known since, either for man or woman" (223).

Setting aside questions of how Lawrence, as well as his publisher, and even the printers who set the type for this scene, got it past the censors a mere quarter-century after the Criminal Law Amendment (Labouchere amendment) of 1885 criminalized any gesture of "love" between men, it might be useful to focus for a moment upon Cyril as a "poet" of friendship.[24] If the poetic in Jakobson's sense is associated with the metaphoric and in Gallop's sense with the masculine, Cyril's position in these two segments of his "poem of friendship" is more feminine than masculine. This is not to say that Cyril is feminine merely because he indicates that his posture is passive,[25] desiring not so much to love as to *be loved* by the clearly active George. Cyril's subject position is rendered effeminate by his own foregrounding of himself as vulnerable. If, in a traditionally patriarchal context, power is associated with the masculine and the metaphoric, to be vulnerable is for either sex to be rendered feminine, as Barbara Johnson suggests when she speaks of Poe's purloined letter as "feminizing" its possessor.[26] Much as Cyril Beardsall may have figured himself as a traveler, or wanderer, he seems, instead, a nestling, nursing his vulnerability, in stark contrast to his sister, Lettie, who envies this same George for his masculine mobility. This text seems split between the cross-gendered siblings: the title's "white peacock" Lettie, who ought to be the "poet," since it is she who celebrates the freedom and mobility inherent in metaphor and transformation, on the one hand, and its narrator, Cyril, who exposes a vulnerability inherent in metonymy and confinement. Ironically, Lettie, who would travel, entraps herself with a husband who subverts her capacity for transformation, while Cyril, who is privileged by being male, would prefer to nestle in the protected valley of Nethermere forever.

The Yet Untrod Path

At the same time, the narrative exposes the feminizing agency of desire in George as well as Cyril. As Lacan emphasized, to be a desiring subject is to be implicated in castration, for to desire is to be made aware of lack, since desire must always be a metonym for that Desire which must always immensely exceed the subject's capacity for fulfillment. In the Lacanian economy of desire constructed by the tropes of metaphor and metonymy, cross-gendering is inevitable, for to be a desiring subject is to be feminized by the vulnerability inherent in lack, while to be the object of the desiring gaze, as Lettie represents herself to George, is to desire to travel, or to escape the feminizing force of confinement, or an object-position. In one sense, George constructs himself as both masculine and feminine, both as desiring subject vis-à-vis Lettie, who is the object of his looking, and as the object of Lettie's, but more importantly, Cyril's gaze.

Part 3 even begins with just such a metaphorizing of Lettie's masculine impulse to travel and Cyril's feminine impulse to feather his psychic nest in Nethermere. Cyril begins this first chapter, "A New Start in Life," with the very metaphor of life experience as travel, only to reveal his own reluctance to set out on such a journey, at least in any meaningful sense of the term. He writes that, following Lettie's departure for a short honeymoon in France, "everywhere was a sense of loss, and of change. The long voyage in the quiet home was over; we had crossed the bright sea of our youth, and already Lettie had landed and was travelling to a strange destination in a foreign land. It was time for us all to go, to leave the valley of Nethermere . . . and to cast ourselves each one into separate exile was painful for us" (237). We have only to look ahead to Ursula Brangwen's revulsion against the deadness of the familiar and her appetite for the unknown, making her unwilling to cease her travels toward her own "Promised Land," to index the painful insufficiency of Cyril to savor, much less celebrate as Ursula will, the adventure of transformation inherent in the metaphor of travel and in metaphoricity itself.

The figure of foreignness operates in the subjectivity of George as a displacement from Cyril, who finds it so inhibiting. Ironically, Cyril focuses upon George's fearful attraction to the foreign, as though he were vicariously experiencing venturesomeness. He says of George, "His one idea was to do the things he was half afraid to do. His passion—and it was almost intoxication—was to dare to play with life. . . . He was afraid to venture into the foreign places of life, and all was foreign save the valley of Nethermere. So he crossed the borders flauntingly, and marched towards the heart of the unknown" (246).

Cyril, on the other hand, physically departs from Nethermere for Norwood, a suburb of London, but it is not a journey in any meaningful sense because his affections remain in the happy valley of his childhood. He tells us: "I suffered acutely the sickness of exile in Norwood." It is, as soon becomes apparent, a longing to "nestle" in the comfortable domesticity of the past. Cyril makes this clear in his domesticating of the natural world itself. He explains: "The hills of Nethermere had been my walls, and the sky of Nethermere my roof overhead" (260). Eventually he can assert: "I had done with the valley of Nethermere. The valley of Nethermere had cast me out many years before, while I had fondly believed it cherished me in memory" (306). At the same time, as a self-styled exile, Cyril has never begun the journey.

Much like its undervalued counterpart *Mr Noon,* this narrative fails to fulfill modernist expectations of closure, resolution, and even clear intent. From the structuralist viewpoint, the text seems unable, or perhaps unwilling, to resolve itself into binaries of metaphor/metonymy, poetry/fiction, male/female. It betrays a cross-gendering of the oppositions dear to the structuralist analysis, as though the text desired more room for indeterminacy and play than an imposed structure of binary oppositions would allow. In the context of Teresa de Lauretis's and other feminist theorists' notions of alternatives to the traditional masculinist narrative paradigm, *The White Peacock* suggests a feminine unwillingness perhaps to accept the imposition of a rigid structure embodied in the investment in closure.

2

De-Oedipalizing *Sons and Lovers*

If ever there was a literary text that deserved to be liberated from biographical readings, *Sons and Lovers* has to be among the first to qualify. Unfortunately, because the second draft, "Paul Morel," no longer exists, it is impossible to compare it with the third and final draft of *Sons and Lovers* to map the extent of the misreading of "Paul Morel" by Frieda Lawrence, who convinced herself that she understood "Freud." Grounded in traditionally simplistic conceptions of the relationship between "biography" and narrative, readings of *Sons and Lovers* have consistently assumed that the revision of "Paul Morel" allowed its author to integrate what could not have been more than the most simplistic notion of the "Oedipus complex" to "unlock the secrets" of the author's own "neurosis" by developing more fully the allegedly autobiographical character's strained relations with various female characters in the narrative.[1] Such a construction of the "romance" of the final stages of this text's preparation posits a sense of the author experiencing an eerie feeling of wonder when Frieda as Freudian detective began to unlock so many "mysteries" of the Lawrence family's dysfunctional condition with the "key" of the Oedipus complex, or the "family romance." Because this so-called Freudian reading of "Paul Morel" was so deeply implicated in

Lawrence's revisions of the text, it might be appropriate to begin with what has constituted the "Freudian" *Sons and Lovers* in its simplest, and perhaps most simplistic, form by turning to Daniel Weiss's *Oedipus in Nottingham* (1962).

Weiss begins to map the Oedipal terrain of *Sons and Lovers* with an examination of Paul Morel's antagonism against/hatred of his father, reminding his readers that in what is probably the earliest draft of the novel Paul plots the death of his father, Walter, after the latter is released from prison, where he served a sentence for accidentally killing the son's older brother. (This is an Oedipal killing of two birds with one stone that Weiss seems to have missed as grist for his mill, to mix metaphors.) The early scenes of *Sons and Lovers,* before the Oedipal son makes his debut, demonstrate the "tumescent" father, Weiss explains, as an expression of the "phallic motif." Walter's "detumescence" had already begun before his son's birth, as demonstrated by his loss of ascendancy in the family. The first haircut the father gives the oldest son, William, is predictably cast by Weiss as a "symbolic castration." The father's acts of increasing violence toward the mother may be viewed in this context as mere expressions of the adolescent son's virginal fantasies of identifying sex with violence, presumably making these episodes of spousal abuse into varieties of "primal scenes." As a modern, working-class "Claudius," Morel as father shrinks, or "detumesces," in the face of his son and rival, upon whom the "queenly" mother bestows the loyalty and affection diverted from her husband. Eventually, the son finds a surrogate for the shrunken father in Baxter Dawes, whose wife, Clara, Paul can never fully enjoy and must return to her "rightful" lover (Weiss 21–25).

The role of mother to this modern Midlands Oedipus is played out by Gertrude. Having cast out her husband from her affections, she turns first to her oldest son, William, who becomes her knightly lover traveling off first to Nottingham and eventually to London as the representative of her own suppressed aspirations for self-development. As forerunner to Paul in this Oedipal scenario, William offers the appropriate conclusion to this family romance: the wages of Oedipal love are death. Crooning a morose "I want a girl just like the girl who married dear, old Dad," sweet William withers away, rather than face a fate worse than death: marrying Gyp, a girl as little like the one his father married as the son could possibly find. Once Paul shows the grieving Gertrude he too can die—almost—of unrequited love for the mother, he is ready to supplant his brother in the role of knight errant performing for her queenly affections.

Having played understudy to William's *jeune premier* role literally all his life, Paul the younger son almost kills himself in the effort at seeking women to love, only to find them inadequate, compared to his first love. Miriam, it turns out, is his mother as "virginal madonna," Weiss explains, in her moral purity and religiosity. As one variety of "devouring mother,"[2] she would put him in her pocket and smother him, presumably enacting in this "Freudian" context a reversal of childbirth, or perhaps a vaginal ingestion? The possibilities here are endless, yet endlessly reductive since the Oedipal son seems to testify to his status as such, whichever way he turns. In ironically finding in Miriam and later in Clara lovers who are like his mother, Paul is presumably Oedipus again, ostensibly fleeing the mother in obedience to the incest taboo, only to bed his mother unwittingly in another guise, like his ancient Greek forerunner, who fled his foster mother only to end up in his birth mother's bed. Following this Oedipal reconstruction, even Clara doesn't stand a chance, because although she is quite different in personality and temperament she is a married woman and therefore sexually initiated, like the mother figure. As Weiss succinctly renders it, "Paul's relationship with Miriam fails because his repressed image of the beloved is fundamentally denied him. Like Ophelia she is sexually desirable, or should be, but her virginity is a supreme article of her desirability. With her as with his mother, Paul cannot act out the desired incest. His relationship with Clara, on the other hand, succeeds and fails in turn because his repressed image of the beloved mother is realized in every essential" (59). Paul succeeds in overcoming his Oedipus complex, Weiss suggests, by adopting the values of the Father. In walking toward that "faintly humming, glowing town" he is, in the words of Weiss, "accepting his father, an idealized image, like Hamlet's father, a 'man,' with all the expansive attributes the generic term allows" (66).

Deromanticizing the Unconscious

This summarized rendition of *Sons and Lovers* à la "Freud" by Weiss could be dismissed as an expression of the rather reductive limits to which so-called psychoanalytic criticism can go in its efforts to apply psychoanalytic insights to literary texts. Unfortunately, Weiss is not alone in his (mis)reading, and it is all too easy to find others who have been fatally attracted to similarly simplistic conclusions. Scott Sanders, a contemporary of Weiss, comments, for example: "For Paul Morel all women appeared as mother and hence are forbidden objects of sexual love" (131). The not-so-hidden agenda of this "Freudianalysis" is patent: analyze the characters as surrogates for the author. Thus, Sanders in reading *Women in Love* asserts: "Just from his suppression of the 'Prologue' and excisions in the text, Lawrence himself clearly felt that defense was necessary. Behind the notion of *Blutbrüderschaft* lurks the less mysterious reality of homosexual love which he was unwilling or unable to acknowledge" (126). It is precisely this kind of interpretive detective work from which this text and others deserve to be liberated.

At the risk of belaboring what may be already apparent, it is imperative to stress the assumptions inherent in these more traditional readings of this text in order to construct a new framework for reading *Sons and Lovers*. First, it is impossible to miss the sense of "application" brought to our attention by Shoshana Felman's brilliant deconstruction of the literature and psychoanalysis binary. Clearly, "Freud," or an exegesis grounded in psychoanalysis as scientific discourse, must end up privileging itself over the literary text, whose function is reduced to serving the explicator's preoccupation with the Freudian Oedipal text as though it had a transcendental "truth" value. Such explication as a variety of "Sherlockholmesing"[3] is grounded, then, in a binary of text and outside-text which in privileging that outside-text inevitably diminishes the text itself. Second, the inescapable knowledge of this text's biographical "origins" locks it into yet another binary—"author" and text. Once again, "author" is inevitably privileged over literary text.[4] The "author" is constructed as an "outside" to which the text serves as mere vehicle; or, to shift figures, the text is a maze constructed by a Daedalus for the clever reader to discover its secrets and bear them to the outside, where they have value. In the case of this "author," "Lawrence," the text *Sons and Lovers* is a Sherlock Holmes story covering the "secrets," or "truth," of his sexuality.

One is tempted merely to begin with H. M. Daleski's sensible general starting point in discussing a key relationship in *Sons and Lovers:* "The clash between Paul and Morel is of course a striking example of an oedipal situation" (51), with Daleski's "of course" suggesting that we need to move on. As an alternative to the "Freudian" readings of *Sons and Lovers,* which the author himself found irresistible, I propose a postmodern psychoanalytic reading of this novel in the context of Jacques Lacan and his readers, as practiced by theorists like Shoshana Felman and Peter Brooks. A postmodern psychoanalytic reading would not be intent upon the "psychoanalytic study of authors, readers, or fictional characters,"[5] as though such "characters" were historical figures. Instead, this "narratology" attempts to apply psychoanalytic insights to narrative and intersubjectivity, or the interchange between "subjects."

Like Freud's, the psychology associated with Lacan's writings is grounded in a notion of the unconscious. For Lacan, however, the unconscious was not Freud's romantically dark and chaotic underworld of irrational drives or instincts, the source of neurotic, even incestuous impulses. Lawrence himself had his reservations about the Freudian unconscious, dismissing it as "the cellar where the mind keeps its own bastard spawn."[6] For Lacan, the unconscious is a fabric or text woven from the infant's reception of auditory and visual images, from birth onward and perhaps even before. The unconscious is a structure of words (even before those words are "understood") as well as auditory and visual images that the infant receives through the ear and eye, but especially the eye. Because it is born "premature," the infant is absolutely dependent upon its female caregiver and spends its first six months restricted to hearing and gazing at what is closest to it. In this stage, the maternal body and objects, as well as the objects of hearing and gazing, become confused. The French psychoanalyst Michelle Montrelay writes: "hearing is very close to the eye, which is seen by the child as an eye-ear, an open hole."[7] In this way, the unconscious becomes associated with all those early images and sensory experiences taken in by the eye and ear. This visual-verbal construct forms the abstract signifiers, or what Lacan calls the "letters" of the body, the effects of outside phenomena through touch, the gaze, sounds, and images. The body is thus eroticized, as these external signifiers become associated with the "letters" of the body, or the erotogenic zones, which Freud termed "mouth, anus, phallus, genitals." As "letters" or erotogenic zones of the (m)Other, voice and eye become erotic organs, or part objects of Desire.

Such a focus upon infancy led to Lacan's theory of the *stade du miroir*, or the "mirror stage." In the attempt here (and elsewhere) to avoid the fate of Freud, whose thinking was regularized into a variety of dogma by his followers, Lacan is typically elusive about the mirror stage.[8] Lacan writes that sometime between the ages of six and eighteen months the infant has a literal encounter with the mirror in which it discovers difference in the mirror image; alternatively, the mother/other female caregiver herself functions as a mirror or reflection of the subject. Whether it is a literal mirror image or a reflection of the (m)other, what is perceived by the infant is the first expression of an other as totalized unity, distinct from the subject's perception of itself as fragmented and dispersed. In contrast to the subject's conglomeration of sense impressions, feelings, desires, as well as its bumbling movements, the mirror image offers something like an epiphanic revelation: the subject perceives the image of the other as static, symmetrical, statuelike—an ideal unity. The subject's jubilation in discovering an ideal outside itself is at the same time the beginning of alienation, a movement away from a natural fusion with the (m)other, the first step toward dependence upon culture. Because he was as much a poet as he was a scientist, Lacan wanted to preserve the ambivalence of the mirror stage so that the mirror can function both as metaphor and as a literal vehicle for the subject's identification with an idealized image outside itself. Because the (m)other functions for the infant in the first eighteen months as a kind of mirror, she becomes implicated in the special sense of doubleness in the developing infant as the child nears the Lacanian version of the Oedipal stage: the subject is at one and the same time a "1" in its Edenic fusion with the (m)other before the fall into language as well as a "2" as it accomplishes the individuation of its move into the register of the Symbolic. This stage of unity and harmony is, therefore, fraught with anxiety since the (m)other cannot be possessed. Indeed, when the eighteen-month-old discovers that its parents do not uniformly respond to its demands, it is ready to move from the Imaginary to the Symbolic.

At eighteen months, the subject also has achieved some mastery of motor coordination, and its psychic energies can now be directed, as Lacan suggests, toward mastery of this foreign language that has had its impact upon the subject since birth. The father, or another male, intrudes upon the mother-child dyad as a representation of the *Nom-du-Pere,* or the Name-of-the-Father. In English, we miss Lacan's punning on the French homonyms *nom* and *non,* or "name" and "no." For Lacan, the Oedipal impulse is not so much the infant's incestuous desire to possess the mother sexually as it is the impulse to preserve symbiotic unity with the (m)other, even though that unity has been paid for with the repression of difference. At the very time, then, that the infant is learning to represent things as words, the Name-of-the-Father (once again, represented by the literal father or some other adult male) is intervening with its "no" to the desire for unity, a prohibition commensurate with the subject's recognition of its own psychic boundaries. In this way, the subject's development from nature to culture, from symbiotic unity to individuation, is inevitably implicated in language and the threat of castration. For Lacan, castration is clearly not a physical threat of emasculation but the metaphorical representation of the trauma of loss, the separation from the mother, the acknowledgment of difference and individuation, experienced by the female child as well as the male.[9] From this point the Phallus is forever a metaphor, a "phallic signifier" (*Écrits* 291) in the Symbolic register, rather than the penis, clitoris, or genitalia as a whole.

Lacan also draws upon the modern linguistic notion of language as both *langue,* or "linguistic and informational meaning," from the conscious, and *parole,* or "truth value meaning," from the unconscious. The former is associated with the Law and the Name-of-the-Father, with culture and reason, with metaphor and the Symbolic; the latter, with Desire and the mother, with nature, with metonymy and the Imaginary. Thus, the conscious and unconscious cannot be separated; both are involved in an inevitable interchange. The conscious, as it is implicated in language, represents the repressed text of the unconscious. Since the unconscious is structured like a language, and metaphor is the means by which a signifier replaces another signifier repressed beneath the bar separating off the unconscious, metaphor indicates both that repression and the possibility for the language of the unconscious to cross the bar, surfacing as veiled within the conscious. Metaphor, in this context, both represses the signified in the unconscious and allows the signified expression in a different form.

In a sense, Lacan deconstructs the polarity of the conscious/unconscious. In this deconstruction, he moves toward a position with which Lawrence would have been sympathetic. In an effort to restore a saner sense of the unconscious as the "good darkness,"[10] Lawrence may have overstated its agency. He was attracted to the notion of conflict and polarity, the fire and water resolving themselves for a moment as the rainbow. Lacan would have been a brother poet in this regard, for he was also aware that one disastrous consequence of polarities is the inevitable privileging of one over the other. Lacan held out for not only the interdependency of the unconscious with other aspects of the subject's psyche but also the notion of the unconscious as the matrix of Desire.

The Oedipal stage, then, for Lacan is the male or female infant, submitting its sexuality to the Name-of-the-Father as the Symbolic order requires accession to language and individuation. Rather than being innate, gender is the result of an alignment with sameness—the mother, primary Desire, the female—or with difference—the Law of the Name-of-the-Father, the male. A subject assumes maleness or femaleness by identifying or not identifying with the phallic signifier. The father stands for the Symbolic order mediating between the Imaginary, associated with the mother, on the one hand, and the Real, on the other. The biological father is the presence signifying the effects of the Real, while the mother is the first real Other, a signifier of primordial unconscious.

Although it is not entirely accurate to identify the conscious with the register of the Symbolic and the unconscious with the register of the Imaginary, it is an attractive identification and difficult to resist. The registers of the Imaginary and the Symbolic coexist for Lacan in the subject without the Symbolic necessarily being superior to or an advancement beyond the Imaginary. The complexity of that schema—suggesting Lacan once again as a poet rather than a scientist—offers the possibilities for avoiding the privileging of the conscious over the unconscious to which Lawrence was reacting so violently in Freud's construction of the unconscious as "the cellar where the mind keeps its own bastard spawn." Implicit in that reaction against the categorizing, dichotomizing impulse of the more scientific Freud is also Lawrence's uneasy accommodation to the moral implications of the "failure" to work beyond the "Oedipus complex" toward moral and sexual health as an adult. In the Lacanian schema, the registers of the Imaginary and the Symbolic are implicated in a permanent interchange: the subject doesn't successfully achieve the register of the Symbolic and forever cast the Imaginary down into the "cellar," for in the Imaginary, or the Lacanian unconscious, we locate the lost territory of Desire, to cast the unconscious in romantic terms. The subject falls into consciousness and the potential for symbolic representation; the price the subject pays for that fall is expulsion from the full citizenship in the register of the Imaginary. This complexity of psychic being à la Lacan would perhaps have been more attractive to a poetic thinker like Lawrence than the Freudian thinking that his followers turned into a dogma for saving sick souls from the ravages of infantile immersions in Oedipus complexes.

It is difficult to avoid drawing the work of Gilles Deleuze and Félix

Guattari into this discussion of the Oedipal triangle—what the two theorists call the "daddy-mommy-me triangle," or "nuclear complex"—even though it is impossible to summarize the complexities of their *Anti-Oedipus* in a few sentences. The "anti-Oedipus" of their title indicates their resistance to what they read as the dogma of the Oedipus complex by which traditional psychoanalysis justifies the repression of desire. They argue that psychoanalysis "injected" Oedipus into the unconscious, and although they accept "an Oedipal sexuality" they reject its production by the unconscious. The triangulation of "being daddy, mommy, or child" initiates the "reign of the 'either/or' in the differentiating function of the prohibition of incest: here is where mommy begins, there daddy, and there you are—stay in your place. Oedipus's misfortune is indeed that it no longer knows who begins where, nor who is who" (75).

Instead of Freud's Oedipus, which adjusts to the repression of desire, Deleuze and Guattari opt for an Oedipus that is undecidable or undifferentiated, in an effort to replace psychoanalysis with a "schizoanalysis" whose "aim is to de-oedipalize the unconscious in order to reach the real problems" (81). Their concern is with finding a means of liberating what they call "desire-production" from the repression inherent in the notion of the Oedipus complex.[11]

Finally, apropos this project, Deleuze and Guattari refer to Lawrence himself while explaining how "Oedipus is a factitious product of psychic repression."

> D. H. Lawrence—who does not struggle against Freud in the name of the rights of the Ideal, but who speaks by virtue of the flows of sexuality and the intensities of the unconscious, and who is incensed and bewildered by what Freud is doing when he closets sexuality in the Oedipal nursery—has a foreboding of this operation of displacement, and protests with all his might: no, Oedipus is not a state of desire and the drives, it is an *idea* that repression inspires in us concerning desire; not even a compromise, but an idea in the service of repression, its propaganda, or its propagation. (115)[12]

They close their useful discussion of the Oedipus complex by writing:

> Oedipal desires are not at all repressed, nor do they have any reason to be. They are nevertheless in an intimate relationship with psychic repression, but in a different manner. Oedipal desires are

> the bait, the disfigured image by means of which repression catches desire in the trap. If desire is repressed, this is not because it is desire for the mother and for the death of the father; on the contrary, desire becomes that only because it is repressed, it takes on that mask only under the reign of the repression that models the mask for it and plasters it on its face. (116)

Infancy

In examining Lacan's writing on infancy, Ellie Ragland-Sullivan draws the reader into some provocative speculation about what contemporary research has taught concerning the physiological construction of gender during the period from the completion of the mirror stage to the age of five. As we now know, concrete and verbal functions are the province of the left hemisphere of the brain, while abstract and spatial functions are the province of the right. The "lateralizing," or specializing, of these left-brain, right-brain functions is not completed, however, until the subject is five, the very age at which "grammar is acquired and a primary sexual identity fixed" (291). In this way, identification with the natural, with the female principle, structures the left brain as concrete and verbal, while identification with the male principle and a movement away from loss structures the right brain as the result of the association with the abstract phallic signifier. Thus, during these years, gender is being constructed physiologically as the hemispheres of the brain are being specialized as more "female," that is, concrete and verbal, or "male," abstract and spatial. Can this hypothesis help to explain, Ragland-Sullivan speculates, the concrete and verbal tendencies of some men who frequently identify themselves with their mothers rather than their lower-class (and often absent) fathers?

It is Ellie Ragland-Sullivan's provocative question about gender orientations of lower-class sons who identify themselves with their mothers that helps to open the text of *Sons and Lovers*. The narrative focuses upon the subject Paul Morel only belatedly, after an extensive description of the parents' courtship and marriage. Dominant in the descriptions of the courting parents are the "erotic organs" of the voice and eye. It is through the mother's eyes that the father is introduced with his "wavy black hair," "vigorous black beard," his "ruddy" cheeks, and "red, moist mouth," the latter noticeable because "he laughed so often and so heartily" (*SL* 17). Through repetition, the narrative stresses how she "watched him fascinated." Other than perhaps "her blue eyes . . . very straight, honest and searching," she is not described as she appeared in his eyes. He is "melted away before her," not because of her physical appearance but because she speaks "with a southern pronunciation and a purity of English which thrilled him to hear." From the beginning, it is her voice that "fascinates" him, while it is "the dusky, golden softness of this man's sensuous flame of life" that fascinates her through her eyes. Although he initiates their relationship by inviting her to dance, it is she who pursues him visually, her eyes ensnared by his beauty—an inversion of the male gaze—while he is fascinated by her voice and the power of language. Years later, when Paul as a young man experiences "strife in love," the narrative allows him to view his father's half-naked body through his mother's still-passionate gaze and to complain to Miriam that she lacks Mrs. Morel's response of fascinated looking. Thus, even before Paul is born, we are introduced to his parents as inversions of conventional gender associations—she is the fascinating speaker, and he, the sensuous object of her fascinated gaze.

The infancy of Paul as the focus of this narrative is framed by the representation of the infancies of the other Morel children. The infancy of William is memorable for the episode of the father's shearing those golden locks that had ensnared the mother's loving gaze. In its staging of this intrusive, prohibiting father holding those shears like the sword of the archangel Michael casting the firstborn out of the Eden of harmony with the mother's body, especially in conjunction with the mother's rare sobbing as she buries her face in his shorn hair, the passage seems almost a parody of popularized Freudian "castration," for William at a year old cannot conceivably have wished to remove his father as a rival in order to appropriate his mother sexually. On the other hand, we can conceive of a preconscious but sentient subject who experiences this threat to the *jouissance*, the sheer physical ecstasy of connection with the mother's body. Much as she will eventually claim to have been silly in this overreaction and admit that the child's hair would have needed cutting anyway, the mother remembers the event for the rest of her life, "as one in which she suffered the most intensely." The birth of Annie, the next Morel child, is not even "announced": she is first referred to in this pre-Paul retrospective when William is old enough to swim naked in the "dipping hole" and Annie to play under the hedge. It is as though Annie as a female simply materializes—as the adult Athena sprang from the forehead of

Zeus. The infancy of Paul, on the other hand, is "special"—even prenatally. In fact, his infancy is so special that the narrative lavishes an inordinate amount of attention on it, marking a radical departure from the conventional "biographical" novel in which the narrative is often impatient to get on to the viewpoint character's young adult life.

The narrative stages a primal scene for the Paul figure in the famous moonlight-and-lilies episode, an aftermath of his parents' row when the drunken father shuts the mother out in the garden. Appropriately, the mother's pregnancy is divulged by the narrative only after she has been ejected from her husband's house. The fetus Paul "boiled within her." Granted this "boiling" takes place in the context of the "shock to her inflamed soul," "seared with passion" and subjected to the cold shower of "great white light." Still, the narrative allows this subject-to-be-Paul the experience of a world beyond the womb, as that phenomenal world has an impact upon the mother's body—a body not yet different from his own. The mother, the narrative indicates, "lost herself awhile. She did not know what she thought. Except for a slight feeling of sickness, and her consciousness in the child, her self melted out like scent into the shiny, pale air." Eventually, "the child too melted with her in the mixing-pot of moonlight, and she rested with the hills and lilies and houses, all swum together in a kind of swoon" (34). In this way, the narrative offers an attempt to recover the experience of *jouissance,* resulting from a memory of limitless joy in the paradise lost of the subject's harmony with the body of the mother. Nowhere else in literature does one find such a transposition of that *jouissance* from infancy back to its prenatal antecedent. In that "swoon" from which "she came to herself" again, the mother perhaps recovers her own unnamed mother whom she loved "best of all," the "gentle, humorous, kindly-soul mother" toward whom Gertrude's father was "overbearing."

In this way, through the fetus she carries, the mother may have recuperated the joyful connection with her own mother, as that loss is replicated in her joy of intense connectedness with him. In the key scene of her holding the newborn up to the sun, a "heavenly father," the mother "felt as if the navel string that had connected its frail little body with hers had not been broken. A wave of hot love went over her to the infant. She held it close to her face and breast" (51). What the narrative offers next can only be read as an uncanny anticipation of Lacan: "Its clear, knowing eyes gave her pain and fear. Did it know all about her? When it lay under her heart, had it been listening then? Was there a reproach in the look?" (51). To these rhetorical questions the narrative is clearly positing an affirmative response: Yes! The prenatal Paul did, indeed, *listen* under her heart, and after birth as well, to the wash of auditory images from without. Even more appropriately, the narrative marks the mother's consciousness as the site of the gaze of her infant's "knowing eyes." The text could not more clearly foreground the centrality of the Lacanian gaze in the mother-infant relationship: "Its deep blue eyes, always looking up at her unblinking, seemed to draw her innermost thoughts out of her" (50–51). That gaze has already been able to read her as co-extensive with the infant subject's being, to know a *jouissance* that it will ultimately lose and futilely seek to recuperate in all later relationships. It is precisely at this point that she thrusts him up toward the sun, as if it, and not the biological father, were her infant's true progenitor, mimicking some primitive ritual in which the newborn's father introduces it to the cosmos. *She* names the subject, confirming, as Gerald Doherty reminds us, that Paul is "*her* son (not Morel's) in the fiction that follows" ("Dialectic" 333). The function of her naming of Paul is to short-circuit the scene that conventionally comes much later in the development of the subject when the Name-of-the-Father initiates the subject into individuation and subjectivity with the prohibitory *Nom/non* of movement into the Symbolic register of language.

This episode of the mother's authorizing the neonate's true paternity ends with a counterpart to the prenatal moonlight-and-lilies episode. The outcome of the dispute between the parents is blood dripping onto the infant's shawl, and then into its "fragile, glistening hair." The father, the narrative indicates, watches "fascinated," and then "his manhood broke" (*SL* 55). The focus upon his "fascinated" gaze at the blood dripping into the infant's hair reinscribes the earlier hair-clipping passage. Once again, well before the Lacanian "castration" scene in which the subject is forced to acknowledge the Name/No-of-the-Father and thereby be initiated into the Symbolic register of language and culture, Walter has proved to be ineffectual in fulfilling that function. What in a traditional Freudian context might be read as a dysfunctioning of the "daddy" in Deleuze and Guattari's "nuclear complex," robbing the infant of the "opportunity" to gain access to the Symbolic and representation seems, instead, a casting of the infant's lot with the Imaginary, or with the "female," or "concrete and verbal" domain as suggested by Ragland-Sullivan.

The engendering of language foregrounds what Paul Delany calls the "positional warfare" of the parents ("Morel Marriage" 161). It is through verbal impotence, rather than drunken violence, that the father breaks his manhood. His wife might have felt sorry for him if he had apologized. She expects him to fulfill his responsibility as the Law of the Name-of-the-Father, to be a master of language, but he cannot: "He had hurt himself most. And he was the more damaged, because he would never say a word to her, or express his sorrow" (*SL* 55). His gestures, action, even his physical bearing may "express his sorrow," but she insists upon representation of meaning in language, in the signifiers associated with her own father, and the Name-of-the-Father. "And so he broke himself" (56). Appropriately for our concern with gender and language, the son will represent his own accession to masculinity through the "baptism of fire in passion" in the dialect of his father.

In this way, the son is not, in a simplistic sense, rendered dysfunctional by the father's failure to function as the Name/No-of-the-Father, for, as we shall see, other males will fulfill that function. Language, if it is to be associated with the "abstract and spatial" aspects of the "male" domain, is in fact more closely connected in the infant Paul with the mother and the female, what Ellie Ragland-Sullivan terms the "concrete and verbal." Perhaps appropriately for the future "artist" Paul, language remains in the realm of what Julia Kristeva terms the "semiotic" rather than the "symbolic," and any discussion of gender and language would be incomplete without at least an acknowledgment of Kristeva's contribution to this discourse.

Because of the male associations of the Name-of-the-Father through whose Law the subject is ushered into the Symbolic register, Kristeva as a feminist reader of Lacan focuses her attention upon the preverbal or presymbolic state, or the "semiotic." Rather than a "principle of an operational state," Kristeva posits the semiotic as "a preverbal functional state that governs the connections between the body (in the process of constituting itself as a body proper), objects, and the protagonists of family structure." She continues: "The kinetic functional stage of the *semiotic* precedes the establishment of the sign; it is not, therefore, cognitive in the sense of being assumed by a knowing, already constituted subject" (*Revolution* 95). A corollary of Lacan's Imaginary register, the semiotic is implicated in *signifiance,* a signifying practice before the advent of the sign and signification. She writes: "Magic, shamanism, esoterism, the carnival, and 'incomprehensible' poetry all underscore the limits of socially useful discourse and attest to what it represses: the *process* that exceeds the subject and his communicative structures" (16). This "signifiance" is an "unlimited and unbounded generating process," an "unceasing operation of the instinctual drives toward, in, and through language" (16). It is the relationship of the semiotic that is, of course, most pertinent here. When Kristeva suggests that the rhythm of the semiotic is "indifferent to language [as signification], enigmatic, feminine, this space underlying the written is rhythmic, unfettered, irreducible to its intelligible verbal translation" (29), it becomes clear we are in a realm where it is appropriate to think of language as gendered; that is, Kristeva is establishing feminine associations with the semiotic and masculine with the Symbolic, presumably within a context where gender is not tied to sex or biological differences. Her work offers a reminder that these binaries have been implicated in hierarchization: just as her "signifiance" has been marginalized by signification, so too the Symbolic has been privileged over her "semiotic." In this way, Kristeva helps to refine the movement of the Lacanian binary of Imaginary and Symbolic registers away from the Freudian binary of pre-Oedipal and Oedipal states whose linearity valorizes a moral injunction for the subject to achieve psychological success and health by moving beyond the Oedipal "stage."

To return to *Sons and Lovers,* however, this text is most importantly deconstructing the binary of the "daddy, mommy [in which is inserted], me." The borders between these traditional gender roles have been rendered indefinite by this narrative, which suggests that the son is not necessarily wounded—recall that the name *Oedipus* refers to the wounds produced by the binding of the abandoned infant's feet—but, instead, he may not have been fully recruited into the Symbolic register. Why must psychic health be equated with absolute acknowledgment of the transformation into the Symbolic—if, indeed, that is possible? Alternately, this is a self-subversive text because it is attempting, on the one hand, to credit the "nuclear complex" at the same time that it suggests that psychic health—as in the youngest son, Arthur—may have little to offer a subject except a kind of healthy nonentity and that at an early stage of development the Paul figure may have been saved from such "health" for the full range of gendered experience, especially the "concrete and verbal" within which his creativity will flourish.

Language Wars

At this point, however, the mother controls the language in the household. When the father comes down from the bedroom to Sunday tea, he eats in a silence that shuts him out from his family. Literally and figuratively, the mother and children speak another language. As the dialogue in the text graphically demonstrates, the father speaks the broad Midlands dialect, while the children are learning their mother's tongue, the Queen's English. Several days later, when the father compounds his alienation by getting caught "stealing" from his wife's purse and threatens to abandon the family, the eldest son, William, uses the most "proper English" to ask, "What shall we do?" When the father returns, he tells his wife: "You may thank your stars I've come back tonight," and, as the narrative indicates, Morel was "trying to be impressive" (*SL* 60). In this way, the mother confirms her mastery through the control of language, coercing her husband into adopting *her* tongue to be "impressive." Paul may be an infant, but these auditory images, and perhaps the sensations and feelings associated with them, have begun to inscribe themselves in the text of his unconscious.

Central to that text is the bilingual context of the Morel household. From infancy Paul has "heard" the *langue* of his father's dialect and his mother's approximation of *parole* even before he could consciously distinguish what the signifiers meant. He has heard the older siblings using standard English. We are insistently reminded of the children's approximation of standard English *until* they launch out into their father's world outside the home. A case in point is the mother's defense of William against the mother of a schoolmate with whom he has been scuffling. The mother's tongue establishes her mastery over her social inferiors. The struggle for power in the family represents itself in part as the conflict of dialects:

> "What!" cried Mrs. Morel, panting with rage. "You shall not touch him for *her* telling, you shall not!"
>
> "Shonna I?" shouted Morel. "Shonna I?"
>
> . . .
>
> "Only dare!" she said, in a loud, ringing voice. "Only dare, milord, to lay a finger on that child. You'll regret it for ever." (68)

Tangential as this concern with the young life of William may seem, it is germane, because he is Paul's forerunner and these battles are being pre-fought for the younger son.

The Law of the Name-of-the-Father generally goes unfulfilled in Walter Morel, its normative representative. Even when the Law seems to be fulfilled, as in the case of the clergyman/godfather who teaches Paul French and German, its functioning represents an extension of the mother. This unidentified individual (perhaps the shy Mr. Heaton whom the father mocked when he came home to find him talking with Gertrude) is "still a friend of Mrs. Morel." It is only for the youngest son, Arthur, that the father functions at least in part as the Name-of-the-Father. Arthur quite easily obeys the injunction to part from the realm of the Imaginary and from the mother. He looks, acts, and talks like a younger version of the father, similarities certainly not lost on the mother, who is allowed to think, "Arthur never knew how deeply he loved her" (286).

Paul, on the other hand, functions with great difficulty in the world of the father, where that difficulty is focused upon the difference between the mother's language, the Queen's English, and the dialect of his father and the townsfolk. Perhaps the best example of Paul's difficulty is the scene of anguish and humiliation in which he must do his "work" of collecting the father's weekly earnings so that the money can be divided among the miners in the father's "butty."

The narrative establishes the appearance of the men in order to clarify the viewpoint of the small and boyish Paul and the threatening adults with whom he has to contend. Mr. Braithwaite, the cashier, for example, is described as "large, somewhat of the stern patriarch in appearance, having a rather thin white beard." Paul is so small that "it was often his fate to be jammed behind the legs of the men, near the fire which scorched him" (94). Braithwaite ridicules him for answering in a voice "small and inadequate" and Braithwaite's clerk adds to the hazing: "Don't they teach you to count at the Board School?" "Nowt but algìbbra an' French," one of the colliers chimes in. The narrative underscores the obvious: Paul "suffered the tortures of the damned on these occasions" (96).

The tortures persist, however, since Paul must wait for his father at the New Inn, where the earnings are to be distributed. The father is surprisingly sensitive to the son's discomfort at having to wait for him in the pub where other colliers are also "reckoning." He speaks "tenderly" to his son and offers him a drink. When Paul goes home "glowering" to tell his mother that he will never go again, he accuses the men of being "hateful, and common," focusing upon their *language:* "Mr Braithwaite drops his 'h's, and Mr Winterbottom says, 'You was'" (97). In this way, Paul acknowledges the effects in his family of what appear to be inversions of Lacan's associations of language with the father and the Name-of-the-Father. "Proper English" in this context is associated consistently with the mother's tongue, as *she* learned her father's. It is the mother who speaks with the authority of patriarchy, not the father. In the hierarchy of dialects, the Queen's English is privileged over all other dialects, including the Midlands dialect spoken by the father and other ordinary citizens of Bestwood. The father's dialect, then, is feminized by its position of powerlessness: it is speech marginalized by what is considered the proper dialect as it is spoken by the middle and upper classes, a written language.

An interesting analog to this scene is provided in Paul's interview at the firm of Thomas Jordan, Manufacturer of Surgical Appliances, who asks him to translate an order written in French and corrects him impatiently when Paul mistranslates *doigts* as "fingers" rather than "toes." Paul is rendered speechless, or impotent, by this representative of the Name-of-the-Father, a figure of authority and yet a "little man." The mother bows to *this* representative of the Name-of-the-Father, as she sits quietly and waits submissively for this necessary business to be concluded. Later, Paul will defend his translation, insisting that "'Doigts' does mean 'fingers,'" and asking, "But wasn't Mr Jordan common, mother?" (121). As in the earlier scene of his turning to her for sympathy after collecting his father's pay, she is surprisingly unsympathetic, stressing that Paul is oversensitive. In her way, the mother emphasizes regard for the Name-of-the-Father. It is the father's ineffectuality as representative of this Name that has earned him her contempt.

The scene is repeated on Paul's first day at work, when he must confront new figures of male authority—this time without the comfort of even his mother's submissive presence. In addition to Jordan, he must deal with Pappleworth, the chief of the Spiral department, who ridicules him for his "execrable handwriting." Like the men in the cashier's office where he collected his father's earnings, Jordan and Pappleworth lament the deficiencies of modern education: "Lads learn nothing nowadays, but how to recite poetry and play the fiddle" (132). Pappleworth embarrasses Paul by asking him yet another time, "Let's see, *what's* your name?" The narrative adds: "It's curious that children suffer so much at having to pronounce their own names" (132). A child like Paul suffers because in supplying his name to these embodiments of the Name-of-the-Father he acknowledges their hegemony over the Symbolic. His only relief from that embarrassment once again is gloating as he reminds himself that Jordan is lacking as a gentleman: "he spoke bad English" (132).

This cross-gendering of language provides one of this text's most fascinating constructions. It grows out of a tension between Lacan's notion of the subject's accession to representation in the Symbolic register through accommodation to the Law of the Name-of-the-Father, on the one hand, and Ellie Ragland-Sullivan's provocative suggestions of the physiological engendering of the brain in early childhood. If she is correct in her construction of the binary of left-brain/natural/verbal and concrete/female *versus* right-brain/cultural/spatial and abstract/male, it may be no coincidence that in this text it is the mother with whom the male subject associates the "verbal and concrete," and not the father. (It may be argued, of course, that as a woman in a patriarchical structure the mother has power only as she accedes to the Law of the Name-of-the-Father.) And to deconstruct what seems a structuralist binary—if that binary has not already deconstructed itself—we need only remind ourselves that no subject is exclusively left- or right-brain, and "gender" in this context is clearly a continuum.

Family Romance

The Lacanian reworking of Freud's "family romance" is evident in a scene that configures Paul's ambivalence toward Miriam, with whom he has established a "Platonic" friendship as an outgrowth of his relationship with his parents. It is spring, and Paul, we are told, has just been promoted to spiral overseer, an indication that he is being drawn into the hierarchy of industrial management. Friday is still "reckoning night for the miners"; the father, however, now "reckons" at home because one member of his butty no longer drinks. The ritual of reckoning takes place in a "masculine privacy" that includes Paul, who moves into the reckoning scene, then back to his own "work," a fabric design for "a curtain or *portière*." When the father heads to the pub and the mother goes shopping, the son is visited by two women: first by Miriam, but more tellingly by Beatrice Wyld, an unrestrained woman who will eventually marry Arthur. Beatrice asks for one of Paul's cigarettes and laughs "wildly," paying for the cigarette with a friendly kiss on the cheek. Paul revenges himself on Miriam as an untouchable soul mate by flirting with Beatrice, using his father's tongue for the first time. "I s'll kiss thee back, Beat," Paul teases, and we suspect that he might have continued to romance this Wyld woman, were it not for Miriam's reminder that his mother's bread is burning.

That Arthur serves as a model for Paul becomes evident in the scene of Arthur's courting of Beatrice. Although the narrative offers a description of Arthur through Beatrice's eyes, we are also being encouraged to view him through Paul's eyes, just as in the earlier scene of Gertrude's still passionate gaze at Walter's upper torso as he washed himself down for the Friday night reckoning. Arthur, we are told, "grew flushed, his eyes were bright, he sang in a manly tenor. . . . He seemed to flaunt his body: she was aware of him so—the strong chest, the sides, the thighs in their close-fitting trousers." And in the very next sentence, dialect is gendered "masculine" in Arthur's replication of his father's speech, as he woos Beatrice: "He liked to lapse into the dialect when he talked to her" (287).

In this critical scene, the narrative reveals Paul negotiating the gendered differences evident in the "daddy, mommy, and me" triangle in a variation characteristic of this narrative. Here, the feminized Midlands dialect of the father and Beatrice, who is to become the youngest son's wife, is juxtaposed with the Queen's English, spoken by Miriam and the mother. These cross-genderings of dialects complicate the conventional notion of family romance or nuclear complex. Much as this son may be seen as dominated by the mother, this mother seems to be functioning as a variety of Phallic Mother, for this Queen's English she speaks is much more clearly a representation of the Law of the Name-of-the-Father. Clearly, her language represents the agency of power. The dialect of the literal father in this narrative is a language of powerlessness, of vulnerability, because it is the discourse of those who occupy feminized subject positions in this text. It is also a feminine language because it is the language of desire, as is evident in these clearly heterosexually erotic scenes. As always in a Lacanian context, to be a desiring subject is forever to be exposing one's lack or vulnerability. Thus it is that in the next passage to be examined the son speaks once again in the feminized discourse of the desiring father.

Coming through to Metaphor

These gender associations of language come together in the memorable scene in Clifton Grove. The son's almost self-conscious adopting of his father's dialect represents a fuller gesture toward an acknowledgment of the Law of the Name-of-the-Father than in the earlier scene of his flirting with Beatrice Wyld. In the Clifton Grove scene, the son begins with merely a shade of his father's language, as in the flirting scene with Beatrice—"Why dost look so heavy?"—then moves to "'Yea, tha does! Dunna thee worrit,' he implored *caressing*" (356; emphasis added). Tellingly, he later says nothing until they have completed their fifteen-minute climb to top of the riverbank, returning to his mother's tongue: "Now we're back at the ordinary level" (356).

When the son's "baptism of fire in passion" comes in the scene of the peewits, the narrative breaks out of its conventional realism—one might say, its "metonymic"—mode and opens up the possibility of metaphoricity. This is a function of metaphor suggestive of what Doherty sees as an opening up of new spaces for transformation ("Dialectic" 329). The narrative makes an effort to move beneath the surface of consciousness into a realm of desire suggestive of the garden scene in which the unborn son Paul "boils" in the mother's womb. Indeed, one senses that this realm outside consciousness parallels the lost *jouissance* of infant and mother: "The naked hunger and inevitability of his loving her [Clara], something strong and blind and ruthless in its primitiveness, made the hour terrible to her" (397). "When he came to," his consciousness is allowed the language to translate this baptism into the metaphors of immersion in the life force, to recognize "in their meeting the thrust of the manifold grass stems, the cry of the peewit, the wheel of the stars" (398). As Doherty perceptively argues, Clara functions as the "catalyst of a breaking of bounds," as metaphor remakes their relationship through its transformative agency (337). The narrative offers Paul equivalents for the empowerment of metaphoricity, the sense of a coming to consciousness as though he were brought to an acknowledgment of the Law of the Name-of-the-Father. Paul must recognize both the irrevocable loss of *jouissance*—the joyful, preconscious harmony with the mother's body—and the inevitable movement into the Symbolic register of language. The passage is crucial because its central metaphors are repeated in the ambivalent ending of the narrative: "To know their own nothingness, to know the tremendous living flood which carried them always, gave them rest within themselves. If so great a magnificent power could overwhelm them, identify them altogether with itself, so that they knew they were only grains in the tremendous heave that lifted every grass-blade its little height, and every tree, and living thing, then why fret about themselves" (398). Thus it is only through metaphor that Paul can be empowered.

The narrative's introduction of the term *identify* is worth noting here. As Diana Fuss reminds us, Freud grounded his notion of identification in metaphoricity, or the "substitution of the one for the other." She writes:

> Metaphor, *the substitution of the one for the other* [her emphasis], is internal to the work of identification. Freud's concept of self-other relations fundamentally presupposes the possibility of metaphoricity—of iterability, redoubling, translation, and transposition. The Greek *metaphora,* meaning transport, immediately implicates the transferential act of identification in the rhetorical process of figuration. Psychoanalysis, at least where its theory of identification is concerned, can actually be understood as a scientific discourse on the problem of metaphorization. (5–6)

Here, the transformative consequences of passion, figured as "baptism," are identified with a "life force" within which the lovers are immersed, as though swallowed up, or, alternately, a force that they in-corp-orate into their bodies. It is perhaps no coincidence that although the narrative indicates the plural in *they,* this transformative identification or access to metaphoricity centers in the male lover, opening up issues of gender associations of trope once again. Freud himself said that identification is "typically masculine."[13]

Riding the train back to town after having abandoned his relationships with first Clara and then Miriam, Paul is overwhelmed by the immense darkness: "In the country all was dead still. Little stars shone high up; little stars spread far away in the floodwaters, . . . the vastness and terror of the immense night" (*SL* 464). He feels like a "tiny upright speck of flesh, less than an ear of wheat lost in the field," a "spark" being pressed into extinction. It is easy to mistake the focus here. Metaphorically, a cosmic darkness is apparently so dominant that life/light seems near extinction. And yet it is not extinguished. "Little stars," "speck of flesh," "ear of wheat," as metaphors of that which counters darkness/extinction, testify to the power of transformation, transference, identification, or metaphoricity itself. In one clear sense, this narrative has decentered the binary positions of mother/father, Imaginary/Symbolic, metonymy/metaphor with which we began. The conflicting dialects of the parents subvert the expected resonances of those binaries; or, we might say that these binaries are not mutually exclusive. The mother in this narrative seems to function more as the representation of the Symbolic order, because it is with her that the son associates language or the agency of representation, while the father is positioned as vulnerable through the agency of desire. Like those positioned as vulnerable, the father can mimic the Queen's English, or his wife's tongue; however, the mother lacks either the desire or ability to mimic his representation of desire. The son has his annunciation of transformation through the father's language, a stigma of desire and its revelation of vulnerability.

This annunciation of the possibility for transformation, or metaphoricity, is implicated in another kind of identification. The trauma of losing the mother has immersed the son in melancholia, which as Freud suggests is a variety of failed mourning. Mourning may be completed when the subject identifies with or incorporates the object of loss. Melancholia is a form of self-consumption, apparent in the narrative up to this point as Paul eradicates all connectedness to others. In mourning, this son passes through identification and transference to the possibility of continuance. And it cannot be missed that this son is literally the agent of the mother's death. Fuss writes: "In identification the subject paradoxically destroys the love object only in order to preserve it: 'better fragmented, torn, cut up, swallowed, digested . . . than lost.' Ultimately, all that remains is the Other's remains; the subject becomes a veritable cemetery of lost, abandoned, and discarded objects" (38).[14] Although this narrative does not authorize the son to tell his own story once the action has been completed, it leaves the impression that Paul is in control of the text. This narrative, then, becomes, to borrow Fuss's metaphor, a "cemetery" of the remains of others as lost objects of love, and in a sense the Other's remains. The capital "O" Other has in its own way been closed off, as the subject moves forward toward the possibility of further transformation.

As Fiona Becket has also argued, Deleuze and Guattari in their *Anti-Oedipus* and, I would add, Kristeva help us to move away from the "doctrinal level," to use Becket's term, at which *Sons and Lovers* has been (mis)read. As I suggest above, traditional readings of this text, including the author's own misreading, have mired the narrative in varieties of structuralist approaches that end up valorizing the masculine over the feminine, the Symbolic over the Imaginary (or Kristeva's semiotic), as well as one dialect over another and one "stage" over another. Close attention to the text reveals, however, that it is much more self-subversive in representing gender using complicated expressions of a cross-gendering in which the traditional categories are decentered to remind readers that what they have been taught to read as mutually exclusive binaries are the ends of a continuum.

3

The Sense of an Ending in *The Rainbow*

No single element in *The Rainbow* has been more problematic than its ending. For some, this narrative lacks closure, and for others, the ending has seemed inappropriate. F. R. Leavis admits in *D. H. Lawrence, Novelist* that "in an important sense, *The Rainbow* is not a finished work," noting the "absence of any conclusion in view" (111, 172). Another reader with reservations about the ending of this text—among other aspects of the narrative—is Roger Sale, one of the earliest to comment on its "narrative technique." Sale is intent upon exploring what he sees as evidences of marked differences between segments of the text written earlier and those written later. He argues that "the reasons for the marked inferiority of the second half, the fact of which is widely enough accepted, have never been stated" and goes on to announce that his aim is to determine "when and how the novel begins to deteriorate" (29). In a similar vein, S. L. Goldberg speaks of the "emotional falsity of the last few pages . . . so glaring that *every* critic has remarked on it" (477, emphasis added). Finally, Scott Sanders expresses similar disappointment with the ending when he discusses Ursula's role as a visionary:

> Yet at the very end of the novel she can imagine no new order, only a sweeping away of the old. This closing glimmer, reflecting a hope-

> fulness which Lawrence was expressing in letters to his new friend Bertrand Russell in the early months of 1915, letters in which he spoke passionately of revolution, seems little more than a gesture on Lawrence's part, for almost every image of the "ordered world of man" which he has presented in the novel has been negative; so he registers the danger of Ursula's temporary rejection of the social, but offers nothing which could give substance to her vision of the "cultivated field." (92)

It is appropriate, then, that we revisit the ending of *The Rainbow* because the ending is *the* element that readers have found wanting in the novel.

The Rainbow ends as it does in large part because of the protracted and complicated process of its production, and no full reading of the novel's technique can be complete without some familiarity with the history of its composition. With the assistance of scholars such as Mark Kinkead-Weekes and Charles Ross, we know that *The Rainbow* was the product of Lawrence's attempt to deal with material similar to that of *Women in Love.*[1] The author wanted essentially to develop the relationship of the Ursula figure with a male figure with whom she would "come through." In order to do so, the Ursula figure needed a past from which to "come through." Successive drafts of this "pre-quel" to a yet unwritten novel reveal the narrative moving backward from Ursula to the generation of her parents and then to her grandparents. In this way, it was the sense of an ending for the characters who would become central to the novel eventually realized as *Women in Love* that generated *The Rainbow.*

The Brooksian Paradigm

Even if readers are unwilling to concur with Goldberg's assurance that "every critic" has found the ending of *The Rainbow* disappointing, or even "hollow rhetoric" (432), few would underestimate the difficulties of its ending. The last pages of the narrative may be read in light of what narratologists like Peter Brooks have theorized about the function of the endings in fiction. In his book *Reading for the Plot: Design and Intention in Narrative,* Brooks posits a theory of narrative desire, or "textual erotics," which offers a provocative framework for a discussion of *The Rainbow.*

In one sense, Brooks is engaged in an effort to recuperate the legitimacy of the term *plot,* which, like the term *character,* has been relegated to the most simplistic discourse about narrative texts. "Plot" for Brooks may be equated with "design and intention in narrative." Plot is the structure that desire in narrative generates in its movement toward "meaning," or truth value—problematic concepts for postmodern readers. This desire of the text constructs the desire of the reader, suggesting the text's autonomy once set into motion. Accordingly, the text's desire for its end parallels the reader's desire for the end of the text, for it is only its ending that can offer the reader the sense of a meaning—illusory as that "meaning" may be—toward which it has been impelled from the outset.

A narrative without an ending, for Brooks, is a contradiction in terms, an impossibility, in the same sense that a life without its ending in death would be inconceivable. Indeed, as Brooks notes, Jean-Paul Sartre asserts in *Nausea* that as a young man he was unable to plot the course of his life until he conceived of the man he wanted to be at his own death; says Sartre: "I became my own obituary."[2] It is the ending, or "death," of narrative, if anything, that confers meaning upon whatever precedes it. As Walter Benjamin writes, "Death is the sanction of everything the storyteller can tell,"[3] because narrative offers its listeners/readers what they can never really know of their own stories—the "endings" that confer whatever "meaning" is possible in narrative. Thus, it may be seen that although Brooks, as we shall see, was influenced by Lacan, it was Lacan the structuralist with whom he (and many others, like Gerald Doherty) was more comfortable, for this Brooksian paradigm for narrative is deeply implicated in the notion that narrative offers "meaning," or that Lacan himself was more interested in the signified than in the play of signifiers.[4]

Narrative is always a repetition, a representation of an action presumably completed by the time the narrating begins. Thus, the ending paradoxically precedes the beginning in a dialectic of opposing times, the time of the action juxtaposed with the time of the narration/reading. The reader of a narrative text moves through its middle with what Brooks calls "anticipation of retrospection." Accordingly, the reader leans forward in anticipation toward the ending because it, if anything, will expose the pattern for which the narrative has been shaping itself in this middle. If it is possible to conceive of a textual unconscious, narrative is thus moved forward to its ending by an instinct, in its Freudian sense of a turning back. In this case, desire for the end is in large part the instinct of the text to move toward the state of quiescence following its last word and preceding its first. On the analogy of the subject's existence in this Freudian framework, narrative is an irritation into consciousness, and into representation, from a state of quiescence and back again following the inevitable ending, or death.

Narrative for Brooks, then, is energized by a dialectic of opposing desires. One is a desire for the end, a kind of death wish, and the other is a variety of Eros, or life wish, if you will. Here, Brooks draws upon Freud's notion of an Eros including sexual desire but exceeding it in a more polymorphous variety, seeking, in Freud's words, "to combine organic substances into ever greater unities."[5] This Eros paradoxically opposes yet serves the desire for the end by postponing it, but only so that it might be the right end. Implicit in narrative is always the possibility of a kind of readerly suicide, a reading ahead to know how the plot will end. At the same time, this "short-circuiting" of desire is counterproductive because whatever meaning the ending may have is implicated in the middle of plot (Brooks, *Reading* 102). This middle is the whole complex of repetitions and bindings, Brooks argues, that can be understood as the erotic. These repetitions and bindings make up the erotic as metaphor, if by that trope we understand the fundamental principle of like-but-different. Thus, plot proceeds through a series of bindings of one element to an earlier element metaphorically, constructing patterns of like-but-different repetitions. This metaphoric like-but-different principle is one of the two structuring principles of unconscious production, according to the Freud of *The Interpretation of Dreams* (1900).

This association of Eros with metaphor and repetition has far-ranging implications for readers of literary texts. As Brooks notes, "To state the matter baldly: rhyme, alliteration, assonance, meter, refrain, all the mnemonic elements of literature and indeed most of its tropes are in some manner repetitions that take us back in the text, that allow the ear, the eye, the mind to make connections, conscious or unconscious, between different textual moments, to see past and present as related and as establishing a future that will be noticeable as some variation in the pattern."[6] This binding or repetition has a dual function, according to Brooks. It connects through the principle of identification, or like-but-different. In addition, it allows the text to offer its reader something of the transformative or transfigurative function of metaphor, allowing us to see clearly in an instant a connection implicit in the very term *metapherein,* to "carry across." Readers familiar with *The Rainbow,* for example, will recall the transfigurative jolt they experience when the narrator indicates that the Ursula and Skrebensky figures are walking where Tom passed with his handful of daffodils on the way to proposing marriage to Lydia; it is the same spot where Anna and Will walked out when they were courting. This metaphor, then, locks together what might otherwise have seemed merely sequential—that is, one generation following another—by lifting the text's readers onto a plane on which they cannot miss the higher significance of the "now" in terms of the "then." Implicit here is a duality in time. The sense of a "now" is transcended periodically by the sense of a "beyond-the-now" that approaches the religious. This beyond-the-now moves both within the mundane, immersed in the material and in the details of the everyday; in addition, it moves within what has traditionally been thought of as the transcendental, so that the quotidian erupts on occasion into what appears to be a meaning beyond daily life.

The sequential or the mundane in this framework ought not, however, to be marginalized or subordinated. As we have seen, the metonymic, or the contiguous, within which Lacan follows Jakobson in conflating the synecdochic, or the detail (or part for the whole), is the powerful counterpart of the metaphoric. Indeed, as Brooks reminds us, the metonymic may at times seem even to outweigh the metaphoric, since desire, for Lacan, was always a form of metonymy, the part-for-the-whole of Desire. In this sense, narrative is drawn forward to its end through a middle of metonymically related elements, the this-and-then-that-and-then-that of plot as a chain of metonyms drawing readers through those metaphoric bindings, or moments of transfiguration, toward the inevitable death of the plot in its transformation through metaphor.

The desire for the end is a death wish, but in a crucially contemporary reading of what has seemed a Freudian cliché, Brooks, like many other contemporary literary theorists, is a neo-Freudian in his focus upon the Freud of *Beyond the Pleasure Principle* (1920), as well as other works less frequently read by American ego psychologists. The *Beyond* represents an especially useful "Freud." It offers the notion of a wish for a recovered quiescence theorized by Freud to be a kind of prenatal state before the subject was "irritated" into life. The *Beyond* has its roots in Freud's struggle to understand experience outside, or beyond, the principle of wish fulfillment he had formulated for the activity of the unconscious. If the dream is energized by an unconscious fulfillment of desire for pleasure, bad dreams—especially the repeated nightmares of traumatized survivors of the Great War's battlefields offering no discernible "pleasure"—understandably rendered Freud's earlier concept of the pleasure principle problematic. The solution to this puzzle came to him, he would have us believe, while he was observing his infant grandson throwing and retrieving a spool on a string, accompanied by the endless repetition of the syllables Freud read as the *oo* and *ah* of the German words *Fort* and *Da,* or "gone" and "there."[7] The repeated throwing and retrieving of the spool seemed to the Freud of the *Beyond* to be the infant's construction of control in the face of the unpredictable departure of the mother. It represented a means of introjecting the mother's absence by stage-managing not only the withdrawal but also the undoing of that withdrawal with her return. Brooks, as a follower of Lacan's post-Freudian reading of the *Beyond,* is less interested in the psychology of the child's exerting control over the undependable mother than the linguistic import of the infant's ascension into the Symbolic. In this way, the toddler's casting away and retrieving the spool as a "Symbol" of the Mother is less important for Lacan than those first words, the diametrically opposed syllables of absence and presence with their implicit conveyance of the subject up into the register of the Symbolic in which language as representation is justified as a means of confronting absence, or Lacanian "lack." The representation of presence in the *Da,* or "there," is made possible by the representation of its grounding in that *Fort,* or "gone." The Symbolic as the potential for representation is the consolation for irretrievable loss, the separation from the Imaginary register in which the subject has been immersed.

It is not too early at this point to note the essentially structuralist system of Freud's discourse, a structuralism Lacan adopts in Freud's writing (and Jakobson's) and usually ends by problematizing. In this context, Brooks too is attracted to the essentially binary implications he reads in the powerful tropological system of metonymy and metaphor. For the purposes of the present project, however, it is necessary first to accept the Freudian/Brooksian binaries and, in the exploration of *The Rainbow* as text, to look forward to a deconstruction of these two tropes, following the lead of Christian Metz in his seminal work *The Imaginary Signifier.*[8]

Central, then, to a Brooksian notion of plot is a dynamic of desire, or "textual erotics," within which the reader is implicated in the text as it is being drawn in opposing directions. The text is of necessity both metonymic and metaphoric, in its movement forward through its contiguously arranged particulars, on the one hand, or metaphorically bound in a series of metaphoric transformations, culminating in its ending, on the other hand. Following the lead of feminists like Irigaray and Gallop who read gender—although not necessarily traditional sex—distinctions in these powerful tropes, it is possible also to read metonymy as "feminine" and metaphor as "masculine" in a kind of narratological framework within which genre and gender are linked through their tropological associations with the metaphoric and the metonymic.

The Rainbow's Two Beginnings

Another of those who might have been included earlier as expressing reservations about the structure of *The Rainbow* is Mark Kinkead-Weekes, one of this narrative's most perceptive readers. Kinkead-Weekes reminds readers of how the "opening chapter of *The Rainbow* is, rather pointedly, divided into two: a first section beginning with a timeless world; a second section beginning with a date"; he goes on to describe at length two diametrically opposed readings of the novel: an "archetypal, [and] a historical view" ("Marriage" 9). Clearly, as Kinkead-Weekes indicates, the "archetypal" has generally been privileged over the "historical view." Why that has been the case and why readers have had their reservations about various elements in this novel, especially its ending, become clearer as we focus upon the dynamic of opposing narrative elements here.

Kinkead-Weekes's two ways of looking at the first chapter and indeed the whole text—the archetypal and the historical—are inherent in Brooks's notions of the dynamic generated by the opposing desires in narrative. It is difficult to begin a discussion of the opening five pages of *The Rainbow,* especially the first two, without hearing Gavriel Ben-Ephraim's pointed reminder that this passage has been "overanalyzed" (132). That probably has been the case in large part because, as Kinkead-Weekes and Ross have demonstrated, these passages date from the later stages of the composition process. It is this belated status that lends the passage its power and justifies the extensive analysis pointed out by Ben-Ephraim almost two decades ago. The passage clearly anticipates the ending of the narrative. More importantly, it establishes what I would denote as the metaphoric/poetic/masculine pole of the dialectic energizing desire in this text.

First, by calling the passage "poetic" I mean to do more than call attention to its rich texture of strong images drawn from the natural world. I prefer to use the term *poetic* as Jakobson and Lacan do in associating romantic/symbolist poetry with metaphor and with the principle of identification or similarity in Freud's schema for the unconscious, in contrast to the association/displacement/contiguity principle. As Ben-Ephraim notes, these first pages celebrate "the untrammeled oneness of man and nature" (132), to employ two terms problematized by a post-modern context. The old-fashioned term *man* is appropriate, for much as we might have once wanted to think we were being inclusive in using the term *man,* it is clearly the *men* here who are more intimately involved in that oneness central to the principle of identification of man with nature, with their suspect metaphysical trappings, each clearly being a cultural construction. It is the men who were at one time immersed in this "intercourse" with the natural world connecting the "rush" of their own "sap in spring" and the throwing of their own "seed" forward each year. It is "the body of the men" that has been "impregnated" with that identification, an interesting cross-gendering within which some "life force" is fertilizing the men who are implicated in its agency (*R* 9–10). This is the metaphoric, or identificatory, move in narrative. It is, however, the metaphoric without the transformative component that we find in the very last, framing pages of the novel. In this context, Kinkead-Weekes is exactly right in reminding us of the need to free gender from sex:

> And one must not talk too glibly of "Men" and "Women." It very soon becomes clear that we are not meant to think of male and female in any simply differentiated way—we shall soon find both impulses, or forces, operating in everyone of either sex, though in differing proportions. Nor can there be any question of choice or preference: it seems self-evident that life at either extreme would be life impoverished. Rather we are to see all human beings as subject to oppositional pulls of these impulses or kinds of consciousness, below the surface of particular character or deliberate choice. ("Marriage" 24)

Kinkead-Weekes lends important support to the beginning of an effort to liberate this text from the simplistic structuralist binaries of men/women, fire/water, and, yes, perhaps even metonymy and metaphor!

Thus, from the very beginning, the text has disconnected gender from sex in its awareness of how the subject ranges from what we have conventionally considered masculinity at one end of the spectrum to femininity at the other. Indeed, it is the women who function at the end of the gender spectrum that is opposed to their traditional sex roles. The Brangwen men look at their world—"The young corn waved and was silken, and the lustre slid along the limbs of the men who saw it" (*R* 10)—in acknowledgment. However, the Brangwen women are the possessors of the traditionally "male" gaze. Furthermore, what they look out at is that "spoken world beyond" into which their heiress Ursula will travel. Ursula's travel cannot be authorized, however, until history, or narrative itself, begins with the first of the named Brangwen men. He must lift himself from the pre-spoken world of the Imaginary, with its illusory unity with the body of nature, into the register of Symbolic representation, to join the Brangwen women who seem to have already metaphorically made that journey toward the spoken world of the vicar and the "*Odyssey*" of local gossip about the "heroes" among them.

Then, in the longer, second segment of the first chapter, the novel begins again, or, to be more precise, begins where *Sons and Lovers* begins at the realist prose of the Jakobsonian/Lacanian polarity. This is clearly the history, or narrative, set in motion by that journey toward representation announced toward the end of chapter 1. If what Kinkead-Weekes has called the "archetypal" functions here as the metaphoric pole, the second beginning of *The Rainbow* is its other pole—the metonymic—with its emphasis upon the contiguous. This contiguous movement begins "about 1840," when the canal was "constructed," sundering forever the earlier and probably illusory sense of connectedness with their world. The consequences of this separation appear next, especially in the individualizing of the Brangwen men, so that now we have "*the* Alfred Brangwen of this period," or the first to have his given name identified. But this is also the metonymic, or synecdochic: in its focus upon details, this later section of chapter 1 is introducing us to the narrative as novel to differentiate that component of this text from the first part, or the narrative as poem. Thus, the narrative introduces the plot aspect, the very aspect that will become so oppressive to so many of *The Rainbow*'s readers, who prefer the poetic or metaphoric to the plot-heavy narrative of grim details and eventfulness more reminiscent of the nineteenth-century realist novel. These two beginnings—one poetic or metaphoric, the other realist or metonymic—introduce, as we shall see, the larger divisions of the novel, the "bifurcation," to borrow Virginia Hyde's term (77), of the book into its two sequential parts.

Negotiating the Metonymic

The opening pages of this second beginning of *The Rainbow* implicate the text in a plethora of detail concerning the first Tom's family—a wealth of metonymic detail reminiscent of its immediate predecessor, *Sons and Lovers*. As in any realist narrative, these details function as selections, or metonyms, of a complexly detailed real world outside the text. Eventually, however, it is the figure of Ursula's grandfather, Tom Brangwen, who becomes associated with detail in a conventionally domestic manner. When he overcomes his resentment against his stepdaughter Anna for having rejected him in favor of his nephew Will, the middle-aged Tom assumes the responsibility of helping the young couple set up housekeeping. "Tom Brangwen was now the fairy god-father"—a strange transgendering of the role—and "was never happy unless he was buying something. . . . Tom Brangwen, with more particular thought, spied out what he called handy little things for her. He appeared with a set of new-fangled cooking-pans, with a special sort of hanging lamp . . . with canny little machines for grinding meat or mashing potatoes or whisking eggs" (*R* 122). And "Anna took a sharp interest in what he bought . . . the little contrivances, which he thought so canny . . . she was always expectant, on market days there was always a long thrill of anticipation" (122). Tom is himself "excited" by this "cupboard love," as he calls it. The narrative itself embraces this excitement in its own preoccupation with detail, extending for over another page devoted to the introduction of what turns out to be an apparatus for wringing out laundry. Clearly, the narrative is demonstrating an effort to recuperate earlier connectedness in this father and stepdaughter through these metonyms of domestic life.

In the context of contemporary gender associations with these tropes, it is not difficult to see these activities of the gentleman-farmer Tom as situated toward the "feminine" end of the gender spectrum, similar to the kind of later-life excitement that we shall see in Will Brangwen's resuscitated creativity in becoming a crafts instructor. The Tom figure has been domesticated, or feminized, by becoming prosperous enough to hire others to do the physical labor. In addition, Tom has never been a traveler in the framework of that metaphor of empowerment. He may be credited with recollections of hearing his English teacher read Tennyson's "Ulysses," with its nostalgic desire to recuperate the lost empowerment of travel into the unknown. In a similar vein, he cannot forget the gesture at travel in his encounters with the foreigner and the woman with whom the young Tom made love. However, traveling for this figure has been restricted to the exploration of the unknown with his wife.

This term *restricted* needs qualification. First, the stage of fulfillment achieved by Tom and Lydia ought not to be underestimated, for the narrative seeks to mark off the possibility of a "coming through" in their generation at the dawn of modern history, within which such a sense of fulfillment is becoming less and less feasible, even as a conception. The narrative does allow Tom one critical variety of travel. It moves him on a journey of cultural exploration, visiting the distant (albeit spatially near) world of his brother's (Will's father's) affair with "an educated woman, a lady, widow of a doctor" (85) in Derbyshire. In this segment of the narrative, Tom journeys to Wirksworth to meet this Mrs. Forbes, on whose person and cottage the text lavishes details Tom might have perceived as a traveler into the unknown: "a drawing room, full of books, with a piano and a violin-stand. . . . The room was of a kind Brangwen had never known" (86). When he asks, "Does my brother like reading?" the woman replies that Alfred is reading Herbert Spencer at the moment and that they read Browning together.

The response to Mrs. Forbes and to the alien territory of the cultivated world in which she has encouraged Tom's Ulyssean brother to navigate is crucially important as the justification for his movement at last into the unknown with Lydia. The narrative allows Tom suddenly to read his post-Edenic world of Marsh Farm not as a bower of bliss but as a bog in which he has been mired: "Brangwen went home despising himself for his own poor way of life. He was a clod-hopper and a boor, dull, stuck in the mud. More than ever he wanted to clamber out, to this visionary polite world" (86). He attempts to console himself with the rationale that "[h]is wife was a lady also." However, "the Marsh" to which he returns forces him to see "how fixed everything was, how the other form of life was beyond him, and he regretted, for the first time, that he had succeeded to the farm. He felt a prisoner, sitting safe and easy and unadventurous" (86). In any case, this Tom figure is positioned as feminine in his confinement to the limits of the farm, a domestic confinement that is the negative pole of the metonymic association with stasis or rest.

Ursula as a Prisoner of the House

The legacy of the Tom figure's feminization in a preoccupation with details is evident also in the heavy burden of this domesticity that eventually rests on the shoulders of the young Ursula, to whom her mother passes the responsibility as eldest child in a family of eight. When Ursula attempts to shed this feminizing burden of concern for domestic detail by taking a job as an elementary-school teacher, she will trade one confinement for another. In response to a feminist daughter who argues for the "right of women to take equal place with men in the field of action and work" the remarks of the mother seem appropriate: "there's a good crop of stockings lying ripe for mending. Let that be your field of action" (329). This response directs the daughter's attention to the details of household management feminizing the traditional woman and less traditional men, such as Tom, with his preoccupation with domestic gadgetry.

But travel to the unknown is made possible by the agency of Ursula's *will.* Balked by the father's obsession with turning his daughters into ladies who need not work, the traveler Ursula settles for the shorter journey of the Brinsley Street School position and what turns out to be just another form of domestic confinement. No segment of the narrative seems closer to the metonymic, or to the conventions of traditional realist fiction. Intent upon liberating herself from domestic servitude—tending the needs of a growing family—Ursula finds herself the servant of Mr. Harby, the master to whom she must account for the details of classroom maintenance.

Much as the young and idealistic Ursula may fantasize about "personalizing" her relationship with her fifty-five charges, this grim narrative, reminiscent of the squalid school scenes in *Jane Eyre* or *Nicholas Nickleby,* offers a fertile site for an orthodox Lacanian to map the Imaginary in sharp conflict with the Real. At the foundation of classroom maintenance is the plethora of details for which Ursula is responsible. The primary obligation is to teach facts, and the narrative insists upon making readers feel this oppression by sharing it. "Seven hats at two-pence ha'penny each?" she must ask the resistant mob of faces (350). "When you say 'their fur is brown,' how do you write 'their'?" she asks in another lesson (358). And the tyranny of Mr. Harby, the master, is implicated in rebellion against a feeling of imprisonment by the task at hand. We are told: "Mr Harby stood

. . . with strength and male power, and a certain blind, native beauty. She might have liked him as a man" were it not for his "bullying over such a trifle as a boy's speaking out without permission" (360). This dislike for him is less the result of his being "a little, fussy man" than the "feminized" position he occupies: "he was imprisoned in a task too small and petty for him, which yet, in a servile acquiescence, he would fulfil" (360). Thus, the narrative allows for sympathy in part with Harby, whose "job was to make the children spell the word 'caution' correctly, and put a capital letter after a full-stop" (360). The outcome is yet another unbinding of gender from sex. As the passage clearly indicates, even a martinet like Harby has been feminized by a patriarchal framework within which empowerment has been engendered as male, regardless of the individual's sexual identity. Women are expected to acquiesce easily to their feminized position as those responsible for the household, whether the household is the family's or the school's.

In this way, the figure of Ursula is constructed as a variety of accountant, a figure synonymous with synecdoche as it has been absorbed into metonymy. Naive enthusiasm about gaining autonomy by paying her own way at home as one means of freeing herself from domesticity will eventually pale under the grim drudgery of work. Here, however, the grounding of what is perhaps illusory autonomy is measured out in shillings and pence. The narrative goes out of its way to emphasize the monetary connection between the Brangwen household and the schoolhouse in a passage foregrounding the narrative's insistence on enumeration and metonymic or synecdochic details. We are told, for example, exactly how much Ursula earns—quite literally down to the last penny!—"four pounds two shillings and one penny"—and she takes her pay home to "put down fifty shillings on the table," without being asked. The mother responds "coolly," "letting it lie." Although she is "hurt" by Anna's reserved response, Ursula feels "free": "she had paid her scot" and had "thirty-two shillings of her own," presumably some of that "gold" she had been "fingering" on the way home (362).

This problematic freedom is adjusted after she has been tested by her pupil Williams. The narrative represents a testing by which she is broken in to her teaching. This long chapter, "The Man's World," abounds in details as Ursula learns to acquiesce to servitude in the prison of St. Philip's School. When the narrative suddenly moves ahead eighteen months to the end of this first teaching assignment, it liberates her from servitude to school teaching to shift the burden yet again to a context of confinement, troped as the weight of synecdochic details to be learned. This generalizing of her experience while studying for the entrance examinations reminds us of another and perhaps a more crucial representation of the metonymic element in this narrative: these jolts forward in time foreground awareness that narrative is impelled by this ceaseless desire to move forward toward the end, as plot represents a metonymy of the-next-and-the-next-after-that.

The Novel's Times

Within the context of the movement of desire toward fulfillment troped as metonymy, a valuable entry to this novel's structure is provided by Roger Sale. Writing of "The Narrative Technique of *The Rainbow,*" Sale explores an element he finds unique to this novel: a deliberate erosion of the "barriers between specific and general time and space," allowing for a sense of suspended time. Sale argues: "This constant movement in time continuums, which is the essential narrative technique of *The Rainbow,* allows Lawrence to describe a large segment of time very quickly, and this, in turn, creates the impression that no time is left undescribed, that the sequence of events and relationships is never broken. . . . The effect is of great movement, yet of a constant thread of 'unstable ego' unifying the movement" (32). Another effect, not explored by Sale, is the shock to the reader in encountering the inexorable movement of time, especially when its passage is not attended to.

It is in these jolts of time that the narrative foregrounds the energy of desire as moments of awareness of the desire of the Other. The center of the metonymic representation of desire in the early segment of the novel is the figure of Tom Brangwen. The years before he "married a Polish lady" are covered with a breathtaking speed, in part because he is the first Brangwen to have stepped out of that slumbering world of immersion in blood-consciousness toward individuation or characterization. Thus, when we get specific references to his age, we are jolted into acknowledging that time has been passing within the text's construction of his life. The narrative offers on succeeding pages the following: "Now when Tom Brangwen, at nineteen, a youth fresh like a plant, rooted in his mother and his sister, found that he had lain with a prostitute" (*R* 20), and "Then, when he was twenty-three, his mother died, and he was left at home with Effie" (22). There follows the generalized rendering of the dampening of his own sexual fires at the Red Lion, and then the critical episode with the woman and her foreign companion at some unspecified age. That is followed by another unspecified time: "Then Effie got married, and he was left in the house with only Tilly, the cross-eyed woman-servant who had been with them for fifteen years" (27), making her old enough, one surmises, to remove her from Tom's tiny constellation of possible sexual partners. The dramatization of the encounter with Lydia on the road begins thus: "When he was twenty-eight" (29). In this way, the text forces the reader to confront the passage of time and with it the incessant impulse of desire. The movement toward the consummation of desire in the Tom figure is represented in at least several senses. However, the reader is also impelled by a desire for the end of this episode, because the chapter title has announced its own closure in Tom's marrying a "Polish lady."

The function of this first sequence of the novel is to establish how the narrative as a whole works. Again and again, the narrative forces readers to acknowledge that time has indeed been passing. The phenomenon is apparent in Tom's midlife crisis, as Anna's declaration of independence forces him to recognize how much of his creative life had been tied up in his effort to turn her into a lady. In the next two chapters, as the narrative focuses upon the coming to womanhood of Anna, readers are suddenly brought into an awareness of how Tom, whom the narrative has encouraged us to ignore, has been aging while she has been growing up. "Was he old?" Tom asks himself. It is a valid question because he cannot be much older than forty-two, the eighteen-year-old Anna having been about four when Tom, at twenty-eight, married her mother. What the jolt of time demonstrates to Tom, and to readers, is that desire persists, regardless of how much we feel we have successfully fed its fires. Tom muses, "What was missing in his life, that, in his ravening soul, he was not satisfied? He had had that friend at school, his mother, his wife, and Anna? . . . What had he known, but the long, marital embrace with his wife?" (120). The passage is among the more painful "spots of time" because it forces the reader to recognize that desire ultimately exceeds gratification.

The point is crucial because many readers have assumed that there is some particular, but unspecified, limitation that holds back even someone like Tom from fulfillment, even though he apparently has "come through" with Lydia. The limitation is universal, however, because desire is always a metonymy of that Desire which we can know, if at all, only through its absence or through desire for a particular object. Such desire known through absence or through desire for an object is grounded in Desire, sealed off in the Imagining with the subject's accession to the Symbolic order. Thus, the sense of failed fulfillment in the Tom figure is not some aberration: to be a desiring subject is to be forever impelled forward to the potential for fulfillment but also to know that desire in Lacan's sense of the difference between "need" and "demand" can never finally be anything but a part of the whole that is Desire.[9]

Hardly has the narrative marked its famous "annunciation" in the relationship of this first couple, represented through Tom's "That's her," than the two are moved toward betrothal and marriage in the short order the reader notes elsewhere in Jack Ferguson's whirlwind romancing of the "horse-dealer's daughter," Mabel Pervin.[10] In one sense this headlong movement toward marriage has been announced by the title of the chapter—"How Tom Brangwen Married a Polish Lady." The chapter follows the paradigm of a desiring subject pursuing Desire troped as desire for an other, a pursuit brought to completion with the promise of fulfillment in the metaphor of marriage. The clearly sexual movement toward consummation breaks through the surface in the narrative's description of Tom's sense that the mechanism of desire has been set into motion and that what he, along with the readers, has been waiting for is "coming": "It was coming, he knew, his fate. The world was submitting to its transformation. He made no move: it would come, what would come" (32). That "fate" is the pattern of desire set in motion by the "look" of recognition, operating in marked contrast here to the gaze, say, of Tom standing in the dark and rain, looking with obsessive attention at the young woman Anna embracing the man who has supplanted the father in the erotic economy of the daughter's desire.

Indeed, with that linked scene of looking, the narrative locks into its essential structure of announcing the potential for the fulfillment of desire and then moving the lovers inexorably forward to their end. In this way, the narrative mirrors the movement of its characters so that the next generation draws attention away from the parents until we are forced to acknowledge the operation of desire in time. The novel itself takes up a generation, as it often does minor characters, moving that generation or character forward to some point of limited fulfillment or death, only to discard the old in favor of the new. (There is a minor shock, for example, when the narrative casually relays the information that Lydia Lensky "had been dead two years now" [342]—a strategy recalling Virginia Woolf's bracketing of the deaths of Mrs. Ramsay and Andrew in *To the Lighthouse.*) Anticipating where the narrative will end in its last pages, the text foregrounds indeterminacy. Nothing is stable or fixed—not character, not the ego, not even Yeatsian "monuments of intellect" or artifacts of "Sailing to Byzantium"—only this unending movement of desire toward its end, so that these characters, the staple of conventional narrative, seem mere gestures of a text, improvising performances in a plot whose end will be death, or the end of desire.

To return for a moment to this phenomenon of the text foregrounding awareness of time's passage, we note that the narrative is playing a variation on this very theme in the case of the early-middle-aged Will Brangwen. Just as Anna's desire to marry Will forced Tom Brangwen to acknowledge how the passage of time is making him reassess the fulfillment of his desire, Ursula's maturing and her desire to journey toward the challenges of experience in the "widening circle" of her world seem to produce a similar assessment of fulfillment in Will. As is the case in family chronicle generally, the text brings readers up short occasionally by enforcing the recognition that the characters upon which the narrative focuses are inevitably marginalized by the exigencies of its larger needs. Thus, the narrative must always find the means to direct attention backward to a character whose plot line has been displaced by a newer interest, often in a younger character. Accordingly, as the narrative has focused upon the maturing of Ursula it has been ignoring her father, with less justification perhaps than its consignment of her mother to the "long trance of complacent child-bearing" (328). These jolts of time, once again, decenter conventional notions of literary characters as substantial phenomena with lives, or existences, rather than being threads within the web of the text.

Such a jolt of time reinforces awareness of the Will figure, for example. Rather abruptly, as though the narrative consciousness has suddenly become aware of having forgotten this figure while attending to the maturing Ursula, the narrative foregrounds Will. Ironically, of course, his function had once been central to the forward movement of desire in this text. Will is in "one of his states of flux," apparently justifying the narrative's renewed interest, as though the illusory stability of a character is sufficient grounds for the abandoning of narrative interest: "After all these years, he began to see a loophole of freedom." Setting aside for a moment this revision of the cliché metaphor of a loophole, it is clear that the narrator wants to emphasize the obvious: if Ursula is approaching the ages of the parents when they married—eighteen for her mother, twenty for her father—then Will is approaching forty. The term *these years* is not exactly clarified by the next statement—"For twenty years he had gone on at his office as a draughtsman, doing work in which he had no interest"—because obviously enough he started his job in Ilkeston the same year he "met" and married Anna. "The growing up of his daughters, their developing rejection of old forms set him also free," the narrative continues (329). Thus, in a sense, Ursula as his oldest daughter has already started to function as a prospective Moses figure, leading her father out of bondage in the prison house of the old ways, or more specifically, his servitude in the lace factory.

It is a feminizing servitude not because the image of lace is associated with the woman's world but because Will has forced whatever small talent he may have once had as an artist into the narrow pathway of the hired engineer responsible for designing the patterns under which the lace-making machines would operate. It is difficult to be at all certain exactly what Will has been doing at work. The narrative offers no help because it never follows Will to work. However, it seems impossible to conceive of a sufficiently large number of lace patterns for him to design; thus, one suspects he may be a kind of early computer programmer, engineering the particular codes that will program the machinery to produce material in endlessly perfect patterns as a mechanized Arachne spinning out lace to cover windows and tables and to decorate women's apparel in a petty bourgeois world intent upon appropriating the semblances of the refined domesticity of its betters. Indeed, Ursula's learning French, for which she may have no practical use, is part of the same lace-curtain gentility of many in her family's class.

In any case, Will finds his loophole and extricates himself from the web of factory life in which he has been netted for some twenty years. It has not been quite twenty years since he last turned his hands to the more artistic endeavors of wood carving, for he was carving the Adam and Eve panel during the months of his courting Anna and he left it unfinished when they married. The panel, it may be recalled, was one casualty of the battlefield in their early married years. When Anna wisely attempts to direct Will's attention back to the panel as a fairly obvious outlet for his desire so that she might achieve some small space for herself in the "physical heat" of their domestic life, he destroys it in spite.

These two decades have taken their toll, as we note in another of those jolts of time when the narrative indicates how Will has returned to his wood carving. This sculpting hardly seems the medium for High Art, and yet it is painful to read: "But now he had knowledge and skill without vision" (330).

The narrative may seem to be offering the Will figure small consolation in becoming an industrial arts teacher or crafts director, but it *is* something. Indeed, anticipating our attention to the metaphorical impulses in this narrative, this something is recorded not only in the minor transformation of his character, as he becomes interested in the crafts movement, but more importantly in a shift in his relationship with Anna. His transformation is first noted by Ursula, to whom the narrative has been directing our attention in the Brinsley Street School block of experience, when she and the narrator note that Will "was coming to his own" (388). And the change of her husband's life, coupled with the move from the small cottage in which they began their marriage to the large house in red-brick suburbia, accords well with Anna's desire for change, now "awake from her sleep of motherhood" (388), and a shedding of the husk of the past.

Before moving on to the transformative function of metaphor, we might summarize this equally important, dual function of metonymy. As the associative impulse of narrative, this metonymic structure is one most commonly understood within plot—the this-and-then-that-which-follows-this. Along with that more generalized strategy of the associative is the appropriated synecdochic part-for-the-whole of detail intrinsic to realist prose narrative that this text is at least in part representing. The family-saga paradigm on which this narrative constructs itself problematizes the Brooksian model for plot, in which ending offers what may be no more than the illusion of meaning anyway. The conventional notion of characters is problematized by an impression of pauses or rests, but no endings. As a result, rather than characters this text offers threads in a texture, a web, within which the character is interwoven and merely moving with one or another thread through the web at the time, while others lack such focus, or at least for a time. It is appropriate that the Will figure is involved in lace making, a weaving of textures that confines threads, since the weaving of texts metaphorically represents the function of metonymy, which we have been reading as feminizing the Tom and Will figures by proscribing their travel. As an important anticipation of where we may end, this text deconstructs the binary of metaphor and metonymy by demonstrating that they are mutually dependent, not exclusive of each other. Indeed, Will's weaving may be read as a metaphor of the metonymic function of a text within which characters have no independent being.

The Transformative Function of Metaphor

Following Peter Brooks's reasoning, metaphor representing the paradigmatic or vertical—in contrast to the syntagmatic or horizontal of metonymy—is the trope of identification or binding. This principle of metaphor as the paradigmatic, or vertical, may seem to suggest the static rather than the dynamic. This apparent stasis of the metaphoric problematizes Irigaray's central metaphor of liberation, or "travel," in her analysis of the economy of tropes, where metonymy is associated with confinement and the feminine. Paradoxically, however, this liberation, or what I have been reading as "travel," is not horizontal, not a linear or contiguous movement toward the object of desire, which would suggest the metonymic, but a vertical movement, a transformation or transfiguration shifting the subject to a different plane. (It is important here to avoid the notion of a necessarily higher plane, since like any polarity this one has the potential for privileging one over the other.) It is the sudden recognition of identity or similarity in the midst of difference that generates the energy of metaphoric binding. Once again, however, such a recognition of similarity ought not to erase the persistence of difference. Indeed, difference is, to use Derrida's term, "under erasure," if that phrase can carry the sense of a presence of similarity within absence. In this way, metaphor, like all the other terms we have been trading in here, carries the burden of doubleness. As we have seen, metonymy functions on a wide range: at one end, it is the trope of Desire energizing a movement toward fulfillment through the part objects of desire; and, on the other, it is the trope of preoccupation with the part. This fetishizing of detail is implicated in a confinement offering little hope of movement toward fulfillment. So too, metaphor, often troped as liberation or crossing the bar, is generally the figure of binding or momentary stasis in the potential for transformation.

This context of metaphor is announced in the courtship and marriage of the "first couple"—"first" in the sense of being the first to be named, as naming offers the illusion of individuality, in contrast to their undifferentiated Brangwen forebears. Its forerunner is in Tom's failed efforts at fulfillment before his famous "look" and apparently involuntary assertion, "That's her." These early adventures are clearly attempts at movement toward the possibility of gratification, if not fulfillment. The narrative follows Tom as he goes out to seek the different. In the encounter with the girl in Matlock with whom he goes off riding into the woods, the narrative tells us: "His heart thumped and he thought it the most glorious adventure, and was mad with desire for the girl" (24). "Afterwards he glowed with pleasure," we are told; however, it is the traveling companion, the "foreigner," who functions as the real object of desire in Tom. The narrative seems to distinguish desire for the foreign man from the homoerotic desire Tom presumably felt for the "boy" with whom he entered into a relationship like that of the biblical David and Jonathan. It is a desire for access to the beyond with which this foreigner is associated. "Brangwen watched with all his eyes" (24) and "Brangwen stared fascinated," in this variation of the male gaze, at the man he loves "for his exquisite graciousness, for his tact and reserve, and for his ageless monkey-like self-surety" (25). Perhaps to rationalize this attraction, the narrative asserts that the foreigner "warmed to" him, "and Brangwen was excited. He was transported" (59). "Transported," or carried across, suggests Tom has been *transformed* by this encounter, positioning the encounter in the realm of the metaphoric.

The transformative effects of this encounter with the other, troped as the promise of his being transported to another world, announce a pattern to be repeated in the courtship of Lydia. Appropriately, the transformation of Tom is presented through metaphor. The narrative indicates that he stares out at the stars from his bedroom, "his whole being in a whirl" (25). Later, when he walks home from proposing marriage to Lydia, the narrative offers a scene in which it is the stars that do the whirling—a scene that Jack Stewart reads as representing "expressionist" inclinations.[11] This excitement at confronting radical "other"ness persists into the next morning when Tom awakes, excited still. The excitement is represented in a marvelously appropriate metaphor: "The girl and the foreigner . . . had set fire to the homestead of his nature, and he would be burned out of cover" (26). The metaphoricity of that figure is foregrounded when Tom reaches home and his resentment at returning to the confinement of a "homestead" that has obviously enough not been literally set afire is troped appropriately: "He balked the mean enclosure of reality, stood stubbornly like a bull at a gate, refusing to re-enter the well-known pound of his own life" (26). Nothing could more clearly inscribe Irigaray's notion of the feminine as metonymy and confinement than this "enclosure" following the promise of liberation.

For days, "a fever of restless anger" continues. Having failed to read the encounter as an annunciation of travel as trope rather than literal journey, Tom "dreamed of foreign parts." Chafing against the bonds of the farm, he drinks himself into oblivion. Or, more specifically, the narrative indicates that he "burned out the youth from his blood," achieving a "kindled state of oneness with all the world." This is a dubious "binding," since, as the narrative makes clear, it is the "end of youth's most passionate desire." This segment of the narrative propels itself forward with breakneck speed, or the speed of desire for the promise of Desire, recuperated in the other. It is a kind of elided metonymy, as the desire flips rapidly through an associative schema of "this-then-that," omitting as many *thats* as possible. The narrative tropes the confusion of being shaken by the other as a "daze" that comes over Tom's mind, resulting from an eruption of fire within him once again: "It was as if a strong light were burning there, and he was blind within it, unable to know anything, except that this transfiguration burned between him and her, connecting them, like a secret power" (38). This "transfiguration" marks the metaphoricity of metaphor toward which the narrative is moving. Movement, then, is not only the linear and contiguous progression toward the end of desire but also its transformation or transfiguration, its *Aufhebung* or lifting upward to a different plane.

Transformation is troped as awakening, birth, and dawn. "He returned gradually, but newly created, as after a gestation, a new birth, in the womb of darkness. Aerial and light everything was, new as a morning, fresh and newly begun" (45). Interestingly, this transformation that has been set in motion is also troped as "trespass," a crossing of the bar, so to speak, but a crossing that is also a violation. In a move reminiscent of Derrida's notion of the *pharmikon* as medicine/drug/poison, "transformation" is not simple because it is also "transgression."[12] The narrative once again tropes as birth the transformation of Lydia into a desiring subject. There is little of the idyllic, Adamic association of Tom's birth as a fully desiring subject in her transformation; it is troped instead as violation: "The first pangs of this new parturition were so acute, she knew she could not bear it. She would rather remain out of life, than be torn, mutilated into this birth, which she could not survive" (53). Each subject represents the unknown for the other to be explored.

The journey remains incomplete for the first couple. That is evident in the introduction of the "broken arch" metaphor shortly after Lydia withdraws into pregnancy, only months after their marriage. The transformation begins two years into the marriage. However, its completion is problematic because the narrative moves him as far into the Unknown as it may be possible for a Tom to be moved. Appropriately, this journey follows his returning home from his visit to his brother's lover, Mrs. Forbes, when Lydia senses that Tom's desire has been aroused to travel down a primrose path similar to his brother's. When each has faltered out statements of the incompleteness of their fulfillment, she bids him, "Come here," and he makes the arduous journey across the room toward a woman whose eyes now reveal she has been "transfigured." His journey to her may encompass the space of merely a few feet between them, but it is an epic adventure into the genuine unknown of the other.

The immensity of the journey is suggested by Tom's resistance to the call to adventure into the unknown. "She waited for him to meet her," we are told, "not to bow before her and serve her. She wanted his active participation, not his submission." In her unwillingness to bow to him and her lack of any expectation that he will bow to her, the Lydia figure anticipates the notion of "star-equilibrium" in *Women in Love*. Tom almost fails to cross the bar into that unknown territory: "it was a torture to him, that he must give himself to her actively, participate in her, that he must meet and embrace and know her, who was other than himself. There was that in him which shrank from yielding to her, resisted the relaxing towards her, opposed the mingling with her, even whilst he most desired it. He was afraid, he wanted to save himself" (90). But the narrative moves him forward toward the "blazing kernel of darkness" so that he is "lit with her in one consummation." The experience of initiation—"[i]t was the entry into another circle of existence, it was the baptism to another life"—is troped once again as travel: "Their feet trod strange ground of knowledge, their footsteps were lit-up with discovery. Wherever they walked, it was well. . . . The new world was discovered, it remained only to be explored" (90).

Following the lead of Brooks, if repetition is a form of Eros, a binding of the present with what has gone before, there is clearly a double sense of metaphoricity here in the statements repeating themselves, as all the while they are representing metaphorical assertions of a carrying-across into another realm and perhaps even representing the power of metaphor to cross the bar of repression that is at the center of representation itself.

Because this passage of Tom and Lydia's initiation was drafted after much of the remaining text had been written, it betrays a sense of belatedness, a self-consciousness of the yet-to-come in introducing the major metaphors of the remaining narrative, especially in its closing passages. The metaphor of travel, or metaphor as travel, is extended in the figure of the doorway—"They had passed through the doorway into the further space. . . . She was the doorway to him, he to her" (90)—to anticipate the failed travel for the second and third couples yet to come. Most important, the closing paragraphs announce the rainbow metaphor of the novel's ending, even though the rainbow is merely implied and the word itself does not appear at this juncture.

The initial link in the chain of arch/rainbow metaphors is forged in the passage of Tom's sense of abandonment by Lydia when she is pregnant with their first child—"He felt like a broken arch thrust sickeningly out from support" (63). Later, it appears in its first major form at the end of this original generation's journey. There the focus is Anna, who, we are reassured, "was no longer called upon to uphold with her childish might the broken end of the arch" of her new father, who felt there was nothing to "thrust" against following his "abandonment" by her mother. The parents have become the "pillar of fire and the pillar of cloud," who meet in the "span of the heavens" so that she is "free to play in the space beneath, between" (91). The passage works on Brooks's "textual erotics" as it binds together this coming through of the first couple with the earlier lack of completion in the man. The text uses, then, the metaphor of the construction of the arch to bind two segments of the text metaphorically through repetition.

It is worth noting also that the text suppresses the term *rainbow.* Clearly, the narrative means us to read this arch, "beneath, between" which Anna can now move toward fulfillment, as the rainbow of the novel's title. Only rainbows can be woven from the delicate conjunction of "fire" and "cloud," or sun and moisture. Undoubtedly, by the time this passage was drafted the title of this text had become *The Rainbow,* and the passage clearly anticipates the rainbow trope of the novel's last paragraphs, where it reaches an apparent apotheosis. In any case, the willingness to allow the title to name the unidentified rainbow here—suggestive of the suppression of the word *clay* in Joyce's story of that title—encourages us to speculate that what the passage is really about is metaphoricity, or the power of metaphor to represent representation itself, as the rainbow metaphor is allowed to function without its signifier.

Fire and Water, but No Rainbow

The rainbow trope, whether or not the actual signifier *rainbow* itself appears in the text, announces the promise of fulfillment in the first couple. The narrative is intent upon positing only such *promise* and nowhere represents *fulfillment,* which is perhaps unrepresentable since lasting harmony and union are constructions of the Imaginary register. Instead, the narrative has already begun to turn attention away from the first couple and toward the next as it rushes into the next generation, like desire impelled toward its end. In the chapter that follows, the narrative begins another rapid movement forward, in this case of the Anna figure, the focus of the first manifestation of the rainbow trope. The pattern recalls the thrusting forward in time in Tom's youth. In the opening sentence, Anna is nine, and four short paragraphs later she is ten and visiting Baron Skrebensky's home several years before Anton is born. It is only a handful of pages later that Anna is eighteen and Will comes into her life.[13]

The narrative announces the second couple's relationship in the corn-harvest segment through the agency of metaphor, making this a clearly "poetic" passage. The Anna figure sets in motion the rhythm of repetition that Brooks would see as central to metaphor. Eventually that rhythm subsumes the corn-harvest segment, for it is she who suggests to Will that they set the sheaves of oats upright. Working in adjacent rows, the figures perform the repetitive activity of stooping, grasping, lifting, carrying, setting down, in a description that continues for two pages before it climaxes in Will's literalizing the erotic rhythm of the activity by stopping Anna for a kiss. As a short, self-bounded episode, this segment of the narrative could not fit the Brooksian, (or male) paradigm for narrative more fully.[14] The repetition of the activity is mirrored in its description, a discourse of repetition that suggests the metaphoric operating within the signifier as well as the signified. The scene also fits the Brooksian paradigm in its rising action as we are led toward the inevitable embrace of the young lovers. The desire for the end, which we share because we are attracted to its inevitability, is not fulfilled until a sufficient number of repetitions of the couple's movements to and fro have provided the erotic bindings through which desire is intensified by the deferral of its fulfillment. His desire is not so much to meet her as to impose his will upon her, to indulge in the illusion of mastery in finally overtaking her, when such illusory mastery is marked with the privilege of his kiss.

And the mastery *is* illusory. As an annunciation of their relationship in the marriage to come, this segment of the text indicates her unwillingness to be absorbed within his desire. "And the whole rhythm of him beat into his kisses, and still he pursued her, in his kisses, and still she was not quite overcome. . . . All the night in his arms, darkness and shine, he possessed it all! All the night for him now, to unfold, to venture within, all the mystery to be entered, all the discovery to be made" (115–16). The man is moved metaphorically along the path into the unknown. Instead of a traveler bent upon exploration as a metaphor for inner discovery, however, Will enacts his name as a conquistador intent upon exploring the mystery of a new world only to possess it. Much as the text metaphorizes the change for Will as another birth—we find, for example, the "birthpain of love"—desire here seems merely the desire to possess: "He wanted her. . . . Something fixed in him for ever. He was hers" (116). This assumption that she wants to possess *him* seems a mirror image of the desire to master her.

Thus, this episode of metaphoric binding through repetition announces relationship in the second couple. She is ready to go home, but he must extract a positive response to his marriage proposal before he will release her. The proposal is phrased as an assertion, then turns into a question when she remains silent—"We'll get married, Anna, shall we?" She says nothing, signing her agreement with a kiss, "clinging to him passionately, in a way he could not understand" (117). His point of view continues to dominate the text, inscribing the male paradigm onto the text of their relationship in an ominously naive manner: "He could not understand. But he left it all now, to marriage. That was the solution now, fixed ahead. He wanted her, he wanted to be married to her, he wanted to have her altogether, as his own for ever. And he waited, intent, for the accomplishment" (117). Thus, this expression of traditional narrative closes the representation of its erotic subtext: desire, postponement, closure in the fulfillment of desire.

The scene of the couple's honeymoon reinstates the dominance of metaphor in the corn-harvest scene of annunciation. The text metaphorizes the honeymoon cottage as a Noah's Ark in which the newlyweds journey into the new world that has been opened up within, the old world they left behind passing away beneath the flood. The language in this scene betrays a sense of belatedness, like the language of the scene in which Tom returns from his visit to Mrs. Forbes and begins the journey of coming through with Lydia. Anticipating the metaphors of Ursula's rebirth in the novel's closing paragraphs, the text introduces the figure of the planted seed and then the fallen chestnut for Will: "a chestnut falling out of a burr, he was shed naked and glistening on to a soft fecund earth, leaving behind him the hard rind of worldly knowledge and experience" (135). It is this metaphor of the "naked kernel" that will dominate the language representing the rebirth of Ursula.

The honeymoon episode is shaped also by the metaphor of the Fall. Unable to bear idleness, Will thinks of his carving of the Garden and acknowledges that his Eve was "too hard and lively," compared to his new sense of a woman's body. He can find no words for the body of his desire but must sign with "a gesture of infinite tenderness" (139). This guilty Adam both feels he ought to be doing something in that "husk" of a world he and Anna have shed yet resents her willingness to return to that "dead world" by giving a tea party. The man seems entrapped within the Imaginary and its polarities of inside/outside or real/fantastic. Within the latter, the text metaphorizes him as two figures from fantasy, one male, the other female: "the youth in the fairy tale, who was king for one day in the year, and for the rest a beaten herd: like Cinderella also, at the feast" (140). Metaphorically, the scene is bound to the scene of the first couple's coming through in order to function as the rainbow arch of promise for the daughter. Here, in contrast, the text makes it clear that this second couple is highly unlikely to offer that promise to Ursula or to any of the other children they will bear.

As the title for this chapter, "Anna Victrix," reminds us, this narrative moves toward the inevitability of a conquest, rather than the transformation or transfiguration implicit in the rainbow metaphor with which the narrative of the first couple had ended. Instead of a journey toward the possibility of fulfillment, this marriage is rendered metaphorically as warfare. "They fought an unknown battle, unconsciously. Still they were in love with each other, the passion was there. But the passion was consumed in a battle. And the deep, fierce, unnamed battle went on. Everything glowed intensely about them, the world had put off its clothes and was awful, with new, primal nakedness" (156). In this Eden after the Fall, the only outcome can be the victory of one and the defeat of the other. The man has not traveled beyond the corn-harvest scene in which he sought to "possess" or "impose himself on her." In the early days of their marriage, the conflict is essentialized in two blunt assertions: "He wanted to impose himself on her" (158) and "She wanted to preserve herself" (157). She now must struggle for her life, until he concedes the impossibility of his aspiration to mastery.

However, "victory" offers no consolation, only an "ashy desolation." With the birth of Ursula, Anna greets Will with "glowing, unseeing eyes" and the assertion, "Anna Victrix." The narrative of their meeting and marrying is closed with a rewriting of the metaphoric ending of the Tom and Lydia segment of the novel. Here, however, the metaphor of travel is foregrounded to emphasize the mother's apparent misrecognition of her womb as the rainbow arch of the future's promise. Just as the man misrecognizes the cathedral arch, in the interpolated chapter immediately following, as an illusory promise of fulfillment, the woman settles into an illusory state of content, figured as the archway through which the children will become travelers. Similarly, quasi-biblical language announces the metaphoric binding of the passage as the representation of closure:

> If she were not the wayfarer to the unknown, if she were arrived now, settled in her builded house, a rich woman, still her doors opened under the arch of the rainbow, her threshold reflected the passing of the sun and moon, the great travellers, her house was full of the echo of journeying.
>
> She was a door and a threshold, she herself. Through her another soul was coming, to stand upon her as upon the threshold, looking out, shading its eyes for the direction to take. (182)

Eager to relinquish the rigors of the journey, the Anna figure is content to provide a Pisgah view of the Promised Land for her children—especially Ursula, the oldest—as travelers to an unknown she herself has forsworn.

The Rainbow to Come

The birth of Ursula marks the beginning of the end. As John Worthen indicates, the dust jacket of the first edition of *The Rainbow* made it clear that it was to be a novel of "three generations of the Brangwen family."[15] This segment of the narrative is metaphorically bound to the preceding segment by the repetition of key elements of the relationship between Anna and her stepfather, Tom. One passage is particularly interesting as another expression of a time outside the conventional linear time implicit in this text. Describing the father's joy when the infant Ursula would toddle down the path to greet him, the narrative indicates that such joyous reunions of father and daughter had the potential for pain also: "Once she fell . . . as she was running with her hands lifted to him; and when he picked her up, her mouth was bleeding. He could never bear to think of it, he always wanted to cry, even when he was an old man and she had become a stranger to him" (198).

Since the Will figure at the end of the novel is hardly "an old man" at forty-three, the text appears to be casting forward beyond the limits of its own chronology, defying our conventional sense of narrative closure. As in the leaps forward in time for Tom Brangwen, this apparently parenthetical remark opens up the conception of time and therefore narrativity as elements that cannot be comfortably bounded by linearity. Thus, linearity in narrative, implicated in metonymic this-then-that, is problematized by metaphoric bindings that subvert the comfortable notion of time running in only one direction.

The text offers a number of other expressions of metaphoric binding in the relationship between father and daughter Ursula. They are, however, bindings not like those in the more salutary relationship of Anna with her stepfather, Tom, but closer to Will's failed efforts to impose himself upon his wife. The text offers the following ominous description of Will's anticipation of Ursula's maturing. "He loved with a hot heart the dark-haired little Ursula, and he waited for the child to come to consciousness. Now the mother monopolised the baby. But his heart waited in its darkness. His hour would come" (194). And when his hour arrives, the text offers more than one episode in which he is allowed to flatter himself with the illusion of mastery in imposing his power on the small, vulnerable, and therefore "feminine" Ursula.

As an expression of the construction of Will's masculinity, the episode with the Nottingham "lass" frames these gender concerns along class lines as well. This "lass"—she has a name, Jennie, but the narrative marginalizes it—is attractive in large part because she is working class. As a result, the man's middle-class status offers him the illusion of power through the privileging of his language over hers in this hierarchical structure: "He made his sentences in sheer, almost muscular pleasure of exercising himself with her" (212). Language, here, is a mere adjunct to the sad aspiration to dominate—the theater in which they meet is the "Empire"—and his motives with her are metaphorically linked to his motives in the repeated scenes of his "play" with the vulnerable Ursula: the assertion that "he wanted to overcome her resistance, to have her in his power, fully and exhaustively to enjoy her" (213) could just as well include his daughter. The text is already forging its connection with the scene of his return later that evening to his wife. Indeed, the text allows Will to connect his "love-making" with the two women: "It was one man who touched Anna, another who now touched this girl. He liked best this new self. He was given over altogether to the sensuous knowledge of this woman, and every moment he seemed to be touching absolute beauty, something beyond knowledge" (214). The terms *sensuous knowledge* and *absolute beauty* will dominate the scene of his Odyssean homecoming. Pathetic as this adventure may be, in contrast to the apparently more genuine journey his father has undertaken with Mrs. Forbes, it is important to the eventual freeing of his daughter from the role of buttressing the "broken arch" of his weight on her vulnerable sensibility. And, contrary to expectation, this construction of a new self in Will propels him and Anna on a further journey in their relationship.

Ironically, the Anna figure welcomes this "strange man come home to her" (217), even though—or perhaps because—she knows that he has had his little "adventure." This "strange man" holds more appeal than "the ordinary mute, half-effaced, half-subdued man she usually knew him to be," and she is "piqued" that he might be "blossoming out into his real self" (217). The text seems to be coming very close to crediting the construction of the subject, rather than the traditional (and illusory) notion of a self. In this way, the text offers a variant of more recent notions that these selves are all constructions of one's relationships with other subjects, perhaps justifying the text's willingness to abandon characters when no further constructions are imminent. Attractive as the flower metaphor may be as a representation of this man's real self, this self is merely a construction of his relationship with Ursula, feminized by her smaller size and emotional vulnerability. The scene seems to be rewriting episodes in the erotic narrative of the couple's representation, as Anna implicitly says of the adventuring Will, "That's him," to represent the appeal of his foreignness. More important, this scene is metaphorically bound to the coming through of her parents in its sense of the participants' transformation.

Dark and tropical as this development in the erotic history of the second couple may be, they are troped as explorers in this seemingly belated passage. "It was all the lust and the infinite, maddening intoxication of the senses, a passion of death," we are told. "All the shameful things of the body revealed themselves to him with a sort of sinister, tropical beauty" (220). At the same time this is a limited coming through for the man, who begins "to find himself free to attend to the outside life as well." The emphasis here is on the metaphoric as transformative and enfranchising, as Will's erotic journey through what he, perhaps more than the narrative, terms "lust" has "set another man in him free." As the text makes clear, almost with a sense of amazement, Will "at length . . . developed a real purposive self" (221). Once again, as the term *developed* itself suggests, this is less a self that had been there all the time than one constructed out of his relationships with the marginalized feminine, allowing him to arrogate to himself this illusion of mastery.

As the narrative of the first couple achieved its closure with the aftermath of Tom's visit to his brother's lover in Derbyshire and the construction of the rainbow arch through which the daughter might make her journey toward the horizon of fulfillment, the narrative of the second couple finds its more clearly restricted closure in what may seem a darker version of coming through, energizing his desire at last for the "outside world." From that world, strangers visit the Brangwen household: first, those visiting the father on business, like beings from another world, and eventually the Anton Skrebensky figure, who is at least half-foreign, the son of Lydia's Polish friend. Ursula's imagination has been fueled by her biblical readings of "those Sons of God who saw the daughters of men, that they were fair" as well as her reading of "the 'Idylls of the King' and romantic love-stories," preparing her for the advent of a more substantial figure than this military engineer, who seems miscast for a role as one of "those Sons of God." He is, however, an "other," one who seems to come from the beyond, and his advent energizes a "new self" for Ursula. Indeed, their first encounter sets in motion the construction of femininity as a reflection of his desire: "She was thrilled with a new life. For the first time, she was in love with a vision of herself: she saw as it were a fine little reflection of herself in his eyes. And she must act up to this: she must be beautiful. Her thoughts turned swiftly to clothes, her passion was to make a beautiful appearance. Her family looked on in amazement at the sudden transformation of Ursula" (272). Like the toddler in Lacan's mirror stage, she constructs an image of an Ursula as the other she sees reflected in Anton's desiring eyes. To be feminine in this more conventional sense of gender, she has no choice but to attempt a self-transformation to approximate that image.

As Skrebensky, the man of the third couple, walks her home from the Marsh, and they stop to kiss for the first time, Ursula perceives another dimension of "his strangeness" in his "breathing heavily, strangely, beside her" (278). To indicate that he is the stranger with whom she will begin her journey toward the possibility of fulfillment, the text dramatically binds this scene metaphorically with the initial stage of the preceding two narratives by including another of the "belated" passages added in the final stages of revision: "Hesitating, they continued to walk on, quivering like shadows under the ash-trees of the hill, where her grandfather had walked with his daffodils to make his proposal, and where her mother had gone with her young husband, walking close upon him as Ursula was now walking upon Skrebensky" (278). The aftermath is crucially different: *she* goes to bed "feeling all warm with electric warmth" (278), and the text lacks any reference to Anton. This difference from the grandfather's returning home—"Big holes were blown into the sky, the moonlight blew about" (48)—or even the father after the henhouse scene—"the youth went home with the stars in heaven whirling fiercely about the blackness of his head" (108)—hardly bodes well for the third couple.

If metaphor may be defined as the same-but-different by which we are encouraged to experience the release of energy when the alien is transformed into the more familiar, the erotic binding of scenes in this narrative also works against the grain of the metaphoric. As this scene of three generations' history of desire indicates, sameness can foreground difference and suggest the evasion of the transformative. Such difference within sameness occurs in Anton's first farewell, an episode linking the tropes of travel and transfiguration. As an officer, albeit a very young one, he has access to a motor car, surely a rare vehicle for desire in the last years of the nineteenth century. The narrative rhapsodizes on Ursula's sheer joy at the movement of desire through "this enchanted world" of the familiar turned magically alien via the automobile, as he sees her "kindle and flare up to the romance of the situation." This journey into desire announces a potential for "transfiguration" ready to be realized when Ursula's lover comes back just before he sets sail for the Boer War. Appropriately, the site offered for the beginning of her "journey" is the wedding of Anna's brother Fred and a schoolmistress, to take place "as soon as corn-harvest was at an end" (285). The Fred figure is yet another casualty of the restless impulse of desire to move forward to its fulfillment in narrative—what I have termed the metonymic—for at the announcement of his coming marriage the reader receives another of those jolts in time: the first couple's younger son, Fred, has grown to maturity completely outside the attention of the narrative—offstage, so to speak—marking his function as incidental to the narrative of Ursula's journey toward the Promised Land. Clearly, by framing the love of the third couple within the context of corn harvest, the text establishes expectations that the annunciation scene of the second couple will be repeated.

That potential is announced, as the young lovers pass the corn stacks, but it is undermined by two interrelated segments of the scene preceding their dancing in the moonlight. The man begins with "the confusion came over him, as if he were losing himself and becoming all vague, undefined, inchoate. Yet he wanted to be hard, manly, horsey" (286–87), in a passage with fascinating implications for more conventional notions of gender. Apparently the "vague, undefined, inchoate" is a feminine morass from which he wants to save his "hard, manly" self-construction. The woman, on the other hand, rejects the invitation to participate in the masquerade of femininity as the mere object of the desire that she first saw reflected in his eyes. She is too attracted to discourse, asking him difficult questions, contesting his soldiery as merely a boy's game. He is rescued for a time from further embarrassment by the intervention of the family on the barge; however, if anything, this intervention only implicates him more fully in an ensuing "battle" for which his history of boyish soldiering cannot prepare him.[16]

The scene with the bargee is critical to the metaphoric element in this narrative in large part because it implicates Ursula in the metaphor of travel. From a passage rendering the idyllically pastoral world of corn stacks and hedges on this side of the canal and the "black agitation of colliery and railway" on the other side, the narrative focuses upon the canal itself and the metaphorical implications of travel it holds for Ursula. As she turns back to Skrebensky, who has after all literally traveled in that world beyond her horizon, she becomes increasingly distraught that his conventional allegiance to soldiering, war, and empire have confined him to a servitude more restrictive than her own. It is in this context that the sympathy with which she responds to the bargee moves her forward on her own journey. The bargee, who has wedded travel with home, bringing his family along with him on his job, offers a step toward the perception that "travel" is indeed metaphoric, for he has traveled more than her soldier lover, who ends up trying to restrain her travel from his position above her on the wharf.

As the narrative makes clear, Skrebensky envies the attention Ursula pays a man so obviously "beneath" him, and it is appropriate that the contest between the lovers for control of the discourse turns on his equivocating on the term *gentle* in her assertion about the bargee. As a prospective mate, her lover fails Ursula by commenting that the wife had obviously been a "servant," and therefore the bargee cannot be "gentle" by birth. Ursula's implicit "wince" at her lover's pettiness speaks her perception of a dead system in which he is implicated; indeed, much of her reaction in the corn-stacks scene is a working out of her sense of how much this man is the prisoner of his traditionalist views. In a passage mixing narrative comment and what appears to be the man's consciousness, we find: "He was envying the lean father of three children, for his impudent directness and his worship of the woman in Ursula, a worship of body and soul together, the man's body and soul wistful and worshipping the body and spirit of the girl, with a desire that knew the inaccessibility of its object, but only glad to know that the perfect thing existed, glad to have had a moment of communion" (294). In a narrative with few expressions of the male gaze, the bargee's admiration of Ursula deserves particular attention.

Ursula's interrogation of her lover's soldiering and her sympathetic response to a social inferior provide a framework for the wedding scenes to follow. Metaphorically, Ursula as a desiring subject is intent upon traveling, or simply moving: "She wanted to let go. She wanted to reach and be amongst the flashing stars, she wanted to race with her feet and be beyond the confines of this earth. She was mad to be gone," and "She must leap from the known into the unknown" (295). Accordingly, she is drawn toward dancing: "The music came in waves. One couple after another was washed and absorbed into the deep underwater of the dance" (295). Her lover, however, cannot genuinely accept this invitation to the dance. Not content to dance *with* her, he insists upon dancing *her* to the rhythms of his own self-confinement in the rigidity and deathliness of the outworn.

In one sense, the two dancers become voyagers on the moonlit ocean of their possibilities together as lovers. She is drawn toward communion with the moon because it offers her liberation into the beyond. He, on the other hand, is all that confines and holds her back from such enfranchisement. He is troped as a "loadstone," a variant of "lodestone," expressing the agency of magnetism or attraction. Instead of a force of attraction or fascination, he is a weight upon her desire to move freely. Ever the embodiment of the conventional, he asks and re-asks, "Don't you like me to-night?" Little wonder, then, that the narrative foregrounds her desperate desire to free herself, to break from this confinement, rendered through metaphors of corrosive salt and sharp metal.

This man just doesn't seem to get it. As they dance, "he must weave himself around her, enclose her, enclose her in a net of shadow. . . . She was bright as a piece of moonlight, as bright as a steel blade, he seemed to be clasping a blade that hurt him. Yet he would clasp her, if it killed him" (297–98). By the end, murder is in the air. "Gradually she began to come to herself" (299), the narrative tells us, and then it moves back into her attempt to reassemble the rent fabric of their conscious beings to cover the perception that he is "dead." Once again, the narrative voice merges with Ursula's consciousness, so there is no way of ascertaining whether the man is indeed spiritually dead, or if it is Ursula who thinks him so. Only after he has left does the narrative flatly indicate: "To his own intrinsic life, he was dead. And he could not rise again from the dead" (304).

Dance binds this episode metaphorically with the scene of Anna's naked ritualistic performance while pregnant for Ursula. In both cases, it is the women who are intent upon liberation or travel, while the men strive to hold them back from that enfranchisement. In both mother and daughter, the narrative inscribes the woman's desperate desire for freedom. It is a desire that, if blocked, will transform itself into a murderous fury of destructiveness. Both of these scenes, then, are expressions of the metaphoric in the transformative, or, even more precisely, the transfigurative quality of the two women's accession to liberation, even though it comes through the destruction of the men who become metaphorized as the confinement associated with the metonymic. (It ought not to be lost on us that Skrebensky is an engineer and a man associated with details, with synecdoche, displaying a fussy concern for small matters such as the class background of the bargee's wife or the price of necklaces.) Unlike her mother, who could not actually dance herself free of Will, Ursula has taken the first step toward her own liberation.

Textual Erotics

All the love scenes in the narrative focusing upon this third couple are replications and bindings that defer and yet prepare for the ultimate transformation in the last chapter. Even before the man comes back into her life, the narrative offers this woman the possibility of another Anton, in the form of Anthony Schofield, the brother of her colleague Maggie. More Greek faun than prelapsarian Adam, this Schofield figure is a mere cul-de-sac for the traveler, a kind of fatal attraction. As he reaches his hand toward the gate to enclose her in this ominous Garden, the text indicates: "She realised with something like terror that she was going to accept," but then, "involuntarily," the unconscious speaks her rejection, "I couldn't" (386). This rejection of his marriage proposal is authorized by the narrative, even though, in another of those long flashforwards, we read: "All her life, at intervals, she returned to the thought of him and of that which he offered. But she was a traveller" (387). This Schofield figure problematizes the Anton figure, as well as the conventional notion of literary personages as characters with some sort of existential value exclusive of the text into which they are woven. Clearly, like his namesake, Schofield is merely another expression of confinement that the woman must turn away from in her traveling. It may be only a traveling *toward* at this juncture, but the narrative moves her past Schofield with a brusqueness indicating that it has some other end in mind—an ending, toward which it leans expectantly.

The metaphoric as repetition binds later segments of the text together as well. The whole complex of Ursula's experience as a university student, beginning as a journey into the unknown and ending with the persistent sense of confinement, repeats the school-teaching segment as merely a representation of imprisonment within the patriarchal structure of masculine power and feminine vulnerability. In addition, the love scenes repeat themselves, and all of them rewrite the corn-stacks scene of years before when one construction named Ursula acknowledged the dying of her lover's soul. Each offers a narrative of failed fulfillment, bound to those scenes that precede and follow; moreover, these scenes also defer what the narrative excites as the desire for the final diverting of the woman's journey from this man's well-worn path.

Like the Ursula figure, the text plays with the romantic notion of accompanying her lover to India. This "delicious make-belief" of a "passage to India" constructs a "tissue of romance" for the latter days of this affair. This willful toying with the metaphor of travel represents one way of troping the metonymic impulse of desire for the fulfillment offered by the ending of traditional narrative. India has its attractions. At the same time, confinement in some tiny niche of Anglo-Indian patriarchy offers only a poor alternative to the "bondage of teaching" in England. In the midst of this romance of the journey, the end of the affair and the closure of this narrative are anticipated by her response to his "When shall we be married?"—reminiscent of his "Don't you like me to-night?" in the prototypical love scene in the corn-harvest segment. Once again, the unconscious "speaks" her, as the text makes clear when it indicates that her "never" comes "out of some far self which spoke for once beyond her" (432).

It is because this Other has had so little opportunity to "speak" Ursula that the end is deferred so long. Because she is a woman in a traditional culture defining femininity in the context of confinement, she is still an inexperienced interpreter of what the Other "means" when it speaks her. Thus, in the final love scene along the coast of Lincolnshire, she tells him, "I want to go," and when he asks, "Where?" she can say only, "I don't know." Even before this scene, Ursula knows that "It is finished" because desire is metaphorically a journey into the unknown, while Skrebensky can offer only the confinement of the known.

The Problematic Ending(s)

Of those readers who complain that *The Rainbow* lacks an ending, we might, in turn, ask, Which of its endings did you miss? In a text where narrative voice subsumes the consciousness of one character, one potential ending informs the closing paragraphs of the penultimate chapter. There, the narrative emphatically cuts away from Ursula to eliminate the Skrebensky figure, whom it precipitously marries off to the colonel's daughter. Indeed, this character proposes marriage the first time he is in his bride's presence—and in a fortnight they are married. "Ursula was not notified of the event," the narrative confides. As an efficient engineer, this former (and dead) lover has organized his future. Ironically, he is launched on "a passage to India," while she continues to represent the promise of travel, even though she appears headed toward a more restrictive confinement.

This confidential information of the former lover's abrupt marriage offers one ending of the traditional novel—a wedding. The sense of an ending for Ursula, however, subsumes the remainder of this text. The confinement of a possible pregnancy engenders her temporary abandonment of the journey: "She had been wrong, she had been arrogant and wicked, wanting that other thing, that fantastic freedom, that illusory, conceited fulfilment which she had imagined she could not have with Skrebensky" (448). The narrative reads out the letter of unconditional surrender to his mastery when she writes: "I shall ask no more than to rest in your shelter all my life—" (449). The promise of freedom balked, this traveler is forced back upon the masquerade of femininity, represented as an acknowledgment of a vulnerability requiring the protection of patriarchy.

Central to the final preparation for the ending of this narrative is the encounter with the horses. The text sufficiently foregrounds its apparent symbolic representation of some fundamental change occurring through the agency of the horses. The passage invites conventionally symbolic readings in which a literary representation has to be a symbol of something *outside* the text. In her essay "To Procreate Oneself," Cornelia Nixon offers an excellent example of the difficulties in reading this symbol. She identifies the horses as a "great symbol," to use Lawrence's own term for a symbol defying the imposition of "meaning," and then proceeds to explicate the meaning of the horses as agents of parturition—midwives to Ursula's giving birth to herself.[17] Nixon helpfully maps the minefield of applying the author's comments from outside texts such as essays and letters and stresses the changing valence of symbols like the horses from earlier texts such as *The Rainbow* to later "Lawrence" texts. Unfortunately, however, she joins the great majority of readers who have opted for the comforting notion of an author whose meanings may change from one text to another within a stage of her/his productivity or from an earlier to a later period, yet an author who remains "Lawrence."

Mark Kinkead-Weekes is helpful in discussing the probably unresolvable question of meaning by reading the horses as an expression of "an intensity of conflicting forces that cannot be denied or reduced and must not be, in Ursula" ("Marriage" 36–37). This reading is especially useful because it posits meaning in "conflicting forces" while avoiding the impulse to identify a series of binaries in which one or the other in the pair is inevitably privileged. Furthermore, this reading focuses upon "forces" that the text constructs as narrative rhythm and avoids the sense of a privileged outside text, or "dehors texte," to borrow Derrida's term.

This segment of the narrative also represents the culmination of the role played by metaphor in the novel. The "bond" of the fetus is shed in miscarriage, as the "dead" lover is shed like leaves, within the binary of confinement/freedom, which is yet another aspect of what the horses are "a symbol of." Earlier, when pregnancy is a possibility, the text asserts: "What had it to do with him? Why must she be bound, aching and cramped with the bondage, to Skrebensky and Skrebensky's world? Anton's world: it became in her feverish brain a compression which enclosed her" (455–56). As the narrative moves toward closure, the text authorizes the shift from the confinement/freedom binary into the metaphoric. It is *within,* not outside, that the transformative journey toward freedom must take place.[18]

That transformation is rendered in large part through the citation of what the Other in Ursula says when it speaks her movement toward freedom in the passage beginning "I have no father nor mother nor lover, I have no allocated place in the world of things" and ending with the metaphor of the nut breaking out of its shell. This nut metaphor is bound metaphorically to its early occurrences in the narrative, preparing for its representation here of transformation as an equivalent for metaphoricity. She is represented within the framework of

> acorns in February lying on the floor of a wood with their shells burst and discarded and the kernel issued naked to put itself forth. She was the naked, clear kernel thrusting forth the clear, powerful shoot, and the world was a bygone winter, discarded, her mother and father and Anton, and college and all her friends, all cast off like a year that has gone by, whilst the kernel was free and naked and striving to take new root, to create a new knowledge of Eternity in the flux of Time. And the kernel was the only reality; the rest was cast off into oblivion. (456)

Although the narrative frames the metaphor of the acorn shedding its dead shell and transforming itself into a new form of life with numerous prose statements of what it represents, no statement can serve as an equivalent for, nor can it diminish, the agency of the acorn metaphor. In a clear sense, it is this metaphoric transformation toward which the plot of desire has been metonymically moving. Furthermore, the organization of movements forward with these metaphoric bindings through repetition retrieves what out of context would seem a trite figure for regeneration.

Indeed, the narrative can work these varieties of retrieval because it offers the (perhaps illusory) sense of the *right* ending. Two marriages in the narrative have been followed by the failed possibility of a third in a rhythm resonating with a sense of closure: marriage, marriage, not-marriage. Marriage with an Anthony who lacks a soul or with an Anton whose soul is dead would deny the trope of travel as the metaphor of transformation or metaphoricity. "Skrebensky" represents "ended-ness": "He was that which was known," she muses, with "poignant affection for . . . that which is past." Instead, she looks to the horizon: "It was the unknown, the unexplored, the undiscovered upon whose shore she had landed, alone, after crossing the void, the darkness which washed the New World and the Old" (457). The journey is in the metaphor, not in our explanation of it, and it is the rainbow at the end of the journey toward which this long narrative has been inexorably moving. That destination is confirmed by the novel's title, the signifier that the narrative has been carrying along on its journey.

Resisting Closure

If the last paragraphs of this discourse leave the impression of an absent ending, it is perhaps because this text has set into motion the binary of conflicting desires—the horses again—with all of that binary's restless impulse to move toward ending yet resist ending. In this sense, Brooks's "textual erotics" may be operating here as well. Brooks's narrative paradigm is a masculine model and a modernist one, too, and as such it is problematized by the ending of the text at hand. In place of narrative closure, this text offers openness, and not merely the open ending. The narrative of *The Rainbow* ends by foregrounding the metaphoricity with which it has been implicated from the outset. The ending *is* metaphoricity within the rainbow trope, with its suggestions of absence/presence of the repressed signified within the signifier.

For what is a rainbow in the realm of the Real? The rainbow is the spectrumizing, so to speak, of light, or fire, within water. In one sense, the rainbow deconstructs the binary of visibility/invisibility, and light can be seen. The rainbow problematizes this fire/water binary, these polar opposites, each of which has the potential to destroy the other. In the rainbow trope, the two seem to offer the promise of resolution, balance, harmony, and so on. However, such union is the province of the Imaginary. The intent here is not to privilege the Symbolic, so much as to reaffirm the agency of the Lacanian Imaginary, Symbolic, and Real as a refuge from the structuralist's binaries. The rainbow, however, is implicated in the Symbolic because it offers only the *promise* of metaphoricity, or transformation. It does not combine in order to *resolve* the conflict of the fire/water, metonymy/metaphor, male/female, and similar binaries. It simply deconstructs the opposition by shifting it to another level through transformation. The ending moves us metonymically toward the fulfillment of Desire, masked as desire, in a metaphor of a sprouting acorn or a rainbow that metaphoricity puts in the place of lack and of that Desire that can never be recuperated. For a moment, the rainbow sutures over the lack by announcing the promise of transformation, or movement onto another plane. And then the rainbow fades.

4

STAGING THE GAZE IN *WOMEN IN LOVE*

In one of the most memorable, and puzzling, sections of *Women in Love*, the narrative authorizes Gerald Crich to make a spectacle of himself by savagely spurring his horse into submission after it has been terrified by the clamor of a passing railroad train. The audience for whose eyes this spectacle has been staged comprises the Brangwen sisters and, of course, the readers who look through, and around, the eyes of the sisters. The term *spectacle* seems appropriate here because Gerald, who performs the illusion of his mastery, assumes the role of author/stage manager as well as star performer. Alternatives such as moving away from the train crossing or demonstrating the mare's skill by jumping her over the crossing gate seem to have been dismissed in favor of this specular and spectacular performance of forcing the horse's absolute obedience to "her" master's will. The scene's theatricality—or, as Linda Ruth Williams[1] provocatively argues, its cinematic construction—is vividly realized through the descriptions of how each of the sisters looks at this spectacle through radically different eyes. The focus of the narrative on Gudrun's looking is reinforced through repeated references to her eyes. For example, we read that Gerald "was very picturesque, at least in Gudrun's eyes," and "Gudrun liked to look at him" (110). Although it would seem at first that Gudrun's eyes are being made to function in a conventionally novelistic fashion as a mere camera recording Gerald's external appearance, the focus on Gerald's eyes and his watching provides yet another indication of the pervasiveness in this text of eyes and the potential for domination in looking at and its reversed mirror image of being looked at.

In staging this scene for its predictably different effects on the two halves of its audience, this narrative equates mastery with exhibitionism, with the construction of a system of self-conscious looking at its spectacle. That spectacle cannot begin until its performer has ensured that its audience is watching. After "looking down the railway for the approaching train," this performer "salutes" his audience, confident that the two women are witnessing the spectacle he is about to script and star in for their benefit. As the mare first begins to recoil from the frightening noise of the approaching locomotive, the narrative indicates that "a glistening, half-smiling look came into Gerald's face." It is a "look" that reflects Gudrun's earlier "ironic smile at his picturesqueness" (110).

When the mare recoils a second time, the responses of the sisters begin to be more radically differentiated. Gudrun's response is the more complex, for she is reacting not only to Gerald's cruel restraint but also to Ursula's humane reaction, voiced in her reasonable question: "Why doesn't he ride away till it's gone by?" (111). Gudrun as watcher appears mesmerized, as she gazes at Gerald "with black-dilated, spell-bound eyes." As the theatrical scene ends, those responses are underscored when Ursula, "frantic with opposition and hatred of Gerald," cries out once again. Gudrun watches, still "spell-bound" and silent, suggesting that the narrative is performing the interaction of psychic states, and not merely recording simple observing in these figures.

The reactions of the two sisters for whose eyes this scene has been performed are further distinguished by the effect that Ursula's voice has on Gudrun, and undoubtedly on Gerald as well. When Ursula cries out the first time "at the top of her voice, completely outside herself," the phrase *outside herself* seems a clumsy misstatement of *beside herself.* The text indicates, however, that "Gudrun hated her bitterly for being outside herself," because her voice "was so powerful and naked." Thus, Gudrun's gaze, which has fastened itself upon Gerald's performance of will-to-power, seems to have immersed her *within* herself so profoundly that Ursula's "powerful and naked" voice is a distracting feature of an "outside" she rejects. It suggests, moreover, that Gudrun has been listening to another "voice," a voice within. Gudrun's voice may sound so different to Ursula, as the narrative records that difference, in part because it is an "other," or perhaps even the Other, that is "speaking" *her.* To underscore the mesmerizing force of that gaze, the narrative likens the scene to one from a "disgusting dream that has no end," yet offers no clear indication of the subject in whose eyes this unending dream is "disgusting."

By the end of this scene, the narrative has established a space within which Gerald the performer and the two sisters as audience have adopted subject positions within a system of the gaze. As Kaja Silverman has suggested, the gaze stands in relation to looking in much the same way as the phallus stands in relation to the penis.[2] By positioning the sisters as audience for this performance of mastery, Gerald as performer constructs one sister as a reaction of horror and the other as an identification with the liberating power of cruelty as it frees the subject from conventional sentiment. In turn, the two observers of this spectacle are constructing each other as binary opposites in this structure of looking and being looked at. As Linda Ruth Williams helpfully suggests, Gerald as performer must veil his function as the object of his audience's looking, even though it is clear from the outset that their watching legitimates his performing of mastery.[3] The painful helplessness of one watcher of Gerald's brutality is balanced by the exhilaration of the other in participating in this trespass against a kind of taboo outlawing such deliberate cruelty. Because the narrative allows the scene to play itself out without cuing its readers as to where they are to position themselves in the scene, the reactions polarized in the sisters are implicated in the narrative. As a result, these polarized reactions "read" a correspondent polarity within readers, allowing them access to both repulsion against malicious cruelty and attraction to the licensing of violation.

The real power of the scene, then, is its theatricalization by Gudrun's imagination after the action of the episode is over, when she apparently loses consciousness momentarily. It is only as the action completes itself—signaled by the approach of the guard's van—that the real power of the scene builds *within* Gudrun, as she reshapes it in her own imagination. As the narrative makes clear, the figure of the guard functions as a surrogate for Gudrun's gaze: he is "staring out in his transition on the spectacle in the road. And, through the man in the closed wagon Gudrun could see the whole scene spectacularly, isolated and momentary, like a vision isolated in eternity" (112). In this way the guard is enlisted as another watcher, along with the sisters; unlike them, however, he is watching not only Gerald's performance, but also Gudrun's. This new watcher and the gatekeeper record her reaction against her watcher's role of silent passivity as she becomes an active, screaming participant in the scene, in her own fashion also "making a spectacle of herself." Springing past the guard, she flings the gate open for Gerald and the mare, crying out "in a strange, high voice, like a gull, or like a witch screaming out." This performance of celebrating Gerald's "mastery" of the show, with the strangeness of her voice and the unexpectedness of her gesture in flinging the gate open with her assertion, "I should think you're proud" (112), seems to surprise even the star performer Gerald in the powerful effect his spectacle has called up in part of its audience.

Looking and Being Looked At

Having introduced the notion of looking at and being looked at, as well as the term *gaze,* in this brief examination of this novel's paradigmatic scene, it is now possible to begin to contextualize this scene within contemporary theorizing about looking. Traditional notions of seeing might impel readers to frame the preceding scene within formalist readings of eye and vision imagery. However, following the lead of Jacques Lacan, recent theorists are more likely to opt for concepts of looking or the gaze in which the unconscious is implicated. Much of the film theory, for example, generated by writers such as Laura Mulvey and Teresa de Lauretis owes an immense debt to the seminal work of Lacanians such as Christian Metz in *The Imaginary Signifier.*

As we begin this discussion of what Lacan understands as *le regard,* or the Gaze, it is important to recall what a strong reader Lacan was of other major thinkers of our century. Because Lacan's thinking is always grounded in Freud, it is impossible to begin any investigation of the Lacanian Gaze without following him in his "return to Freud." In this case, we may follow Lacan back to Freud's early study, "Instincts and Their Vicissitudes" (1915). There is an uncanny appropriateness in beginning with this key text because the three central instincts Freud hypothesizes along with their "vicissitudes," or reversals, are all evident in the scene of Gerald and the mare. The first is probably the most obvious—the sadism explicit in Gerald's performance of cruelty in mastering the mare. Freud sees the interrelations between sadism and its "vicissitude," masochism, in terms of three stages: (1) the instinct begins in an impulse to exercise control or to master another person as an object; (2)

the instinct reverses itself by relinquishing that other person as object and a turning back upon the subject as passive object; (3) the completion of the three stages occurs in the search for another subject in relation to whom the original subject might become a passive object (127). The "instincts and their vicissitudes" may be understood as a continuous shifting pattern of oscillation between opposing positions, similar to the silhouettes in an optical illusion, so structured that one can see, for example, either the vase or the two profiles, but not both simultaneously.

It is Freud's discussion of the second major instinct and its vicissitude that Lacan found most useful to his formulation of the Gaze. Freud sees similar stages in the interrelations of the visual, or "scopic" instinct and its reversal. What seems a simple act of looking is merely the first of three stages in the visual experience. At first, the act of looking, like sadism, is an effort to control another subject as an object. In its second stage, looking turns back upon the subject or some part of the subject as though that part were an object viewed. Finally, another subject is introduced in the third stage as a viewer for whom the first subject can function as object. In this way, the watching subject may achieve control over the object, only to become the object observed and therefore mastered (129). To understand either position—looking at or being looked at—one or the other must be "repressed." When one position is "repressed," or erased, a trace of that position remains as a ghost of the absent, repressed opposite, producing an oscillation between positions. This notion of oscillation creates a post-structuralist context of binaries whose traces of each other undermine any illusion of exclusivity.

The extremes of the visual drive and its opposite are represented by what Freud calls the "scopophiliac," or voyeur, and the "exhibitionist," who seek to arrest this oscillation by permanently canceling or repressing the opposing position. The voyeur, accordingly, chooses to repress the exhibitionist's passive, watched position in order to become the active watcher. To achieve control and to deny object loss, the voyeur must avoid being seen, for to be seen is to become an object. Rather than accept loss as a principle of absence, the exhibitionist chooses to conceptualize loss as a thing. In the process, the loss is turned into what Robert Con Davis calls a "phantom presence—a fetishistic totem—that, in reality, negates . . . the structural position the loss should have created. Exhibitionism is a positioning whose significance is always to show and never to be shown—that is, never to be shown any loss" (987).

It is important at this point to follow the eclectic Lacan back to one of his sources, Jean-Paul Sartre's *Being and Nothingness*. This gesture of a "return to Sartre," so to speak, is authorized by Lacan's discussion of the Sartrean *regard*, or gaze, in his essay "Anamorphosis" from *The Four Fundamental Concepts of Psycho-Analysis*. For our purposes, this detour to Sartre's *Being and Nothingness* is useful because it allows Lacan himself to offer his own revision of the Sartrean *regard* as the Lacanian Gaze.

Lacan begins his "return" with the assertion that Sartre's discussion of the gaze represents "one of the most brilliant passages of *L'Être et le Néant*." He proceeds to rehearse Sartre's definition of *le regard* before offering his own revision of it. As Ellie Ragland-Sullivan points out, Lacan seeks to distinguish the gaze from the simple fact that "people see with their eyes" (94). According to Lacan, *le regard* for Sartre is "the gaze by which I am surprised—surprised in so far as it changes all the perspectives, the lines of force, of my world, orders it, from the point of nothingness where I am," leaving the subject as a "scotomized" object (*Concepts* 84). Lacan continues: "In so far as I am under the gaze, Sartre writes, I no longer see the eye that looks at me and, if I see the eye, the gaze disappears." Lacan counters that Sartre is wrong: when the subject invites and succeeds in obtaining the gaze, the gaze does not disappear simply because the subject becomes aware of being its object. Painters (and it seems appropriate to add here artists generally and writers in particular), Lacan goes on to say, "have grasped this gaze as such in the mask." Lacan concludes, "The gaze sees itself—to be precise, the gaze of which Sartre speaks, the gaze that surprises me and reduces me to shame, since this is the feeling he regards as the most dominant. The gaze I encounter—you find this in Sartre's own writing—is, *not a seen gaze, but a gaze imagined by me in the field of the Other*" (*Concepts* 84; emphasis added). Lacan's introduction here of the Other points toward his formulation that "the unconscious is the discourse of the Other" and his grounding of the gaze in the earliest stages of the human subject's development.

As Ragland-Sullivan indicates, Lacan's definition of the gaze is grounded in its agency as "one of the first structuring mechanisms of the human subject." Infants "introject," or take in, the gaze before they have gained the power of seeing and before they have any sense of otherness, the "other" being still synonymous with themselves as subjects. Within the mirror stage, the gaze plays a central role; however, before the eye begins to see, "prespecular objects of Desire become permanently enmeshed in a network of inner vision" (94–95). With the advent of consciousness, "seeing oneself seen" becomes central as the subject develops a sense of "self" implicated in the notion of being seen by another. As Ragland-Sullivan phrases it, "The other's look or words have connected with the repressed discourse linked to the Other's gaze. . . . By linking the gaze to the earliest moments of the formation of the subject, Lacan has made it a part of the primordial unconscious system of representations, which are later reflected in consciousness" (95).

It is impossible to leave this scene without acknowledging once again the perceptive contribution of Williams to this discussion of looking. In her study *Sex in the Head: Visions of Femininity and Film in D. H. Lawrence,* Williams examines this scene of Gerald and the horse at great length to argue that this and other Lawrence texts are interestingly divided against themselves. Grounding her discussion in the film theorizing of writers such as Christian Metz and Laura Mulvey, who clearly bear the mark of Lacan's thinking on the gaze, Williams demonstrates how Lawrence texts anticipate many of the staples of cinematic representation, even though their author went on record—in his later writing, it might be emphasized—as being vehemently opposed to film. As her title cleverly indicates, Williams seeks to associate Lawrence's abhorrence of film with his phrase "sex in the head," representing bad or cerebralized sexuality. At the same time, Williams points out, he was also drawn to scenes in which he "perversely" focused the attention of the reader, through the narrator/camera's eye, upon icons of male beauty. For Williams, Lawrence's "looking at" men operates "perversely" because he resorts to the construction of female agents to do his gazing for him. Williams is interested in using Lawrence's texts as a means of reading the author's sexuality and often cannot resist engaging in rather sensationalist discourse—she calls Lawrence a "cine-phobe and macho misogynist," for example.

Because the Williams study shares so many interests with this one, it can also point up some useful contrasts. First, *Sex in the Head,* despite its brilliant application of film theory to Lawrence texts, hearkens back to more traditional varieties of biographical criticism. It reads the text as a representation of its author, in this case subtly attempting to "out" "Lawrence" by recycling the outmoded views of Kate Millett, namely that the author exploits female characters in his fiction to represent his "homosexual" desire, preserving some of Millett's insinuation of the "perversity" of such desire. Secondly, this approach seems "feminist" in a similarly dated manner with its reliance upon now-discarded presumptions of "masculinity" and "femininity." It is precisely this essentialism—implicit within structuralism, especially with its grounding in biographical criticism—from which the examination of Lawrence texts so desperately needs to free itself. This effort to read the sexual desires or orientation of the author in the texts, nourished by obsessive attention to the "life" of their author, can end only by perpetuating the reductiveness of older readings, despite their borrowing from contemporary theorizings in film studies.[4] As we shall see, Williams's traditional, or essentialist, notions of gender as inextricably linked to sex or biological differences keep us from seeing that gender is implicated in positionality within the structure of the gaze, so that, for example, Gudrun is positioned as "masculine" as an avid watcher, while Gerald is "feminized" by her gaze, just as at other points Gudrun can vehemently resent her positioning as the "feminine" object of the miners' looking, and their wives' looking, and Gerald can function in a more traditionally "masculine" position as the watcher, as we see in the "Water-Party" section. The notion of "cross-gazing" implicit in Williams's approach is grounded in the essentialist assumption of gender as fixed and discrete, rather than fluid and variable as the Lawrence texts themselves so brilliantly suggest. Accordingly, these texts await less reductive readings that respect the complexities of gender construction, rather than interrogating the texts for evidences of some illusory so-called truth concerning the author or as a representation of a notion of life outside the text.

Although the episode in which Gerald performs his illusion of mastery for the eyes of the sisters offers a most dramatic representation of specularity and spectacle, the episode is not unique. Indeed, from the very beginning *Women in Love* is dominated by constructions of looking at and being looked at. The novel's opening scene ends with the assertion that "The sisters found themselves confronted by a void, a terrifying chasm, as if they *looked* over the edge" (10). To divert their attention from further regard of that void—their future—Gudrun, the incipient watcher in this text, suggests that they go for a walk: "Shall we go out and *look at* that wedding?" The walk to the church becomes painful to Gudrun, "exposed to every stare" of these "uneasy, watchful common people." At the same time, of course, she invites their stares with her brightly colored stockings. Her reaction to the comment of one spectator is particularly worth noting. The narrative indicates: "A sudden fierce anger swept over the girl, violent and murderous. She would have liked them all to be annihilated, cleared away, so that the world was left clear for her. How she hated walking up the churchyard path . . . *in their sight*" (13; emphasis added).

In this episode Gudrun's being-looked-at-ness is set in marked contrast to Ursula's lack of self-consciousness; even though Ursula is similarly positioned, the situation calls up no such response in her. Thus, in its positioning of Gudrun, the scene offers a good example of the Sartrean *regard* when he asserted "*Le regard de l'autre, c'est l'enfer,*" or "Hell is the other's gaze" (Ragland-Sullivan 94), or even "Hell is other people." Gudrun's reaction of "surprise" at being positioned as the "scotomized" object of others' looking is the product of her ignoring the exhibitionist effects of those bright stockings. The revulsion against being looked at by these ghoulish spectators is so great that she almost misses the opportunity to be a spectator herself at the Crich wedding.

More important, she almost misses the first of several close encounters with Gerald Crich. The wedding party and its spectators offer something in the way of a model for subsequent scenes, such as Gerald's with the mare, in which viewpoint characters are positioned as watchers of others who are themselves spectators. At first, the scene provides Gudrun with a diverting spectacle, and the narrative even foregrounds its own theatricality: each guest seems "a complete figure, like a character in a book, or a subject in a picture, or a marionette in a theatre" (14). Soon, however, we discover why Gudrun has been brought to her position as spectator, for it is Gerald upon whom her gaze "lights." He has "the strange, guarded look, the unconscious glisten," which becomes the signature of his personality. The statement that she "lighted on him at once" suggests a linkage of staring or gazing with an aggressive, almost predatory assault upon Gerald.

This predatory aspect of the gaze, traditionally associated with the male, has been gendered "masculine" because the position of the one who looks is empowered by the gaze structure. When Gudrun says, "I shall know more of that man," it becomes clear that seeing is at least a double phenomenon here, for gazing at/familiarizing herself with Gerald will be her way of knowing him. In this way, she will "know" Gerald in an essentially Western mode of knowing. As Williams notes, Gudrun's apprehension of Gerald is a mode of knowing traditionally reserved for the male eye, which knows the love object to be pursued as a complex of surfaces in which the eye becomes ensnared. At the same time, it is not a question of Gudrun masquerading as a male to know, and to anticipate possessing, the object of desire through the gaze, nor a question of Gudrun representing a female impersonator looking at a male as a means of sanctioning homoerotic desire. What is at issue here is the engendering of positions in the gaze structure as masculine or feminine based on the power inherent in the gaze. Because patriarchy has empowered men and because the gaze empowers the looker position, it is no accident that looking has been the province of the masculine.

The implication of Gudrun in the system of looking and being looked at is problematic. From Freud, we have learned that exhibitionism and scopophilia or voyeurism are inversions of each other. As part of the gaze structure, each position is the opposite of the other, and yet as Lacan would see the two, neither is distinct from the other and neither has an essence but is only a construction of positionality. At this point Gudrun becomes involved in the gaze by training her eyes upon Gerald as an object of desire. Clearly, the gaze is reading her voyeurism, implicit in her aversion to being looked at. This is an aversion that the narrative has just dramatically foregrounded in her revulsion against being stared at by the "watchful common people" on the way to the church. However, the text offers at least one notable exception. In the memorable section of the "Water-Party," where Gudrun's dancing takes on a more clearly performative character as she succeeds in dancing Gerald's cattle away, the construction of the gaze produced by her exhibitionistic performance complicates any simple analysis. Gudrun as self-immersed performer becomes aware of the cattle that have suddenly appeared as a powerful and potentially lethal audience to her performance. Appropriately, she draws their looking to her performance as a representation of her awareness that she is vulnerable as the object of their looking, and yet she overpowers these beasts which are outside the system of the gaze by performing her gazing at them. Although they cannot return her gaze, clearly her looking can read in them the power of the male gaze she appropriates by seizing the position of gazer. Eventually, her performance shifts once again with her awareness that she is being watched by not only Ursula but also Birkin and especially Gerald. Because she is aware—before he informs her—that these are *his* cattle, the dancing away of the cattle becomes a performance primarily for his eyes, in much the same way that the scene with the mare was staged for hers.

In the first encounter, however, Gudrun is positioned as the looker. As the object of her gaze, Gerald is positioned as the power of fascination: "There was something northern about him that magnetised her" (14). What the gaze seems to be reading in her is "violent and murderous" impulses, suggested by her recognition that Gerald's "totem is the wolf." His "clear northern flesh and his fair hair" are metaphorized as "cold sunshine refracted through crystals of ice." In this way, Gerald's "god" is Apollo, the Greek god of light, order, and knowing through the eye, the same Apollo whose totem was also the wolf. The visual representation of Gerald draws upon the earliest graphic evidence of classical Greek civilization—the kouros, or "Apollo," the "beautiful boy," to use Camille Paglia's term, the first sex object of Western desire.[5]

Gudrun's bizarre reaction to gaining knowledge of Gerald by looking at him suggests the extent to which the power of the gaze may be reading the unconscious in her. As she stares at Gerald, who seems at this point not yet aware of the role chosen for him as love object/exhibitionist in this staging of the gaze, Gudrun is being read as an active, even aggressive, and potentially sadistic watcher: "She was tortured with desire to *see* him again, a nostalgia, a necessity to *see* him again, to *make sure* it was not all a mistake, that she was not deluding herself, that she really felt this strange and overwhelming sensation on his account, this *knowledge* of him in her essence, this powerful *apprehension* of him" (15; emphasis added). If her reaction seems "orgasmic," it is the result of the abruptness of her lighting upon Gerald as her potentially perverse soul mate in this dramatization of Freud's notions of the "instincts and their vicissitudes." The crucial term in the passage just cited is *apprehension*. *Her* visual knowledge of *him* is an "apprehension." This knowing through the eyes is, thus, at one and the same time a perception and a conception, indicating her mental construction of what she sees in him. It is, moreover, an arrest and a foreboding, suggesting the impulse to fix him as an icon of her desiring eye, with all the repercussions of such imposition upon another human subject.

This "apprehension" of Gerald's body offers an opening for the helpful insights of Peter Brooks in *Body Works*. For Brooks, the intense pleasure this text credits in Gudrun's looking at the body of Gerald, clothed or nude, represents "epistemophilia," a term he borrows from Toril Moi to indicate what he sees as "an erotic investment in knowing," especially knowing through the gaze (53). "The body held in the field of vision," Brooks generalizes, "is par excellence the object of both knowing and desire, knowing as desire, desire as knowing" (99). As we shall see in the "Diver" section, this narrative is implicating its readers, along with the sisters, in a kind of epistemophilia, as it focuses the gaze on the body of Gerald in a process of denuding it, exploring its privacy (and potentially its "privates"). The text, thus, invites a complicity in the desire to break out of one's own bodily isolation, as Georges Bataille suggests, in a gesture of erotic looking, a looking that is ultimately for Bataille "the affirmation of life all the way into death" (quoted in Brooks, *Body Works* 8). In the case of Gudrun, however, this pleasure in looking seems an act of appropriation, a gesture toward possession, rather than a pleasurable binding of one's being with the other's. It is perhaps no coincidence that in the next scene in this sequence, Gerald's body is literally denuded—*la mise à nu,* to use Bataille's term—as the text exposes the secret and private in line with Brooks's argument that the novel as form from its very beginnings has been implicated in staging varieties of denuding for its readers' visual imaginations (28–29).[6]

Gerald as Exhibitionist

The next encounter in this chain of episodes linked through their foregrounding of looking and being looked at occurs in the "Diver" scene. The narrative positions the sisters as ready audience by having them walking once again, this time near Willey Water. Suddenly, their casual looking at the landscape is interrupted by the intrusion of "a white figure" running from the boathouse and diving into the water. Significantly, the diver is identified at first only as male. As a man who has taken possession of the watery world, this "white figure" calls up Gudrun's envy, for this *he,* even if not Gerald, has the privilege of swimming nude in such a public place. As audience for this performance the sisters stand "watching" the diver. Clearly, the episode functions as a preparation for the subsequent scene of Gerald's performance with the horse toward which this encounter is inexorably moving, for their reactions are radically differentiated. As in the scene with the mare, the more visceral Ursula has no envy whatever of the "cold" and "wet" freedom of the swimming "white figure," while Gudrun, as the clear focus of the narrative's attention, stands "watching . . . as if fascinated." Eventually, the narrative indicates that the sisters "could *see* his ruddy face, and could *feel him watching them*" (47; emphasis added). At this point, the function of Ursula seems once again to be little more than a casual, cheery contrast to the "fascinated" Gudrun. Ursula's statement of the obvious—"It is Gerald Crich"—rings upon the ear like the naive reaction of a child, in contrast to Gudrun's "I know." As in the earlier wedding scene, Gudrun *knows* Gerald through her eyes, as they once again establish their fix upon his body. Clearly, the text is representing a "knowing" and a "desiring" through the eyes, in line with Brooks's insights concerning the attraction here of Gerald's body and his awareness that his body is the object of the other's gaze.

What follows is an ingeniously staged performance of looking and being looked at. Part of what "fascinates," or even mesmerizes, Gudrun is Gerald's absolute self-containment. He is performing not only a state of self-content in the isolation of this watery world, which in "Water-Party" he will inform the sisters is *his* water; he is also performing a celebration of something very much like narcissistic self-sufficiency. He appears to be wrapping himself in an aura of glamour. Like the star of film or rock music, Gerald has charisma, and he grows to relish its effect on others. The effect on Gudrun is made clear in a passage demonstrating the operation of the gaze:

> And she stood *motionless gazing* over the water at the face which washed up and down on the flood, as he swam steadily. From his separate element he *saw* them, and he exulted to himself because of his own advantage, his possession of a world to himself. He was immune and perfect. He loved his own vigorous, thrusting motion, and the violent impulse of the very cold water against his limbs, buoying him up. He could *see the girls watching him* a way off, outside, and that pleased him. He lifted his arm from the water, in a sign to them. (47; emphasis added)

Obvious though it may be, it is worth repeating that Gerald's reaction here, and elsewhere, lifts him out of the context of the Sartrean *regard,* for as soon as he becomes aware of Gudrun's looking he acknowledges her gaze and seems to relish the performance of his construction of masculinity for her desiring eyes. Clearly, there is a "seen gaze" here, to use Lacan's term. However, that more conventional gaze is also implicated in a "gaze imagined by me in the field of the Other," a gaze performed in the unconscious as well.

The nakedness of Gerald's body is also worth noting here as a preparation for the bohemian scene to follow in London. In the London scene, his nakedness becomes a source of embarrassed self-consciousness to Gerald. In the context of the self-conscious nudity of the other men, who seem intent upon making a statement rather than merely expressing an impulse toward physical intimacy among friends, Gerald's body is covered to protect it from unwanted looking by those whose conspicuous display of their bodies even Gerald is reading as an inducement to expose his for their voyeuristic purposes. In that scene the evasion of what Gerald perceives as his own "being-looked-at-ness" replicates Gudrun's discomfort in the scene with the ogling miners. In both scenes we are offered expressions of the Sartrean *regard* in which the consciousness of being looked at triggers an aversion to the look of the other. On the other hand, in the nude wrestling scene, although Birkin also strips off his clothes, it is Gerald's nakedness upon which the narrative focuses, almost as though he were a classical Greek statue in motion.

To return to the scene in "Diver," it is interesting that Gerald's nakedness is veiled from the view of the sisters once they have identified him. At the same time, Gerald seems to be experiencing an autoerotic pleasure in exercising the exclusively male privilege of swimming nude, a privilege that "ladies" of this time would be reluctant even to acknowledge as a desire. But it is his complete nudity as maximum exposure to the external world that is essential here. The complete enclosure of his body by cold wetness defines the contours of his form as a sculptor shapes the surface of a statue. And Gerald thrills to this radical self-containment, as though he were an *objet d'art,* self-consciously enjoying the knowledge that his audience is aware of his hard separateness.

Once again, the elements of performativity and the sense of spectacle make it difficult not to read this scene as "cinematic," but in a very much current sense of the term. Recent film theorists have argued that it is time to adjust what have become traditional understandings of looking in film. Laura Mulvey, who established many of those now-traditional understandings in her seminal essay "Visual and Other Pleasures," posited that film technology is structured by the male gaze at the female object of its desire, within which the actor's looking is a representation of the spectator's with the camera's eye as its instrument. That understanding of the engendering of film has seemed increasingly problematic to recent film theorists, in part because that construction of the gaze has difficulty encompassing the question of how female spectators function as members of an audience in which the female subject is object of the cinematic system of looking. More importantly, Mulvey's theory of looking in cinema seems to have no means of responding to an ever more insistent question in film theory: what are we to make of the male subject as object of the gaze, especially as loosening movie codes have allowed more of the male body to be exposed to the camera eye? And beyond that, what are we to make of the male actor who often seems to be performing the spectacle of his own construction of masculinity for the desiring eyes of some unclearly defined audience? In this context, this narrative breaks new ground by allowing this performative element in Gerald Crich, who is in a clear sense "making a spectacle of himself" for the eyes of the reader. If these scenes of Gerald's performing his masculinity seem contemporary, it may be because he is positioned by the text as the contemporary film actor is often positioned—as one who self-consciously exposes his body for the desiring eyes of his audience.[7]

Gerald's audience in the "Diver" scene is a radically split one, as the two sisters once again react to the spectacle he is making of himself in diametrically opposed responses. Ursula continues to be the casual, sociable onlooker, laughing at her own cleverness in comparing Gerald to a Nibelung. Indeed, she seems to be almost self-consciously enjoying the ironic appropriateness of this comparison of Gerald to a figure in the *Nibelungenlied,* where Gudrun's Teuton namesake plays a crucial and destructive role. Gudrun, in contrast, is deeply implicated in the gaze: "Gudrun said nothing, only stood still *looking* over the water" (47; emphasis added). Her silence and immobility, set off by Ursula's bubbly talk and Gerald's mobility, underscore the power of the gaze. By watching Gerald's exhibitionist activity as though he were an object generated by her watching, Gudrun is being read by the Other, by the unconscious as it works through Gerald, as object and as other. And he too is being read by her gaze, as becomes clear in the statement: "They *watched* him. He waved again, with a *strange movement of recognition* across the difference" (47; emphasis added). The word *difference* seems at first a lapse for *distance;* however, it is ironically apt here, perhaps the narrator's Freudian slip, since the "difference" between Gudrun as the one who looks and

Gerald as the one who revels in his "looked-at-ness" collapses upon itself as both are implicated by the gaze.

That subversion of "difference" through identity helps to prepare for the clearly sadomasochistic overtones of the later scene of Gerald and the mare. As a narcissist with exhibitionist tendencies, Gerald, like Gudrun his soul mate, is a complex mixture of conventionally masculine and feminine characteristics. He "exults" in the masculine freedom and mobility he is performing, the metaphoric "thrusting with his legs and all his body, without bond or connection"; at the same time, as exhibitionist or object of the watcher's gaze, he is positioning himself in a passive and thus feminine position of vulnerability or susceptibility to Gudrun's active, assertive, and eventually sadistic control. In her gaze, he reads a celebration of his own masculinity, and yet he needs a confirmation of his mastery in the slavishly devoted and envious eyes of the other to whom he gives up power. Thus, he can know power only by sadistically exulting in the knowledge of his own male freedom and mobility by performing them for the benefit of the oppressed female's eyes. Perhaps he even senses the perverse potential in his relationship with the slavish Minette, whose self-humiliation foretells his own in the last stage of his affair with Gudrun, who flaunts the power that has devolved upon her through Gerald's admission of a "feminine" dependence upon her.

Gerald's awareness that the sisters know that he is naked in the water, even though they are unlikely to see much of his body, implicates his performance in a variety of autoerotic desire, similar to Birkin's nude scene in the woods, which occurs in the narrative just before Gerald's scene with the mare. When, as a consequence of Hermione's attempt to smash his skull with the lapis lazuli paperweight, Birkin staggers into the park and follows his impulse to strip away the clothes that are his obvious connection with civilization and lie down in the primroses, he is alone and unobserved (except by the narrator and the reader, of course). The point is worth emphasizing because this scene in Ken Russell's film of the novel, along with the nude wrestling scene, is likely to rupture the illusion of cinematic realism when the spectator, unlike the reader, is made aware that s/he is cast as observer, or even voyeur, in the very public space of the movie theater. Because reading is a solitary act and because the narrative moves the action onto a symbolic level, the scene can call up desire in at least some readers. That the scene arouses desire in Birkin is made clear in the sentence that the Cambridge editors have restored to the text near the end of the scene to validate his sense of harmony with the greenwood: "He knew where to plant himself, his seed" (107). Although Gerald may be similarly aroused by the "isolation" in which he "exulted," "happy, thrusting with his legs and all his body," there are clear indications that if he experiences autoerotic pleasure it is the result of the spectacle he has made of himself for the sisters, performing the freedom of swimming nude, an act from which they are foreclosed by social constraints.

The gender constructions of the two principals in this scene, Gerald and Gudrun, demonstrate how Lawrence is in many ways our contemporary, almost a century later. Indeed, the scene is much more lucid in a contemporary postmodern context than the conventionally modernist one in which it is usually read, in large part because it points to the construction of gender in terms of positionality. Gerald is at one and the same time both the performer of masculine power and freedom and the feminine object of the gaze. Similarly, Gudrun as a woman has been empowered through the agency of the gaze because it is clearly for her eyes (and indirectly the reader's as well) that Gerald is performing his masculinity. This scene is an excellent point at which to raise these issues, in anticipation of the nude wrestling scene, for example, where the conjunction of *two* nude men alone together not only in proximity but full physical contact with each other makes it extremely difficult to fend off the now-clamorous judgments of a thinly disguised homosexual episode.

It seems important, then, early on to establish some of the indeterminacy, fluidity, and aversion to fixed categories that have become associated with the slippery term *postmodern. Women in Love* offers such a powerful and complex narrative in large part because it defies the fixity and determinacy conventionally associated with a novel such as *Sons and Lovers*. Here the gender of the characters seems more "allotropic," to use Lawrence's own famous term for indeterminacy and fluidity in his fictional creations. Although many readers continue to be uneasy talking about fictional "characters" with the confidence of a generation ago, this novel seems to be offering us more of the improvisational elements in its characters: the narrative is again and again constructing their gender by moving them into contexts in which their positionality engenders them. This indeterminacy and fluidity may be more difficult for traditional readers to tolerate because they may want, in anticipation of, say, the gladiatorial scene, to find some truth of the character's sexual orientation or gender suddenly unmasked in a moment of self-exposure. Instead, the text appears more intent upon demonstrating how subjects perform their gender according to the context, or how they move through continual reconstructions of their gender according to their position vis-à-vis the other subjects in the scene.

Gerald as Watcher and Watched

It is interesting too that this "Diver" scene is connected with the "Water-Party" episode, in which the sisters have their turn at enjoying the "male" freedom of swimming nude, admittedly in a remote area where they do not expect to be seen. The scene is yet another theatricalization of the gaze, beginning with Gudrun's recounting of the "vile experience" of watching impoverished boys diving into the muddy Thames for coins tossed to them by passengers on a steamer. The narrative indicates that Gerald "*watched* her all the time she spoke, his eyes glittering with faint rousedness" (161; emphasis added), perhaps because of her cruel disdain for the poor. This indication of Gerald's "faint rousedness" after watching *her* performance of aristocratic disdain would seem to indicate that Gudrun has no monopoly on looking. Like Gerald, Gudrun is a hierarchist, who privileges *his* diving over the loathsome grubbing for money of poor boys in the mud. Birkin, if he recalls his earlier conversation with Gerald at Breadalby, might find some amusement at Gudrun's performance of disdain, since Gerald's questions about the social status of these Brangwen women led Birkin to twit him for snobbery: "Class-barriers are breaking down!" (94).

This "Water-Party" scene makes an extremely important contribution to the economy of the gaze by helping to free it from Williams's generally reductive and exclusionary focus upon the male gaze supposedly cross-gendered to reveal the author's secret desires. As they row away, *Gerald* becomes the watcher over the water.

> Her voice was shrill and strange [like her voice as she throws open the gate for him and his mare], calling from the distance. He *watched* her as she paddled away. There was something child-like about her, trustful and deferential, like a child. He *watched* her all the while, as she rowed. And to Gudrun it was a real delight, in make-belief, to be the child-like clinging woman to the man who stood there on the quay, so good-looking and efficient in his white

> clothes, and moreover the most important man she knew at the moment. She did not take any notice of the wavering, indistinct, lambent Birkin, who stood at his side. One figure at a time occupied the *field of her attention*. (164; emphasis added)

In repeating references to Gerald's looking at Gudrun as she recedes into the distance, the narrative marks the power of the gaze in the couple's relationship as that gaze allows the subject to read the discourse of the Other within the other.

The gaze plays a significant role in the scene of Gerald and Birkin's intrusion upon the privacy of the sisters. The famous scene of Gudrun's doing Dalcroze exercises and becoming aware of the Crich cattle follows Ursula's suggestion that the two swim in the nude. The positioning of the cattle as "watchers" of her dancing underscores the theme of hypnotized staring in this text. Clearly, the cattle are a projection of her preoccupation with evading the stares of ogling men, since these cattle are not milch cows but "bullocks," or steers, literally a sort of prospective "beef cake." Her sadistic display, generated through her implication in the gaze as she watches these castrated males, suggests that she is being read by the Other as a complex mixture of scopophilia-exhibitionism and sadomasochism. Obviously enough, she enjoys the "helpless fear and fascination" of the cattle, "breathing heavily" with a quasi-sexual arousal. Appropriately, *her* exhibitionism with his cattle, positioning Gerald as voyeuristic watcher, confers a power upon him that she deeply resents: "She was *watching* him all the time with her dark, dilated, inchoate eyes. She leaned forward and swung round her arm, catching him a light blow on the face with the back of her hand. . . . And she felt in her soul an unconquerable desire for deep violence against him" (170; emphasis added). He recoils in surprise from what is a mere gesture of violence, "and a dangerous flame darkened his eyes." Like Gudrun, "fascinated" by his exhibitionism with the mare, Gerald is rendered speechless, his heart nearly "bursting with a great gush of ungovernable emotion." If Gudrun's reaction to his cruel mastery of the mare can be (mis)read as an "orgasm," surely this "bursting" represents Gerald's coming.

Gudrun's implication in the gaze is so intense that she is slow to shake off its effects. As a watcher who resents the feminizing position of being stared at by men, she attempts to escape from the mastering of Gerald's eyes: "She stood negligently, staring away from him, into the distance." All the time, he is "*watching* her closely. His eyes . . . lit up with intent lights, absorbed and gleaming" (171; emphasis added). When she attempts to avoid his gaze by moving away, Gerald pursues her, admitting that he loves her. It is appropriate to the more traditional masculinity Gerald is performing that he can tell Gudrun he loves her *only* after she has played her traditionally feminine role as object of that pursuit and asked him not to be angry with her. In this sadomasochistic arena of struggle for power, he shows himself up, to her at least, as one of his steers by "swooning" in response to her mocking tolerance of his overture. The conclusion of this episode reconfirms the interrelation of the scopophiliac-exhibitionist and sadomasochistic drives in a chilling passage foretelling the cataclysmic relationship to come for the two:

> "It's all right, then, is it?" he said, holding her arrested.
>
> She *looked at the face with the fixed eyes,* set before her, and her blood ran cold.
>
> "Yes, it's all right," she said softly, as if drugged, *her voice crooning and witch-like*. (172; emphasis added)

More than in any of the preceding scenes, Gudrun has indeed apprehended Gerald through the gaze: her eyes have read the Other in him as other. Within his performances of mastery, he advertises his desire to be mastered. If scenes such as these have mysterious power over even the most sophisticated readers, that power inheres in the intensity of our gaze as we watch these visually realized, theatrical episodes in which the gaze is reading our unconscious. For the male reader at least, Gudrun is a variety of Medusa, that dread image of the powerful female, fascinating, bewitching, and petrifying Gerald and those who gaze at her along with him. But clearly for male as well as female readers Gerald is specularly attractive in his energetic performance of traditional masculinity, a performance made ironic by our recalling his self-evident pleasure in also positioning himself as the object of the desiring gaze of others, focused in the eyes of Gudrun.

Yet another link between scenes in which looking is prominent may be found in Gerald's exploration of the cul-de-sac offered by Minette, an exaggeration of Gudrun's performance of a potential for submissiveness on the road toward slavishness. When Minette and Gerald first meet, the encounter is rendered through repeated references to her looking at him and his quite self-conscious suffering of her gaze: "Still she stared into his face with that slow, full gaze which was so curious and so exciting to him. . . . And he was aware of her dark, hot-looking eyes upon him. She had beautiful eyes, dark, fully-opened, hot, naked in their looking at him" (64). Once again, it is difficult not to find analogies here with the construction of looking in film. Especially relevant in this context is "fetishistic looking" as John Ellis defines that phenomenon in his book *Visible Fictions*. Ellis writes:

> Fetishistic looking implies the direct acknowledgment and participation of the object viewed. This contrasts with the voyeuristic emphasis on the film pretending that it is not seen whilst all the time constructing itself for the viewer. With the fetishistic attitude, the look of the character towards the viewer (i.e., down the camera) is a central feature. Each participant, the absent actor and the present viewer, gaze at each other. It is the gaze of longing, asking for the impossible abolition of the distance that separates the spectator and fiction. This implies a lack of the secure knowledge that the voyeuristic attitude gives the spectator over the fiction. It implies an equality, a directness, and a level of delicious frustration. It also implies a lack of change and of action. The voyeuristic look is curious, inquiring, demanding to know. The fetishistic gaze is captivated by what it sees, does not wish to inquire further, to see more, to find out. (47)

Although Ellis is talking about film, his perceptions help us to open this text to explore its tendency to position Gerald Crich as the object of what Ellis calls the fetishistic gaze. The narrative foregrounds Gerald's awareness that he is food for the hungry eyes of another, in this case, Minette. At the same time, an unidentified narrator is also observing this scene of looking for the benefit of the reader, who, like a spectator in the film theater, is looking through the narrator as through the lens of an unobtrusive camera, perhaps with a desire for which Minette's rather slavish adoration of the male is a more obvious substitute.

The gaze is suspended for a short time by the intervention of Minette's lover Halliday, but it resumes with references such as "She looked at him steadily with her dark eyes, that rested on him and roused him so deeply" (67). And as is so often the case in this text, the gaze is also implicated in epistemophilia, the desire to know: "She wanted to know. And her eyes seemed to be looking through into his naked organism" (67). In one sense, the looking here is at least double, if not multiple. Perhaps as a statement of her limited expression as a *female* agent of looking, Minette is left at the level of voyeuristic looking, to borrow Ellis's term, and once her curiosity to "know" is satisfied she looks away while the longing look of the narrator/reader lingers on. The operation of desire is clear in the assertion that "she wanted the secret of him, the experience of his male being" (60).

The wedding scene and "Diver" episode are further linked by the dance scene at Breadalby. This Breadalby scene provides further evidence of the novel's theatricality as it positions Gerald as an audience for Gudrun's and Ursula's performances as Ruth and Naomi, respectively. Gerald's female counterpart here is Hermione, who "loved to watch" (91). (We recall Birkin's stunning accusation in the "Classroom" scene: "what you want is pornography—looking at yourself in mirrors, watching your naked animal actions in mirrors" [42].)[8] In the Breadalby scene, both Gerald and Birkin are positioned as watchers, but with a difference. Gerald is "excited by the desperate cleaving of Gudrun to Naomi," with its "female, subterranean recklessness and mockery," while Birkin sees not only the "brilliant frustration and helplessness of Ursula," but also the "dangerous power" of her "powerful womanhood." Birkin, we are told, "was unconsciously drawn to her. She was his future" (92). At the same time, Gerald and Gudrun continue to struggle for position in the scopophiliac-exhibitionist pattern, while Ursula and Birkin struggle on the level of words. Gerald's performance and Gudrun's reading of it in the "Coal-Dust" episode, then, represent a reaction against their positions in the Breadalby scene, just as the "Water-Party" will reverse "Coal-Dust."

In between these episodes in which Gerald and Gudrun shift positions in the scopophiliac-exhibitionist pattern, we find another expression of the gaze. First, we need to note that Gudrun's fascinated watching of Gerald's exhibition of "mastery" over his mare is followed by an inversion of the scene of the sisters walking to the Crich wedding. There, Gudrun is offended by the silent staring of the miners' wives at her because of her brightly colored stockings. In the scene following Gerald's equestrian performance, Gudrun is stunned by the fascinated watching of two miners who break their silence to disagree on whether five minutes with Gudrun would be worth a week's wages. Almost to reassert her mastery as a watcher, Gudrun is allowed to see a miner washing himself, "naked down to the loins, his great trousers of moleskin slipping almost away" (115). This watching, reminiscent of Connie Chatterley's peeping at Oliver Mellors washing himself at the outset of their relationship, restores her more usual, "male" position as watcher. The gaze overtakes Gudrun and Gerald in the episode that immediately follows their encounter in "Coal-Dust."

The Master Mastered

The "Sketch-Book" section of this text seems to have as its sole purpose the further implication of Gudrun and Gerald in a deadly contest for mastery. The scene is the Willey Water of "Diver" in what has become a pattern of juxtaposing in a variety of metonymy/metaphor; that is, these segments of the text are associated in terms of being like and yet different from each other. The narrative returns to remap the water of "Diver" in which Gerald was earlier immersed; this time, however, he is clothed and in a boat, as he will be in "Water-Party," where he is both on and in the water. Furthermore, Hermione functions as a female counterpart for Gerald in this scene, composing with Gudrun, who is sketching yet another triangle, like the earlier diver and the mare triangles. When Gerald reaches for the sketchbook to examine the text on which Gudrun has been working, his memory of her "last words" allows him to regain the mastery he experienced in that scene when "she was compelled by him." Her gaze reads this illusion of mastery in his face, and she is overcome: "her mind went dim and unconscious" (120). Although this segment of the narrative is not extensively developed, it clearly demonstrates the function of the gaze, as Gudrun's looking at Gerald's face in a moment of illusory mastery becomes a way of establishing that his face is "reading" her unconscious. The scene ends with a further extension of the power of the gaze, as Gerald watches her dismissing Hermione for apologizing profusely after carelessly dropping the sketchbook into the water: "He *watched* her with an insight that amounted to clairvoyance. He *saw* her a dangerous, hostile spirit, that could stand undiminished and unabated. It was so finished, and of such perfect gesture" (122). Thus, the text allows Gerald to read in Gudrun a corresponding narcissistic self-containment. She too has "charisma," in that "finished" and "perfect" theatrical "gesture" of brushing aside Hermione's fussy attempts at apology and laying the blame instead on Gerald. The gesture celebrates Gerald's "aristocracy" as one who is above the law, disdainful of conventional sanctions against cruelty to animals and with insufficient regard for the perishability of sketchbooks. Once again, it is looking rather than the words accompanying that looking that is worth noting: "She *looked* at him, with her fine blue eyes, and signalled full into his spirit . . . her voice ringing with intimacy almost caressive now" (122). "The bond was established between them, in that *look*," the text indicates, a "diabolic freemasonry." Little doubt remains that "she had a power over him," a power confirmed by her establishing visual mastery, or the illusion of mastery, over him as the watched exhibitionist in this oscillation of the gaze. The scene offers a brilliant expression of that oscillation between looking and being looked at which Robert Con Davis so accurately sees as the basis of the gaze: a system or "theater" of positionality in the visual text that can be understood in post-structuralist terms as "a decentered set of positions [which] never—at any stage—reaches an end or comprises a totality."[9]

The gaze clearly functions early on in this text as a kind of annunciation of the struggle for mastery between Gudrun and Gerald. The demonic undercurrent of their relationship is suggested in the "Rabbit" chapter, as the text focuses Gerald's looking at the welts on Gudrun's forearms and perceiving "her sullen passion of cruelty" (240). The earlier performance of Gerald and the sisters with the mare is evoked by the sound of Gudrun's "high voice, like the crying of a seagull, strange and vindictive" (241). Again and again, the narrative focuses upon Gerald and Gudrun's looking, especially their exchange of the gaze, which allows each to read the Other in the other: "Gudrun looked at Gerald with strange, darkened eyes, strained with underworld knowledge, almost supplicating, like those of a creature which is at his mercy, yet which is his ultimate victor"; "Glancing up at him, into his eyes, she revealed again the mocking white-cruel recognition"; "She looked at him and saw him, and knew that he was initiate as she was initiate"; and finally, "Her eyes looked up at him with shocking nonchalance" (241–43).

The gaze is represented again in the scene of Gudrun and Gerald joining the couples "spooning" in the underpass. The mastery of Gerald over the courting miners, who bring their women here, allows her to "sleep" for a time in passive submission to that illusory mastery. The narrative begins with simple looking—"She looked up, and in the darkness saw his face above her," with "a white aura," as though Gerald "were a visitor from the unseen"—then develops into an expression of epistemophilia as her fingers become extensions of her eyes: she would "know" him as "Eve reaching to the apples on the tree of knowledge" (331). In stark contrast to the segment of this narrative representing the movement toward marriage in Birkin and Ursula's relationship, darkness is clearly not the province of Gudrun and Gerald's erotic contest. Darkness forestalls the elaborate staging of the gaze on which Gerald and Gudrun depend for their shifting performances of positions of mastery and submission.

When the narrative moves to the sexual consummation of Gerald and Gudrun's struggle for mastery, the text foregrounds another representation of the gaze in Gudrun's elevation into a hyperconsciousness, figured by the narrative as wide-eyed sleeplessness. The narrative represents her powerful wakefulness, as she "lay wide awake, destroyed into perfect consciousness . . . with wide eyes staring motionless into the darkness" (345). This is no simple insomnia of a woman whose lover has too quickly spent himself. Instead, the narrative makes clear that the darkness of the room impedes epistemophilia: "She wanted to look at him, to see him" (345). Further references to this desire to look at him follow, with a repetitive insistence that seems to mirror Gudrun's desire to know and therefore to master Gerald through her eyes. What the narrative is intent upon establishing here is that Gudrun, roused into this state of "violent active superconsciousness," spends an entire night under the imprisoning weight of Gerald's body, gazing into a night whose darkness reads her own. The process is troped as the drawing of a "glittering rope of knowledge out of the sea of darkness . . . from the endless depths of the unconsciousness" (346). As those who are drowning supposedly see their lives passing before their eyes, Gudrun sees her whole past, but as a rope she has to haul out of the dark sea of her unconscious.

Another Kind of Looking

The other major construction of looking occurs as an apparently stark contrast to the lethal force of the gaze in the segments of this text representing the context for mastery in Gudrun and Gerald. Indeed, the representation of looking in Ursula and Birkin functions so much like conventional expressions of lovers' looks as to be barely noticeable. Simply put, Birkin performs the role of watcher and Ursula en-acts the role of the watched: "en-acts" is appropriate because she is performing as Naomi in Hermione's staging of the biblical story of Ruth. The relationship of Birkin and Ursula begins with a reversal of the watcher and watched positions of Gudrun and Gerald. At Hermione's drawing-room theatricalizing of the Ruth story, Birkin is described as "watching [Ursula] like a hermit crab from its hole" (92). What he sees, however, is Ursula as "a strange unconscious bud of powerful womanhood. He was unconsciously drawn to her. She was his future" (92). This last assertion *She was his future* echoes Tom Brangwen's *That's her* in the earlier novel. The narrative here renders overt the looking that remains implicit in the Gudrun-Gerald relationship. First, in the more normative Birkin-Ursula relationship, it is Birkin who looks at Ursula, in a fairly conventional expression of the male gaze. However, once we grant the presence of the male gaze there seems little of the power of the gaze in this externalized rendition of looking. That is, the narrative is merely asserting what it elsewhere stages as the gaze in the Gerald-Gudrun relationship: Ursula's subjectivity is being penetrated by Birkin's look at the same time that Birkin seems aware Ursula as other is "reading" the Other within himself. Generally, however, following this cursorily rendered looking, the Ursula and Birkin figures are noticeably lacking in the complex structure of looking and being looked at in which the Gudrun and Gerald figures are implicated.

There is one notable exception, however. Immediately following the "Rabbit" chapter, in which Gerald and Gudrun have sealed their demonic "love" through mutual exposure and visual penetration, Ursula comes upon Birkin stoning the moon's reflection on Willey Water. Before she is aware of his presence, however, Ursula herself suddenly senses the moon as a variety of "watcher": "It was like a great presence, watching her. . . . And there was no avoiding it. . . . she suffered being exposed to it" (245). As a result of that exposure to the moon as watcher, Ursula seeks shelter from the oppressive moonlight in the shade of the "tree-hidden bank." After positing her reaction against the moon's reflection on Willey Water, the text generates another watcher, whom Ursula as watcher uncannily recognizes immediately as Birkin. Because, as the narrative indicates, she is exhausted of any concern for anything, she watches for a long time without revealing her presence to this other watcher. Given the oppressive agency of the moon as an anthropomorphized watcher, Ursula accepts the position of voyeur in this scene, even though the narrative leaves no doubt that, while watching Birkin, Ursula is very much aware he might do "something he would not wish to be seen doing" (246). In this way, the scene stages the gaze in a manner very similar to that of the episode of Gerald on his horse. Here again, we have an intricate layering of watchers. Escaping the moon that she feels is watching her, Ursula looks at Birkin, who is gazing at the reflection of moon. Thus, the moon's reflection is closing the circle of looking, in which the text's readers are also implicated as the narrative encourages them to visualize the scene.

Unlike its counterpart of Gerald on his horse, this scene theatricalizes looking without the object of the gaze—Birkin—being aware of his position. The system of looking thus approximates Sartre's *regard,* because as soon as Birkin recognizes that he is the object of Ursula's looking he shrinks in a gesture of exposure, similar to hers when she seeks the shade as shelter from the moon's powerful "eye." It is only when she can no longer bear the intensity of his reaction as he stones the moon's reflection on the water that he becomes aware of her presence. Before that happens, however, she gazes in silent, unmoving fascination at the evidence of the moonlight's powerful effect on him. What she is looking at clearly becomes a visual text he unwittingly fashions for her gaze. For her as watcher, this text of stoning the moon's reflection is clearly reading the Other within her. Were that not the case, she would not expose her position as watcher, thereby surrendering the power inherent in that position, in order to erase the visual text. It is as though Birkin has been constructing that text on a child's Magic Slate, and Ursula, who can bear no more, lifts the transparent cover sheet to make the text disappear.

The awkward, uneasy, but also welcome lapsing back into consciousness for both watcher and watched here is mirrored in the reader, positioned as watcher of this visual and dramatically visualized text. The relief readers experience is grounded in the perception that this text is also reading them. Ursula and Birkin's uneasy relief is evident in the staccato dialogue through which they reconstruct everyday consciousness after the intensity of their joint but separate lapsing out. Just before she breaks the spell of his unconscious violence against the moon's reflection, the narrative indicates that "Ursula was dazed, her mind was all gone" (248). The same might have been said for Gudrun as Gerald completed the performance of mastering his horse. Once again, the text in its metonymic movement forward has reached a point of transformation. Ursula has read something in this text that Birkin was performing by stoning the moonlit water. In the same way, once she makes her presence known to him, he is forced to acknowledge his own reading of/by the visual text of that moonlit water.

As in other scenes of metaphoric transformation within this text and

The Rainbow, we are teased into explication. What was the moonlit water reading in Birkin? What was Birkin's stoning of the moon's reflection reading in Ursula? If we return to the beginning of this "Moony" chapter, we note the strange circumstance of the narrative beginning with two brief sentences to indicate Birkin had gone to the south of France and nobody had heard from him; it then focuses upon Ursula's present state of hard indifference. "Mostly her heart was closed in this hidden, unconscious strain of contemptuous ridicule," the narrative generalizes, then adds: "But the strange brightness of her presence, a marvellous radiance of intrinsic vitality, was a luminousness of supreme repudiation" (244). It ought not to be ignored that Birkin's stoning of the moon's reflection satisfies Ursula's aversion to this light, as is made clear in her curious desire to escape it early in the scene, as though it were some kind of watcher. Ursula may also be demonstrating an unspoken desire for what Maurice Blanchot in his essay "The Gaze of Orpheus" calls the "*other* night," a darkness behind the darkness of the night. In this way, the gaze may be reading Ursula's aversion to what the moonlight represents, as she watches Birkin's increasingly desperate, and futile, effort at erasure.

The promise of the darkness of that "*other* night," posited by Blanchot, is offered in the lovemaking in the "Excurse" chapter. In the parlor where they have had their tea, Ursula and Birkin make love, in a fashion, but their lovemaking seems the inverted image of Gudrun and Gerald's. Looking and being looked at are foregrounded, yet they are implicated in a renewal of vision. Here the gaze reads in each looker an absence of hierarchical power and a depth of tenderness released by the power of metaphoricity.

> She *looked* at him. He seemed still so separate. New eyes were opened in her soul, she *saw* a strange creature from another world, in him. It was as if she were *enchanted,* and everything were *metamorphosed.* She recalled again the magic of the Book of Genesis, where the Sons of God *saw* the daughters of men, that they were fair. And he was one of these, one of these strange creatures from the beyond, *looking* down at her, and *seeing* she was fair.
>
> He stood on the hearth-rug *looking at* her, at her face that was upturned exactly like a flower, a fresh, luminous flower, glinting faintly golden with the dew of the first light. And he was smiling

faintly as if there were no speech in the world, save the silent delight of flowers in each other (312–13; emphasis added).

These are eyes that do not look at another to exploit the vulnerability of the other; they are eyes that see in the other the rainbow promise of the Unknown, or alternately a "New Heaven and New Earth."

If this scene represents the *annunciation* of the potential for metaphoricity in the Ursula-Birkin relationship, its realization occurs in the night scene in Sherwood Forest. Since "it was pure night," the regime of looking and being looked at has been utterly suspended, and only darkness and silence reign in this kingdom of tenderness and touch. "Quenched, inhuman, his fingers upon her unrevealed nudity were the fingers of silence upon silence, the body of mysterious night upon the body of mysterious night, the night masculine and feminine, *never to be seen with the eye,* or known with the mind, only known as a palpable revelation of living otherness" (320; emphasis added).

Clearly, this text is bent on grounding the Birkin-Ursula relationship in the unspoken darkness of an unknown into which the narrative wisely bars its readers from following, even though it continues to offer enigmatic references to the two journeying together into a world outside the realm of looking. On board the night boat to the Continent, for example, Ursula discovers what she had been saving herself for: "In Ursula the sense of the unrealised world ahead triumphed over everything. In the midst of this profound darkness, there seemed to glow on her heart the effulgence of a paradise unknown and unrealised. . . . the paradisal glow on her heart, and the unutterable peace of darkness in his, this was the all-in-all" (388). Unlike the Gerald-Gudrun relationship, this marriage has no farther to go in a world of looking; it is the "other" relationship—the struggle for mastery between Gudrun and Gerald—that awaits its transportation into the menacing otherworld of an Alpine realm of brilliantly intense light. This "North," Jack Stewart reminds us, is a world of "*water,* ice, . . . blue-eyed Teutons, . . . light, spirit, intellect" juxtaposed to the "South" of "*fire,* sun, warmth, . . . darkness, the body, . . . earthliness" ("Art" 135). The Tyrol, then, is a dramatic locus for the potential of a rainbow harmonizing "North" and "South."

The Prince of the Light

Because the text has grounded that "other relationship" of Gudrun and Gerald in looking, the movement of the narrative from the grayer, dimmer world of England to the dazzling light of the top of the world can do little but call up a sense of impending disaster. The narrative implements that disaster by positioning the artist Loerke, who is also a sculptor, in the text as another representation of looking, a variety quite similar to what the narrative has exposed in Gudrun. From the moment the narrative allows Loerke to step onto the brilliantly lit stage of the Alpine cul-de-sac in which Gerald constructs his destiny, this smaller, gnomish figure is represented as another watcher: "But Loerke was *watching* closely, with his uncanny, full, suspicious *eyes.* Something in Gudrun seemed in accord with him. . . . She too was *fascinated* by him, *fascinated,* as if some creature, a rabbit or a bat or a brown seal, had begun to talk to her. But also, she knew what he was unconscious of. . . . He did not know how, with his full, submerged, *watchful eyes,* he could *look into* her and *see* her, what she was, *see* her secrets" (426–27; emphasis added). Because as a watcher, it is his "quick, full eyes, like a mouse's" that are his defining feature, the rest of his body need not be large, for it exists only to support the agency of his looking. The "fascination" in which her looking is implicated is noteworthy again: this is the ensnaring of the look in the object of such "fascination" that it seems to bind the looker in her position of irresistible watching. Such fascination in its own fashion deconstructs the usual notion of the gaze being a position of power, or masculinity, for here the object of this fascinated watching seems more clearly the power position.

As the prince of this dazzling world in which the look reigns supreme, Loerke is accorded a mocking, gnomic, subversive power to form a bond with Gudrun and eventually push Gerald out into the cold. The narrative focuses upon the immense power of the mountains, which become a visual text in which Gudrun reads a potential for liberation ultimately dwarfing what she read in Gerald's performance of mastery in the spectacle of the mare. It is she who envisions her "consummation" awaiting her "over the strange blind, terrible wall of rocky snow, there in the navel of the mystic world" (410). Once the narrative has removed her sister and Birkin, who take flight to the warm South beyond these mountains, and she is no longer inhibited by the sanctions they represent for her, Gudrun can enter into a kind of mystic communion with the mountain peaks, with the knowledge that part of the pleasure of that communion is its exclusion of Gerald. The difference in the looking of these two represents the difference in their reading of these mountains as visual text: as

Gudrun's eyes gaze at the snow-capped peaks, rosy in the reflection of the setting sun, the narrative offers her an annunciation, while Gerald is a tourist who refuses to share her consummation. Indeed, the narrative foregrounds the radical difference of her gazing and his cursory looking: "To her it was so beautiful, it was a delirium, she wanted to gather the glowing eternal peaks to her breast, and die. He saw them, saw they were beautiful. But there arose no clamour in his breast" (446). The power of her looking and his resentment of that power are foregrounded in the subsequent interchange, as she finally turns her eyes back to him, expressing her judgment: "That was the most perfect thing I have ever seen" in "cold, brutal tones." When she laments that he has seen fit to undermine her aspiration to achieve communion with the mountain peaks, his response is telling: "'One day,' he said, softly, looking up at her, 'I shall destroy *you,* as you stand looking at the sunset'" (447; emphasis in the text).

This contest over her looking at the sunlit peaks has a gentler counterpart in the aftermath of Gudrun and Gerald's first lovemaking in the Alps. Although the narrative is fairly restrained in describing this so-called lovemaking, the effect on Gudrun seems more like having been raped than made love to. Curiously she cannot hear his protestation of undying love because she "lay looking at him as at something she could never understand, never: as a child looks at a grown-up person." He kisses her eyes closed "so that she could not look any more" (402). It is difficult to conceive of a more representative set of gestures for Gerald's performance as Gudrun's lover: either he must kiss her eyes closed or he must destroy her for looking at whatever she finds in the external world—mountain peaks, for example—as a reflection of her innermost being.

This deadly world of intense light over which the watcher Loerke reigns has its power over Birkin and Ursula, who may have come through but who are in the end no more impervious to the dominance of cold light. In the Alpine scene of dancing, drawing together earlier scenes of spectacle such as Gerald and the mare, for example, or Gudrun with the bullocks, Birkin is positioned as audience for Gerald's performance of love as erotic conquest with the Professor's daughter, who seems immediately "fascinated" with her "conqueror." If, as Mark Spilka reminds us, love between men in this kind of "Love Ethic" is the "step beyond marriage which makes marriage possible" (153), this spectacle of erotic conquest may be reading Birkin's arousal by Gerald's performance of traditional masculinity.

In one of this text's rare concentrations on looking in the Birkin-Ursula relationship, the narrative draws attention to "the odd little fires playing in his eyes." Ursula is "frightened of him, but fascinated." Interestingly, she is "fascinated," with its suggestions of his having captured her by forcing her to focus her eyes on him. Then the narrative emphasizes the mutuality of these gazes as it indicates that "before her eyes, as in a vision, she could see the sardonic, licentious mockery of his eyes." And to confirm that Birkin is staging a performance of his male animal mastery to which Ursula transfers responsibility, the narrative makes explicit her visual confirmation of his performativity: "He knew all the time what he was doing, she could see it in his smiling, concentrated eyes" (412). It seems impossible to exaggerate the significance of his position here as active initiator of the gaze, along with her willing surrender to its agency in him.

This unusual staging of the gaze in the Ursula/Birkin relationship undermines the tempting binary of the two couples, one of which is perverse and the other normative. Ursula's reaction to Birkin's suggestive licentiousness is especially worth dwelling on. The narrative insists upon Birkin's performance as the master of looking in this scene. "The sardonic suggestivity that flickered over his face and looked from his narrowed eyes, made her want to hide, to hide herself away from him, and watch him from somewhere unseen" (412). After several more references to their exchange of looks—"The flickering fires in his eyes concentrated as he looked into her eyes"—the narrative credits a defensive gesture regarding "bestiality" in Ursula's consciousness. It is a gesture that may be grounded in the narrative's subtle suggestions of anal intercourse. In its repetition of references to "shame," the text recalls the lovemaking of Will and Anna after his return from a bit of philandering with the factory girl in Nottingham. Surely, it cannot be dismissed as mere coincidence that these two texts foreground the exploring of "another kind of love" just after a spectacle of erotic conquest, whether performed or witnessed by the lover bent upon liberating himself and his partner from "shame." In any case, some sort of suspension of "paradisal knowing" in this "normative" couple seems to have been produced by this staging of the gaze, itself the product of this Alpine world of brilliant light.

The counterpart of this scene is staged in Gerald and Gudrun's bedroom. The narrative abruptly turns from its exploration of Ursula's meditation on "bestiality" to indicate that Gudrun too "had been watching Gerald" as he performed his easy mastery over the Professor's daughter. While watching Gerald's performance, Gudrun has been reading in it Gerald's need for continuous "erotic conquests" to construct his masculinity. Rather than being appalled by his obsessive philandering, Gudrun finds in it another confirmation of his vulnerability to her "epistemophiliac" inclinations. In their bedroom, Gudrun stages one variety of the gaze by performing her nightly ritual of brushing her hair before a mirror, which the narrative deliberately exploits for its complication of simple looking. She is the master of the gaze because although he is looking into the mirror he is not gazing as she is. His performance seems much more reminiscent of Sartre's *regard* because he is unaware of being looked at. "When she looked up, she saw him in the glass, standing behind her, watching unconsciously, not consciously seeing her, and yet watching, with fine-pupilled eyes that *seemed* to smile, and which were not really smiling" (414; emphasis in the text). Gudrun is strangely overcome by anxiety. As in the "Moony" episode, in which Ursula breaks the tension of having read the Other in Birkin's stoning of the moon's reflection, Gudrun struggles to find something to say in order to return Gerald and herself to everyday consciousness. Once again the narrative focuses upon her eyes: "her eyes were so bright with strange nervousness, she felt he could not but observe. But she knew also that he was completely blind, blind as a wolf looking at her" (414). This seems a bizarre self-contradiction: Gerald is "looking at her," but at the same time he is "blind." Clearly he is not actually looking at her so much as he is being read by the Other. In this fascinating play with a mirror, the narrative seems to be rereading Lacan on the mirror stage, for as Lacan has made clear, the subject need not look into a literal mirror but may discover an other to reflect the subject's aspiration to wholeness.

The narrative continues to explore Gudrun's agency in this economy of looking as she watches Gerald unselfconsciously looking at her. The passage is marvelously provocative in its representation of looking: "She could see him, in the mirror, as he stood there behind her, tall and overarching—blond and terribly frightening. She glanced at his reflection with furtive eyes, willing to give anything to save him from knowing she could see him. He did not know she could see his reflection. He was looking unconsciously, glisteningly down at her head" (415).

In this context, because Gerald is unaware that Gudrun is looking at him, Gudrun can preserve whatever power the look confers on her only so long as she maintains her position as furtive looker. Should Gerald consciously look *at* her, her power would vanish. Furthermore, the narrative confers on Gudrun the privilege of *knowing* that she can be that kind of looker only if she is unobserved. Beyond that, the narrative goes on to stress how Gerald's dominant corporeality as he stands behind her is so oppressive that she is only a few minutes away from caving in completely and groveling at his feet! Only her quick wits save her, as she sends him on an errand to look for something in her bag, a bag she had never allowed anyone else to go into. Now she can turn around with "her dark eyes blazing with uncanny, overwrought excitement," for the balance of power has swung to her, without Gerald's ever having become aware of how he was a mere hair's breadth away from achieving her total subjection.

The narrative allows Gudrun to awaken first the next morning and watch the sleeping Gerald, whom she reads as a potential Bismarck and the instrument of her ambition. Based in this reaccession to mastery over Gerald, she is prepared for the next encounter in which looking confirms her ascendancy. The narrative allows him to perform his conventional masculinity by asking her whether the toboggan ride was too much for her. However, she has so clearly regained her mastery that she can evade the conventionally feminine response he sought: "She looked at him with her brilliant eyes, that seemed to have undergone some transfiguration" and replies, "It was the complete moment of my life" (420–21). Hardly the response a lover might expect, Gudrun's comment echoes her earlier transfigurative experience with the mountain peaks lit by the setting sun. "Gerald's eyes became hard and strange," as he spends more of his time skiing—alone, since Gudrun doesn't ski—and thereby opening a space for Loerke to perform his own mastery as the prince of this realm of dazzling light and looking.

The narrative focuses upon Loerke as an alternative construction of masculinity to Gerald's. As Ursula remarked when the party arrived in the Tyrol, "It makes one feel so small and alone" (398), and thus it is appropriate that Loerke, the smallest and most alone of them all, should be master here. His dominant feature, once again, is his eyes: "like a troll's, or like the eyes of a lost being, having a strange, dumb, depraved look of knowledge and a quick spark of uncanny fire." Immediately after this assertion, the narrative adds that as Gudrun tried to engage him in conversation, Loerke evaded contact with her, "looking at her with his watchful dark eyes" (422). Interestingly, Ursula succeeds where Gudrun fails, even though the narrative makes clear that it is the latter in whom he is interested. Gudrun finally engages him in conversation when she intrudes upon his description of a frieze on which he is working. Because friezes belong on temples, not factories, this conversational lead opens up not only Loerke's perversion of Art to serve the Machine but also the final representations of the look in this novel—looking at works of art.

Looking at Art

Looking at art, of course, is not new to these closing chapters. The narrative has already introduced such observation in the bohemian context of Halliday's arty gathering, where the *au courant* acquisition of the African statue allows that work of "primitive" art to "read" Gerald, who, we learn, "hated the sheer African thing" (79). In a more important way, Gerald's reading of the statue allows for Birkin's reading of the "fetish" at least in part as a response to Gerald's extreme reaction against it. In the interpolated passage in "Moony," Birkin theorizes about the great polarity in which the fetish represents the "African way" of immersion in sensuality, in juxtaposition to the "Northern way" of mind-consciousness, dominant in Gerald and Gudrun. Much as the narrative validates how extensively this fetish as work of art has read Birkin's struggle to metaphorize the polarity of dark, African sensuality and bright, northern consciousness, his actual reading of the artifact is not represented in the extensive manner of the text's theatricalizing of the subsequent looking at Loerke's art.

From what seems a whole portfolio of illustrations of Loerke's work, the narrative focuses upon one of his productions to offer an expression of this text's *ekphrasis,* or looking at art in a print text. This illustration represents the statue of the nude girl on a horse, which Loerke seems to be proudly exhibiting as a demonstration of his mastery. This text within the text is central to the structuring of the last major expression of looking in the novel because it provides a telling example of the agency of art reading the Other in the lookers who try to read it.

In one sense, the scene in which Loerke directs the sisters' attention to the illustration of his sculpture of the girl on horseback rewrites the scene of Gerald and the mare in order to authorize Loerke as the prince of light. As in Gerald's spectacle, Gudrun is the agent of the gaze, while Ursula seems only to be looking in the Sartrean manner. Gudrun gazes at Loerke's "soul" by probing his personal history with her "large, grave eyes, that seemed to draw the confession from him as the marrow from his bones . . . to open some valve in his veins, and involuntarily he was telling" (425). Almost immediately, however, he recovers mastery in the scene by turning his gaze toward her, "watching closely, with his uncanny, full, suspicious eyes" (426). As in the Gerald performance, she is "fascinated" with Loerke; at the same time, she sees his power over her, even though he seems unable to: "He did not know how, with his full, submerged, watchful eyes, he could look into her and see her, what she was, see her secrets. . . . He knew her verily, with a subconscious, sinister knowledge, devoid of illusions and hopes" (427). And it is in this context that the looking at art becomes a displacement for Loerke's looking into Gudrun's innermost being.

The text allows us to look over Gudrun's shoulder at the reproduction of Loerke's representation of the small, naked girl upon a "massive, magnificent stallion, rigid with pent up power" (429). Gudrun's looking at the reproduction allows the work of art to read her: "Gudrun went pale, and a darkness came over her eyes, like shame, she looked up with a certain supplication, almost slave-like" (429). On the one hand, Gudrun knows that Loerke reads that "slave-like" response in the context of the "slave-like" model for the sculpture who was forced into performing for the artist/master. Furthermore, Gudrun must know that Loerke will read the "certain dark homage" to the work of art she is performing as an expression of her own recognition that she has become locked into a hopeless master/slave struggle with him. She may try to affect independence, "throwing back her head and looking at him with affected coldness"; however, Loerke "still gazed at her steadily, and his dominance was not shaken" (429).

The narrative enjoins Ursula to reenact her earlier role in the scene of Gerald and his mare at the railway crossing. She speaks for the horse again—not the reproduction of a horse in Loerke's picture of his sculpture but the real horse from which the artist was working. "Why did you make the horse so stiff?" (430). In one clear sense, the narrative is requiring Ursula to induce Loerke to speak for his art as a *representation* or as a textuality privileged over the "real" from which it begins: "It is a work of art, it is a picture of nothing, absolutely nothing" (430). In this modernist context where art has absolute value over the Yeatsian "fury and the mire" from which it is generated, Ursula is forced to play the role of a fool who rushes in where angels fear to tread. As in the earlier scene of Gerald and the mare, Ursula loses by exposing her anger at the exploitation of the natural world. In exasperation at Loerke's cool disdain for anything outside Art, she argues that his world of art and the real world are not separate as he proposes. Instead, his art reads him: "You can't bear to realise what a stock, stiff, hide-bound brutality you *are* really, so you say, 'it's the world of art'" (431). The narrative even draws Gerald in to support the views proposed by Loerke and Gudrun.[10] With Ursula and the voice of more traditional notions of art in retreat, Gudrun can take hold of the reproduction and credit Loerke for the depth of his understanding of the young model. It is her homage to Loerke that ensconces him finally as the prince of these brilliant heights, and characteristically the text indicates that homage through looking: "She lifted her eyes slowly, with a hot, flaming look into Loerke's eyes. His soul was filled with her burning recognition, he seemed to grow more uppish and lordly" (433).

This scene may not seem major enough to serve as the one on which this discussion of looking and being looked at should end. However, this scene is essentially the thematic climax of the action, and all that follows is its denouement. In the very next scene, Ursula persuades Birkin that they need to escape to the warm South, and Birkin never hesitates a second in agreeing to leave immediately, even though Gerald will be abandoned to the primacy of Gudrun's rule with her consort, Loerke. The scene of looking at the reproduction of Loerke's sculpture has imposed a tragic structure on the text, and the characters seem almost self-consciously enacting roles in a tragic action whose outcome cannot be changed. The narrative has already confirmed Birkin's allegiance to Ursula, while Gerald has failed to support her reading of Loerke's art at which they have been looking.

In actuality the narrative offers one further scene of looking, the scene of Birkin's looking at the frozen corpse of Gerald, no longer a performer but certainly an object of desire still.[11] In its understated fashion, the corpse metaphorizes Gerald's being as a "denier." The text clearly distinguishes between the love that Birkin felt for his dead friend and the disgust that he feels in looking at the frozen carcass Gerald has chosen to become rather than return that love. As Birkin stares at it, the corpse becomes a text that reads coldness and heartlessness in Birkin as well, and he must turn away from the frozen body to seek out the place where Gerald left it. Birkin climbs to the top of the pass well beyond where Gerald stopped and looks "south to Italy." It is not a "way out," he decides, but a "way in again," and when he turns away he accedes to a sense of the ineffable beyond his powers to explore: "Either the heart would break, or cease to care. Best cease to care. Whatever the mystery which has brought forth man and the universe, it is a non-human mystery. . . . Best leave it all to the vast, creative, non-human mystery" (478). But Birkin must return to look at Gerald once more, and this time the option is not to "cease to care."

In looking at Gerald's frozen face the second time, Birkin posits a sort of humanist's faith. He tells Ursula that he believes it is possible to be joined in some indeterminate afterlife with the spirits of those by whom we are loved. It is in this context that Gerald's nay-saying, which freezes the life from his body, comes to take on its largest metaphysical dimensions. If Gerald's choosing death were not sufficient to leave Birkin bereft, his withholding of love is to leave his survivor's spirit bereft for eternity, for as Birkin's meditation makes clear he believes that Gerald has missed the opportunity for a special kind of immortality: "Those who die, and dying still can love, still believe, do not die. They live still in the beloved" (480).

Grim as Birkin's gaze at Gerald's face may seem, it is one of the relatively few positive expressions of looking in the novel. This is a loving gaze that demonstrates how the one who looks or reads the text of the gaze's object ends up becoming read by it in turn. As Birkin stares at Gerald's face in death, he reads the depths of his own loss in Gerald's refusal to return his offer of love. That unrequited love between the two men parallels the love to which Ursula and Birkin appear to have come through, as both give way to the mighty contest between Gerald and Gudrun for mastery. The energy of that contest, rather than the coming through of Ursula and Birkin, overpowers all else, and the dominance of the Gerald-Gudrun duel to the death is nowhere more clearly demonstrated than in the staging of the gaze in the representation of their relationship.

5

Mr Noon as Postmodern Text

The posthumous novel *Mr Noon* makes its appearance in this examination of Lawrence's longer fiction in a postmodern context, both for its contribution to postmodern reading practices and as a variety of postmodern text itself. Its position in the Lawrence canon is problematic, since it is clearly not major in the same sense that one could claim for the other novels examined in this project. Few would argue that this novel would even have been published if the text had not been produced by "Lawrence." It is, however, for its usefulness in problematizing traditional notions of "author," "text," and "canon" that *Mr Noon* earns a place here.

To contextualize its appearance as a text, the story of its loss and recovery offers some useful background for a reading of *Mr Noon* in a postmodern context. Postmodernism, as Fredric Jameson argues—or postmodernisms, to use the plural, as he prefers (*Postmodernism* 2)—is the cultural representation of late capitalism, and as such it has telling effects upon textual production. The text's appearance was made possible only after part of the manuscript was acquired by the Ransom Humanities Center of the University of Texas, and after the Cambridge University Press, which had already begun its production of "authoritative" editions of the complete Lawrence canon, decided to include the novel among the author's other texts. No one with a professional investment in the project would have pretended that this text would ever occupy a central position in the Lawrence canon, and even the notion of such a canon continues to be grounded in the criteria of modernist aesthetics, or formalist values. At the same time, the commitment to the publication of *Mr Noon* was clearly an expression of a system within which its value as an item of textual production and consumption lay in part in its provenance as a recovered text, its appearance marketed as rivaling the publication of the computer-assisted Gabler edition of Joyce's *Ulysses*. Furthermore, *Mr Noon* was culturally constructed as yet another autobiographical fiction, offering new insights into the "life of D. H. Lawrence," very much in line with what has been a tradition of reading "Lawrence" biographically. Clearly, this text serves as one more example of the modernist tradition that invented the Author as that quasi-transcendental signifier of "meaning." It is a system within which texts have value in measure of their function as signifiers of the "lives" of their authors/producers. Or, as Lee Edelman has troped this reading practice in relation to the problematic constructing of a "queer criticism," the text is a closet whose door we open or a box whose lid we raise to disclose the secret "meaning" it holds. In any case, from the outset *Mr Noon* clearly represented a text whose value was grounded in its newness—as though it were a repackaged detergent, distinct from other products in the publisher's line, and offering hints of a newly reconstituted "Lawrence."

The text appeared in 1984, long after the death of the author, largely due to the vagaries of what now begins to seem like a medieval textual production. The stage of textual production during which *Mr Noon* was generated is archaic; as an extended prose narrative the text would have had to have been written by hand and then mechanically reproduced using the current technology of the time—a typewriter. At this earlier stage of technology a narrative such as *Noon* could also be directly composed on a typewriter. However, like its handwritten counterpart, a text composed directly on a typewriter would have had to be mechanically reproduced, since it would be inconceivable that a writer could draft a first version of a text with one or more carbons to produce multiple copies in an age of textural production before word processing and photocopying. Thus, the difficulties of antiquated technological generation of texts could produce this sort of "romance" of a lost text drafted but never finished.[1] The "new" novel of 1984 was new by virtue of a long second segment, its first segment having appeared as a shorter fiction, also entitled "Mr Noon," a half-century earlier but also after the death of the author.

Mr Noon as Unfinished Novel

The other feature of this text, and one which might serve as the focus of its reading in a postmodern context, is its status as an "unfinished" novel. One starting point for an exploration of its "unfinished" status is offered by Peter Brooks in *Reading for the Plot*. Brooks argues that narrative has traditionally depended upon the "sense of an ending" to persuade (we might suggest, delude) the reader into the (mis)perception of "meaning," so that a narrative that, for whatever reason (or lack of reason), exposes its lack of an ending would undermine conventional expectations of "meaning." What, then, are we to make of a text such as *Mr Noon* that breaks off in midsentence, in one sense literalizing the "death of the author" because he never returns to complete the manuscript? Much as it would be interesting at this point to unpack that exposure of lack at/of the end of a narrative, that discussion must be deferred, for this text also offers provocative areas to explore in its problematizing of what the reading practices called "Lawrence studies" have been preoccupied with: namely, the irresistible binary of "Lawrence" the "author," on the one hand, and the texts also denoted as "Lawrence," on the other.

Among the earliest reviewers of *Mr Noon* was Michael Black, who is also a member of the Cambridge University Press editorial board. Anticipating that many of this novel's readers will find it "awkward," Black adopts a defensive posture. He asserts: "We have to remember that this is an unfinished novel, and particularly that, for good or ill, it hasn't been subjected to Lawrence's usual repeated and drastic process of revision."[2] This assertion could not provide a more appropriate opening to our discussion of postmodernism and modernism, or more specifically an interrogation of *Mr Noon*'s postmodern status, for Black is clearly approaching this text from the traditionalist/modernist notion of the work of art as finished. In fact, there may well be something quintessentially modernist about this conception of finishing the text. One example comes immediately to mind in the tremendous investment of energy made by W. B. Yeats to finish his poems. Part of the legend growing up around major Yeats poems is their having undergone dozens of revisions, as the author imagined constructing himself in the texts produced, as a mask or symbol like the singer upon a golden bough in "Sailing to Byzantium." One need not look too far beyond such modernist icons as Yeats to find apt expressions of this essentially modernist notion of the collected works of art as the segments of the Artist's being, the artifacts or monuments constructed by the Artist as his or her legacy to the future. One also recalls Virginia Woolf's struggle to finish her great novel *To the Lighthouse,* which she indicates she accomplished when she found that gesture of the famous brush stroke for her dilettante artist Lily Briscoe to provide just the right closure to her word picture. To complete this extended analogy, one cannot help recalling arguably the greatest modernist, James Joyce, each of whose works represents a significant advancement upon its predecessor, the last of which, *Finnegans Wake,* being so much a culminating segment of his life's work that once the author had finished it there seemed nothing else for him to do but die.

Black, of course, means more than one thing by denoting *Mr Noon* as "unfinished." The novel stops in midsentence, leading the reader to ponder how much further the narrative might have extended itself beyond this point, where it stops rather than ends. At this point, we could explore some of the ways in which plots reach their "sense of an ending," to borrow Frank Kermode's title. If we follow the lead of Peter Brooks we might argue, indeed, that *Mr Noon* is not a narrative at all because it lacks an ending. In his system of "textual erotics," as we noted above in the discussion of *The Rainbow,* a narrative without an ending has no plot, because it is the ending alone that confers meaning upon all that precedes it. Otherwise, we have the inconclusiveness of endless life, without the ending of death to indicate what it meant. That, some might argue, is exactly what the text of *Mr Noon* is offering: a "textual erotics" that could conceivably go on forever, without a climax—certainly a horror within the context of what I term the male narrative paradigm.[3] This is not the "open-ended-ness" that we have been taught to expect, and even enjoy, in modernist novels such as *Ulysses,* where only the naive would credit as substantial any of the speculations about whether Molly Bloom will serve Poldy *his* breakfast in bed or whether he will be able to risk conceiving another child with her—speculations grounded in the misapprehension that these characters have an existence as something other than threads in the text(ure) of prose narrative.

These considerations lead us around to the more meaningful ways in which Black probably means that this narrative is unfinished. An open ending is feasible in a narrative whose readers have been prepared for the possibility that one or more endings could be in the offing. *Mr Noon* is unfinished in the sense that the absence of an ending restricts the narrative from offering any cues concerning the direction in which readers are being taken. In another sense, however, it seems legitimate to ask whether part 2 as a unit of narrative is any more inconclusive than the last chapter of *Women in Love*. In other words, if we abandon ourselves for a moment to the illusion that these characters exist outside the text, we might ask, as less experienced readers, will Birkin find a blood brother whose love will allow him to find completeness in his marriage to Ursula? Will he find such a man and then encounter enough opposition from Ursula that the marriage dissolves? Most readers are more than willing to accept such inconclusiveness because they are aware that the exploration of those questions would entail another novel and that this one has been about a man discovering the possibility of true marriage as the balance of his love for a man and his love for a woman. And that discovery is sufficient to give readers the sense of an ending. As we approach the consideration of the last chapter of *Mr Noon* we would do well to keep that in mind.

No, it is much more likely that by the term *unfinished* Black wishes to denote the absence, as he suggests, of this author's retooling of earlier drafts of a novel such as this one, a style Lydia Blanchard calls "occasionally rough" ("[On *Mr Noon*]" 154). It is because it lacks this very kind of revision that *Mr Noon* is narratologically interesting, however, perhaps even postmodern, for its abandoned state makes it impossible for its reader to avoid an awareness of its textuality. Indeed, as Joyce Wexler argues, all the longer prose fiction after *Women in Love* might qualify as postmodern.

"Self-Consciousness" and the Foregrounding of Textuality

If Wexler is right and much of Lawrence's later work may be classified as postmodern, the grounds for such a claim of postmodernity can be found in what Blanchard has seen as the increasing "self-consciousness" in this author's texts. Much of what might have been revised out of this text would be those expressions of an implied argument between the narrator constructed for this text and a fairly explicit implied reader. This implied reader and the response to *her* of the first-person narrator, a "Lawrence," seem to be generating the energy by which this narrative moves itself forward. This is, of course, not to say that this novel has no semblance of a plot, for surely this is a rendition of the narrative of "coming through." It *is* to say that we encounter a far different "textual erotics" from what Brooks has in mind—a struggle whose climax can be anticipated in the narrator and reader's coming into harmony with each other, however briefly, keeping in mind, of course, that such harmony is always a problematic construct.

Central to the possible classification of *Mr Noon* as a postmodern text, then, is the way in which its foregrounding of textuality is enhanced by what appears to be an assault upon one of the conventions of the traditional novel—a "gentle reader," whom the narrative addresses as a surrogate for prospective readers. Although directly addressing the "dear reader" goes back to the very origins of the novel in the eighteenth century, this text's parody of the strategy, especially as it becomes a verbal assault upon the actual reader, demonstrates that the intent here is not merely to poke fun at bourgeois conventionality but to undermine the reader's implied assumptions about fiction and the purpose of reading. Indeed, of those who have written on *Mr Noon,* Philip Sicker has come as close as anyone to classifying this novel as postmodern when he terms it an "anti-novel" (a term used by Maria Aline Ferreira as well) like Laurence Sterne's *Tristram Shandy.* Within the parody of a literary convention, then, we see "Lawrence," the "laughing prophet" in Black's words ("Gentle Reader" 175) reveling in the sheer joyfulness of having licensed himself for the first time to speak, even to "preach," openly rather than covertly as he may have assumed his readers had seen him straining to do elsewhere in his fiction.

"Lawrence" here requires what the British call "scare quotes" because a major postmodern gesture in this text is its self-conscious play with the fictional construct called "Lawrence" that this text is producing. As the editor's notes make amply clear, readers are confronted in *Mr Noon* with the especially problematic relationship in modernist writing between author and autobiographical text, both of which are equally "ficted" constructions, to borrow Norman Holland's term (304). This narrative exudes a rhetorical exuberance in its self-conscious violation of the conventions and boundaries of modernist aesthetics, which so often turned the work of art into a "well-wrought urn" hermetically sealed in the silence of its self-enclosed world. One has only to imagine the devastating effect on the reading of *To the Lighthouse,* for example, if Virginia Woolf's narrative voice should suddenly adopt the "dear reader" strategy.

Part 2 of *Mr Noon,* unlike the more conventional part 1, contains many long and increasingly raucous passages of direct address to a "gentle reader." Blanchard counts over sixty such occurrences ("[On *Mr Noon*]" 157). In these passages of direct address, the identity of that "gentle reader" shifts perceptibly. Once again, it has been speculated that these passages appear in the published novel only because of the death of the author before the text could be finished. In any case, these passages clearly demonstrate the text's frustration with its audience—however that prospective audience might have been construed. Examination of part 1, however, the segment that *had* in fact been revised before the death of the author, suggests that the foundation had been laid there for this assault upon the reader. As early as the second chapter, the narrative contains addresses to the "dear reader" amid the explanation of the social custom of "spooning." These addresses to the "dear reader" seem generated as an effort at denying the reader any refuge in ignorance of the custom on the basis of unfamiliarity with the colloquial term:

> Dear reader, have we not all left off believing in positive evil? And therefore is it not true that the seducer, invaluable in fiction, is dead? The seducer and the innocent maid are no more. We live in better days.
>
> There are only spooners now, a worldful of spoons. Those wicked young society people, those fast young aristocrats, ah, how soft as butter their souls are really, tender as melted butter their sinfulness, in our improved age. Don't talk of lust, it isn't fair. (20)

The narrative fully demonstrates how the "spoon" that teases up male sexuality can turn a "Galahad of sentiment" into a man who is less lover than rapist. Certainly, the Noon figure of this part is someone reckless of consequences, and the narrator cautions: "Beware, gentle reader! For if in the course of soft and kissy love you once get out of the melting spoon-mood, there is hell to pay, for both you and for her" (27). The "hell" that is apparently about to be paid at the end of this segment is the social embarrassment of unwed motherhood—if the offending lover cannot be coerced into marriage. The narrative, however, devolves into a parody of farce by producing a fiancé with a silly name—Walter George Whiffen—

whom the Emmie figure allegedly had forgotten about while spooning with Noon. The "gentle reader" is informed that Emmie is now Mrs. Whiffen, and "all went happy ever after." Clearly, it is this narrator who is functioning as a more important figure in the text than the depthless Noon figure. This narrator continues: "As for Mr Noon! Ah, Mr Noon! There is a second volume in store for you, dear reader. Pray heaven there may not be a third" (93).

This element of play with the novel's characters represents yet another hallmark of the postmodern narrative. Speaking of the "curious detachment" of this author from a narrative with such inescapable "autobiographical roots," Sicker writes that Lawrence "hovers over his creations, not as Joyce's unseen god, but as a highly visible puppet master, pulling strings to move the narrative forward and alternately teasing, berating, and lecturing his audience" (192). The analogy aptly supports the postmodern structure of *Mr Noon*. If this narrative employed that notion of the artist as "unseen god" playing with his creations, the reader might be struck by the painful irony of this context of divine insensitivity to the consequences of such "play." Here, however, the focus upon the textuality of the text undermines such attachment, creating the sense of depthlessness so often associated with the postmodern text. Thus, the Joycean artist/god as "within or behind or beyond or above his handiwork, invisible, refined out of existence, indifferent, paring his fingernails" (*Portrait* 215) is one expression of the modernist paradigm, just as the artist/"puppet master" may be read as a signature of the postmodern. In a similar vein, Blanchard in her essay on "The New Audience of *Mr Noon*" comments on "Lawrence's analysis of the fictionality of his own fiction" and later speaks of its "[a]nticipating the playfulness of a novel like *The French Lieutenant's Woman*" (224, 231), a novel generally conceded to be among the early expressions of postmodernism.

Ungentling the Reader

When the reader turns to the opening pages of that "second volume," the narrator explicitly foregrounds this novel as a text that "he" is "writing" and that the reader is reading. The narrator's tone suggests a radical change in the narrative's perspective on the reader. The Noon figure is awakening in his bedroom in Munich, the reader is informed with a deliberate abruptness, as though the text is intent upon startling the reader into a sense of the psychic transformation "Noon" has undergone.

The irony here is grounded in the assumption that this Noon figure is a fictional character who represents a historical or real person, when the context indicates that Noon is no more than the construction or "ficting" of a textual thread that can be transformed as capriciously as the text requires, since the traditional notion of mimesis has been abandoned or preserved only to be played with. Indicating an awareness that the reader expects him to add that the bedroom is in a brothel or similarly disreputable place, the narrative becomes more aggressively defensive in the face of the presumed strictures of reader expectations: "Oh, I know you, gentle reader. In your silent way you would like to browbeat me into it. But I've kicked over the traces at last, and I shall kick out of the splashboard of this apple-cart if I have any more expectations to put up with" (98).

It would seem that the gender of the gentle reader has become more decidedly female, since the narrator suggests that "she" might want to go up to her room to change into something more comfortable to enjoy the remainder of the narrator's story.

Increasingly, the reader is mocked for "her" conventional "gentleness." It is as though Noon's former spooning partner Emmie had been lifted out of her milieu of passionless propriety as Mrs. Whiffen to function as the bourgeois matron/reader of part 2, a woman looking to fiction for a few thrills to compensate for domestic boredom. When, for example, the narrative reveals the Noon and Johanna figures finally permitting their passion free rein, the narrator refuses to allow the narration to be interrupted by the "gentle reader," who might be pruriently concerned with what is transpiring behind the bedroom door. The passage indicates, among other things, an awareness in the narrative of the humor in "preaching" the gospel of sensual love:

> Oh thunder-god, who sends the white passion of pure, sensual desire upon us, breaking through the sultry rottenness of our old blood like jagged lightning, and switching us into a new dynamic reaction, hail! Oh thunder-god, god of the dangerous bolts—!—No gentle reader, please don't interrupt, I am *not* going to open the door of Johanna's room, not until Mr. Noon opens it himself. I've been caught that way before. . . . I am busy apostrophising Jupiter Tonans, Zeus of the thunder-bolt, the almighty Father of passion and sheer desire. I'm not talking about *your* little messy feelings and licentiousnesses, either. I'm talking about desire. So don't interrupt. Am *I* writing this book, or are you? (137)

This last assertion, or rhetorical question, certainly offers another postmodern confirmation of the narrative as illusion, to be punctured here by foregrounding its textuality. The earlier assertion of having been "caught that way before," however, indicates that "Lawrence" exceeds even that by-now-conventional strategy by reminding the reader that this is a novel by "Lawrence," the scandalous writer whose work has offended public morality before. In this way, the narrative draws the "Author" on stage, as Byron occasionally does in *Don Juan* in a similar postmodern gesture.[4] Like Byron, "Lawrence" seems to be enjoying the element of play grounded here in an indeterminacy of boundaries that the reader is apt to find unsettling: Is this the narrator "Lawrence" speaking, or the author "Lawrence" speaking? If this "narrator-Lawrence" can be "ficted," to use Holland's term, is "author-Lawrence" enjoying the game of contributing to the ficting of his own authorship? And is this radical departure from the more clearly determinate "Lawrence" of the earlier, "serious" novels anything but unsettling to those readers with the "serious" interest in preserving the notion, or illusion, of a Lawrence that may be changing, or "allotropic," yet always in the end unitary and determinable?

At another juncture, the narrator browbeats the reader into resisting the appeal of a sentimental reaction. The passage once again demonstrates that the narrative is willing to risk the undercutting of its seriousness, especially in a key episode in the movement of the Gilbert and Johanna figures toward "true, terrible marriage." Following Gilbert's "annunciation" of his life with Johanna, described as "such a lovely sense of fulfilment in the future; peace like a river flowing . . . into the sunset," the narrator turns upon the "gentle reader" to remind her once again that this text is not a sentimental romance. He says, "After this very nice little peace-like-a-river touch, I am going to let the cat out of the bag. For I'm sure if I don't, you'll be yelling and saying that I promised you two turtle-doves in a cage. Gentle reader, I have *not* got two turtle-doves in a cage for you. I'm sorry, but I'm not a dove and pigeon merchant" (185). What Noon has found is a "peace not made up of quietness or of lovey-doveyness," but a momentary truce in the struggle between "indomitable opposites." The "gentle reader" is told: "And till we fight our fights like splendid royal tigers, in the wonderful connubial rage, we are nothing" (187).

In order to glimpse the vision that might save them from being "nothing," readers of this text must be offended, mocked, angered. Essentially, then, readers have to be *un*gentled by the narrator. This conflict between narrator and reader recuperates the conflict inherent in the vision of love as the rainbow resulting from a brief moment of conjunction between the mighty opposites of fire and water, light and cloud. Readers, too, must be drawn into psychic conflict in order to know how its power can generate relationship. The narrator asks:

> But why the devil should I always *gentle-reader* you. You've been *gentle reader* for this last two hundred years. . . . Time you became rampageous reader, ferocious reader, surly, rabid reader, hell-cat of a reader, a tartar, a termagant, a tanger. . . .
>
> Therefore you sniffing mongrel bitch of a reader, you can't sniff out any specific why or any specific wherefore, with your carrion-smelling, psycho-analysing nose, because there *is* no why and wherefore. (204–5)

The figures here of a dog sniffing out the dead meat of concealed motives could not offer a more appropriate trope for an aversion to traditional psychoanalytic readings, whether the subjects of those readings are "patients"/analysands or "authors"/literary "characters."

Once readers have completed the regimen of "un-gentling," this narrative suggests, they are ready to be "gentle" in a radically new way. Now they can be gentle or tender toward the vulnerable subjectivity of the other, recuperated in the "sex embrace" within the pursuit of "true, terrible marriage." It is a pursuit without closure, as becomes apparent in the final pages, because conflict will always be implicated in a genuine relationship. Thus, the narrator can turn now to a reconstructed "gentle reader": "Marriage, gentle reader, rests upon the root-quivering of the awful, surpassing sex embrace, full and unspeakable. . . . This is the real creation: not the accident of childbirth, but the miracle of man-birth and woman-birth. . . . Spasm after spasm we are born into manhood and womanhood, and there is no end to the pure creative process" (226). In this way, the reader is being ungentled to acknowledge that relationship represents process, ongoing and unending. And, as this crucial passage indicates, rebirth "exists" as a phantom possibility, as was apparent in the closing paragraphs of *The Rainbow.* Identity can never be fixed and finally defined. It is not grounded in the discovery of some hidden self—like Holland's "lost glove"—but in the interaction with the other, and perhaps with the Other as well. This marriage bed is a battlefield of "indomitable opposites," with only short-term truces—truces that are always to come and never to last. Lovey-doveyness must give way to a notion of inevitable ambivalence.

In the closing pages, the reader "changes gender" one last time. This gender shift, like other elements of this text, is yet another indication of how problematic modernist conceptions of fixed identities and literary conventions can be, if rigidly imposed. In any case, the "ungentle reader" is now male. "Do not imagine, ungentle reader, that by just chasing women you will ever get anywhere. Gilbert might have had . . . a thousand really nice women, and yet never have cracked the womb. It needed the incalculable fight such as he fought, unconscious and willy-nilly, with his German Johanna: and such as I fight with you, oh gentle but rather cowardly and imbecile reader: for such, really, I find you" (291–92). This last assertion seems this text's clearest statement of an impulse to erode the conventional boundary between the "outside" and the "inside" of the text by addressing the audience directly and, what's more, confirming that the "dear reader" is not simply a quaint narrative strategy to serve as the object of parody but a means of dramatically drawing the prospective, actual reader into the text to pay stricter attention to what the narrator conceives of as its message.

The Lack of an Ending

The novel ends inconclusively with the Noon and Johanna figures apparently having come through to Italy and to the affirmation of their unfinished *pursuit* of "true, terrible marriage." The text's lack of closure is only another reminder of the artifice inherent in what I have called the male narrative paradigm. In one clear sense, this ending, or lack thereof, is much more like the alternatives to the traditional paradigm mapped by feminist theorists of narrative such as Teresa de Lauretis and Kaja Silverman.

De Lauretis interrogates the traditional paradigm in an effort at legitimating its alternatives. The plural, alternative*s,* is critical to her project because she is intent upon avoiding the simplistic binary thinking of a single "female narrative paradigm" to counter the "male narrative paradigm." Perhaps because Brooks's *Reading for the Plot* appeared the same year as her own book *Alice Doesn't,* de Lauretis turns to the writing of Robert Scholes for an example of the theorizing about the traditional narrative paradigm that she reads as "masculinist." Scholes writes, "what connects fiction . . . with sex is the fundamental orgastic rhythm of tumescence and detumescence, of tension and resolution, of intensification to the point of climax and consummation. In the sophisticated forms of fiction, as in the sophisticated practice of sex, much of the arts consists of delaying climax within the framework of desire in order to prolong the pleasurable act itself" (quoted in de Lauretis 108). De Lauretis responds: "Those of us who know no art of delaying climax or, reading, feel no incipient tumescence, may well be barred from the pleasure of this 'full fictional act': nor may we profit from the rhythm method by which it is attained" (108). Her wit ought not to diminish the power of the insight de Lauretis is foregrounding here: namely, the conventional notion of rising action, brief climax, and falling action is deeply inscribed with masculine desire. And here we would do well to specify the "engendering" of the rhythm as "masculine" rather than as "male," for gender constructions obviously do not maintain what we have perhaps deluded ourselves into reading as the distinct boundaries of sexual identity.

This theorizing of de Lauretis is informed by the writing of Jurij Lotman, the Soviet semiotician. Lotman explored the binary he read in the origins of myths as cultural texts, on the one hand, and what we consider narratives, on the other. For Lotman, myths are implicated in a cyclical movement of time, linked with seasonal rhythms. Lotman generalizes: "Because linear-temporal categories, such as beginning and end, are not pertinent to the type of text thus generated, human life is not seen as enclosed between birth and death, but as a recurrent, self-repeating cycle which can be told starting at any point" (quoted in de Lauretis 116–17). Story or narrative, as it is usually understood, is implicated in a rhythm of linear time with its apparently inevitable beginning, middle, and end. This linear rhythm or structure functions as the "other" of myth's cyclic patterns in this structuralist binary, Lotman suggests. Although the linear has become the convention for narrative, it is worth noting that it is a structure grounded in the anomalous. Lotman writes: "And it is the latter which, organized according to a linear, temporal succession of events, generated oral tales about incidents, calamities, crimes, chance occurrences—in short, anything contravening, or in excess of, the mythically established order of things" (quoted in de Lauretis 118). Within Lotman's structuralist thinking, two mutually exclusive "times" are posited, and as a binary they have been especially attractive to writers such as the feminist Julia Kristeva, who posits a "Women's Time," in which "*repetition* and *eternity*" (her emphasis) inform "female subjectivity," as presumably "linear time" informs male subjectivity (191).

De Lauretis's effort at exploring alternatives to the traditional narrative paradigm finds support among other feminists such as Marianne Hirsch, whose study *The Mother-Daughter Plot* focuses upon the rewriting of that paradigm by nineteenth-century women practitioners of realist prose fiction. Hirsch asserts: "Female plots . . . act out the frustrations engendered by these limited possibilities and attempt to subvert the constraint of dominant patterns by means of various 'emancipatory strategies,' the revisions of endings, beginnings, patterns of progression" (8). In borrowing the term *emancipatory strategies,* Hirsch acknowledges her indebtedness to Patricia Yaeger's *Honey-Mad Women,* the term *emancipatory strategies* appearing in Yaeger's subtitle. What Hirsch would read as a "female" narrative replaces the "retard, postponement," and "deferral" of the male narrative paradigm with "continued opposition, interruption, and contradiction" (102).

If we can decenter this female-male binary by restructuring these gender differences to acknowledge their functioning in both women and men, these insights regarding the engendering of narrative seem especially relevant to the issues involved in the (non)ending of the *Mr Noon* text. Indeed, these insights help us to revisit the question of unfinishedness to pose the next logical question: *why* was this text unfinished—perhaps even unfinishable? The question leads into the minefield of biography, since for the traditionalist the answer is obvious: in the time it was generated, the text that became *Mr Noon* was unfinishable because it could not be published.[5] The text makes no effort to hide the fact that is a kind of roman à clef, whose characters are portraits of real people, with predictable resentments about the prospect of having their closets opened had this clef text appeared at the time of its composition. Stepping back from the minefield at least for a time, it is worth speculating that this text was unfinished in part as a gesture of an unwillingness to resolve its "continued opposition, interruption, and contradiction" into the male narrative paradigm with its "retard, postponement," or "deferral."

All this is only another way of returning to one feature of narrative in *Mr Noon* that it shares with at least *The White Peacock, Sons and Lovers,* and *The Rainbow:* this sense that the narrative is not organizing itself as though it knew its own ending, so to speak. Here, we might recall Brooks's important insight that in the traditional model the construction of "plot" can begin only after the action has completed itself. Within this construct, narrative must have a particular end toward which it is constructing itself, or else it has no so-called meaning. Brooks's theorizing about the ending of narrative may, finally, be tautological, for it assumes an ending that must seem as though it was "there all the time." However, it was *not* there from the beginning because narrative constructs itself page by page. In a sense, Brooks traps himself within the structuralist's binary of "action" and "plot." That is, Brooks can argue that the ending always exists before plot begins only because he can believe in an "action," an "outside-text" that is inevitably privileged over narrative. Narrative in this context must always serve as the handmaiden of an action that, if not part of an allegedly real outside world, must masquerade as such in supporting mimesis.

Confronting the Biographical

If *Mr Noon* was unpublishable at the time of its composition because of its patent roman à clef status, it was allowed to join the canon of Lawrence's works in large part for the very same reason. Indeed, the extensive textual machinery for the novel in the Cambridge edition incessantly reminds the reader of the text's (auto)biographical roots. In this way, it becomes extremely difficult, if not impossible, to read *Mr Noon* without being aware that this is a "ficted" version of the "real world" and historical figures and events. It is as though this text is constantly decentering itself by reminding us that its "outside" in the "real world" is always already *inside* the text, or conversely that whatever lies outside the text is, like what is inside, a reading or writing.

At the same time, this binary of "real" and "ficted" that seems to be clearly privileging the real outside over against the reconstructed, or imagined, inside—if that outside/inside binary has not already deconstructed itself—is also working in the opposite direction. That is, not only is the text being subordinated to the life of one or another historical personage, but the ravenous hunger of the real seems to set itself upon the ficted as a representation of the real outside of the text. Thus, the text of *Mr Noon* becomes a mine of presumed (auto)biographical material and whatever the text reveals of the Noon figure is assumed to be a revelation of the author's life. Here, in microcosm, is a concentrated representation of what seems to be the notion that it is the life of the author that is the ultimate interest, and not the text.

A classic example is the (in)famous *New York Times* review of *Mr Noon* by Diana Trilling, one of the surviving practitioners of the modernist criticism that flourished over a half-century ago. Probably concluding that this text would never have been published unless it was by "Lawrence," Trilling ignored much of the novel to focus upon the text as a document of self-exposure. In her reading of *Mr Noon* as autobiography, Trilling foresaw devoted readers of Lawrence feeling "betrayed" because the "priest of love" (monogamous, married love, presumably) had concealed from the community of his faithful followers the "truth" that Frieda had been "unfaithful" to him before they were even married. Once again, the Trilling essay represents the impulse to privilege the author's life, or biography, over the fictional text.

It is ironic, then, that Trilling misses the point of *Mr Noon*'s postmodern gesture toward textual "play." Two generations before Trilling would have an opportunity to (mis)read this text by identifying its first-person narrator with the author, this narrative anticipates that reading practice and exploits its comic effects, as Byron brilliantly does in (re)constructing himself as the author/narrator of *Don Juan*. The text of *Mr Noon* constructs an open secret in its negotiating of the relationship with the prospective reader by offering a narrator who is assumed to be such an obvious thinly disguised "Lawrence" as "author." What is more difficult to see in this (mis)construction of the "author" is the implication that the "author" is *always* a textual (mis)construction. The naive belief in a "Lawrence" who exists as a kind of transcendental signifier within the grand narrative of his life is deconstructed by this text itself, as it suggests that the unnamed but tacitly understood "Lawrence" it is constructing behind its narrator is no more than another web of words.

Back of the biographical impulse in Lawrence studies, then, is this presumption that the identity of "Lawrence" exists as an "outside" that is as discoverable as a lost glove. It is an identity that implies a modernist mode of thinking in that regard. In this context, the "Lawrence" of one text—say, a letter or an essay—may be applied to another text such as poem or narrative, allowing whatever (mis)reading the applier chooses. This is an especially pertinent issue in reading difficult narratives such as "The Woman Who Rode Away," frequently misread as being the production of the very same "Lawrence" of those notorious letters and essays with apparently misogynist points of view. Following Roland Barthes and Michel Foucault, who write on the "death of the author" with the completion of the text, we might move another step down that road and underscore their implication that the author is a construction of the text whose only existence is in that particular text, and that all other texts by the same author are the constructions of siblings.

In her recent introduction to Lawrence, Linda Ruth Williams reminds her readers that few writers in the twentieth century have had so much attention directed to their lives. In her words, "With the exception of suicides such as Virginia Woolf and Sylvia Plath, whose deaths have too often been the inscribers of their lives and the critical filter through which their work is read, perhaps no other twentieth-century writer has been so strongly interpreted through the lustre of biography" (*D. H. Lawrence* 1). She continues: "The two primary movements in critical theory this century which have argued against attributing authorial intention to the text—I. A. Richards's practical criticism of the 1930s, and the 'death of the author' poststructuralism following, in particular, Roland Barthes's work in the 1960s and 1970s—seem to have had little impact on readings of Lawrence . . . despite the fact that it was Lawrence who wrote 'Never trust the artist, trust the tale'" (1–2). Chronicling the establishment of this privileging of what was conceived of as Lawrence's "thought" over the texts, Williams acknowledges her own sense of self-division in an assertion that impinges upon my own project: "However, because of this overbearing bio-critical history, it is with some trepidation that I frame this introduction to Lawrence with his facts of life, since this has been exactly the way in which life-infused readings have come to predominate" (3). Perhaps this "case study" of Williams's struggle with "this overbearing bio-critical history" ought to have been prefaced by acknowledging her as one of the most perceptive writers on Lawrence to have appeared on the scene in the past decade. The effort initiated by F. R. Leavis in the 1930s "to win clear recognition for the nature of Lawrence's greatness" (quoted in Willams, *D. H. Lawrence* 2) has produced a construction of "Lawrence" from which a scholar like Williams may dissent but ultimately feel drawn irresistibly into maintaining by rehearsing the "life" as an introduction to "the key issues which continue to dominate his work" (4). Until readers acknowledge that "Lawrence" and his writings participate equally in a constructedness, biography will continue to be privileged over narrative. Again and again, writers on Lawrence texts cite the author's injunction, "Never trust the artist. Trust the tale," and then proceed to call upon the Lawrence of the letters and essays as an expert witness to support their readings of the fiction. And the biographies of "Lawrence" proliferate.

6

Revisiting Mellors's Penis in *Lady Chatterley's Lover*

The first page of Kate Millett's (in)famous chapter, "D. H. Lawrence," in her polemic *Sexual Politics* offers the reader an uninterrupted citation of the scene focusing on the penis of "Lady Chatterley's Lover," Oliver Mellors. Millett (ab)uses the passage as the opening shot in her assault on what she sees as its author's implication in patriarchy through his "quasi-religious" celebration of the phallus as the instrument of male mastery. The Lawrence text itself seems to authorize a preoccupation with the penis as a symbolic representation of the phallic, often using the terms interchangeably and thus permitting a confusion that allows a hostile reader like Millett an entry for her exploitation of this text in yet another rehearsal of the myth of an Author who can be (re)constructed through his texts. A similar confusion of the penis with the phallus persists a generation after the publication of Millett's second-wave feminist polemic. Thus, the time seems right to organize a return to the issues of sexuality and gender raised by *Lady Chatterley's Lover* in an effort at reading it anew in a more sophisticated context of gender theorizing.

Writing Desire

The theorizing of Jacques Lacan offers a useful starting point for recuperating the Lawrence text in large part because of the major contribution made by Lacanian theory to the contemporary discourse of gender construction. Lacan is especially useful[1] because his central idea of the phallus as a signifier of desire within the Symbolic order offers the means of freeing gender theorizing from the structuralism inherent in the biological essentialism within which traditional feminists such as Millett and her generation became trapped. The subject for Lacan is always born into a world of language to which it gains access through its transformation within the Symbolic order. That transformation takes place in Lacan's rewriting of Freud's texts on castration. Lacan departs from Freud's notion of castration, especially as it has been popularized as the male subject's anxiety concerning the loss of his penis. For Lacan, castration represents the subject, female as well as male, having to relinquish the dyadic relationship with the mother in a castration that constructs the Phallus as a signifier of Desire in the Symbolic, a Desire fully known only within the Imaginary through immersion in the (M)other, but lost now as the price of admission to the Symbolic register. As earlier noted, the movement into the realm of representation closes off within the unconscious what the subject experienced within the Imaginary realm, but especially that *jouissance* of completed desire from which the subject is forever cut off. It is that *jouissance* as the fulfillment of desire for which the phallus becomes a signifier. Because the phallus is at one and the same time a signifier of plenitude and lack, it is appropriate to read Lacan's phallus in a post-structuralist context of instability, where it is neither the signifier of plenitude nor of lack, of Desire or Castration, but only a signifier in a realm where it is impossible to conceptualize one without the other, or where there are no sharp (structuralist) outlines.[2] In this regard, Lacan's phallus functions much as Derrida's "trace," a signifier of absence within a ghostly presence.[3]

To equate the phallus with the penis is, from the vantage point of the Symbolic, to remain entrapped within the Imaginary register, in which the subject was once content with fantasy identifications with the (M)other and all the other binaries with their illusory resolution into a spurious unity. As earlier noted in the effort to rescue the text of *Sons and Lovers* from its Oedipalizers, Lacan offers a salutary move away from the misconception of the subject working through the Freudian Oedipus complex to adult health, not merely as the achievement of the goal of personal development, but as a moral obligation. Once again, Jerry Flieger is helpful in her deconstruction of the structuralist impulse to see the Symbolic privileged over the Imaginary in Lacan; she writes: "What each of these instances of the desiring circuit finally underscores is that the Imaginary and the Symbolic are not distinct developmental phases in human life but are interacting registers of a continuing intersubjective drama" (112–13). In this way, Lacan's Imaginary and Symbolic orders escape the entrapment in linear thinking intrinsic to Freud's background in nineteenth-century biology, with its assurance of mastering one's fate by successfully working through the oral and anal stages to the genital, thereby achieving "health" by successfully working through the Oedipal stage.[4]

To return to Lacan's notion of the phallus, however, it is crucial to pay attention to his effort to separate it from the penis and to stress that he means the phallus to be understood as a signifier and not a body part. Lacan writes:

> In Freudian doctrine, the phallus is not a phantasy, if by that we mean an imaginary effect. Nor is it as such an object (part-, internal, good, bad, etc.) in the sense that this term tends to accentuate the reality pertaining in a relation. It is even less the organ, penis or clitoris, that it symbolizes. And it is not without reason that Freud used the reference to the simulacrum that it represented for the Ancients.
>
> For the phallus is a signifier, a signifier whose function, in the intrasubjective economy of analysis, lifts the veil perhaps from the function it performed in the mysteries. (*Écrits* 285)

This distinction between the penis and the phallus, as David Savran has pointed out, is crucial to the difference between Lacan's notions of the Symbolic register to which the subject is raised by the power of representation through language.[5] Within the Symbolic order the phallus is a privileged signifier, distinct from the male sexual organ and its biological function within the Real.[6]

> The phallus [Lacan continues] is the privileged signifier of that mark in which the role of the logos is joined with the advent of desire. . . . it can play its role only veiled, that is to say, as itself a sign of the latency with which any signifiable is struck, when it is raised (*aufgehoben*) to the function of signifier.

> The phallus is the signifier of this *Aufhebung* itself, which it inaugurates (initiates) by its disappearance. That is why the demon of . . . shame arises at the very moment when, in the ancient mysteries, the phallus is unveiled. . . .
>
> It then becomes the bar which, at the hands of this demon, strikes the signified, marking it as the bastard offspring of this signifying concatenation. (*Écrits* 287–88)

Thus, it is only when the phallus is perceived as signifier, only when absence or lack can signify presence, that signification can take place.

It is this notion of the phallus functioning only when "veiled" that marks Lacan's most provocative contribution to contemporary theorizing about gender as well as signification. Lacan seems to be constructing the phallus as the "master" metaphor in line with Irigaray's anxiety about the sex-linked identities of Lacan's tropes.[7] In any case, like metaphor, the phallus operates only when it is repressed or kept down below the "barre" through which Lacan, as we have seen, represents a signifier holding down another with its signified. And yet this repression is what raises or empowers the phallus, as metaphor marks its signified as that "bastard offspring of this signifying concatenation."[8] It is this tension between veiling and unveiling in this text with which the discussion below is concerned, for that tension offers a useful entry to a text that seems preoccupied with unveiling the mysteries of the phallus, both by uncovering the penis with which the phallus is often (mis)associated and by bringing into "literature" those words and explicit descriptions of desire that have been traditionally suppressed.

The Text(ure) of Wragby

If the phallus is a signifier for that *jouissance* from which the subject feels bereft, the immersion of *Lady Chatterley's Lover* in textuality could not be more appropriate. At its center is Wragby, the stately home of the Chatterleys, and, as such, a web of textuality, or words. Wragby is a locus of clever talk, the discourse of upperclass British society for which "sex is just another form of talk, where you act the words instead of saying them" (*LCL* 33–34). In this context, even the figure who seems most liberated—verbally at least—Tommy Dukes, can claim, for example: "Oh, intellectually, I believe in having a good heart, a chirpy penis, a lively intelligence, and the courage to say shit! in front of a lady," only to demur in the next breath: "No, my heart's as numb as a potato, my penis droops and never lifts its head up, I dare rather cut him clean off than say shit! in front of . . . *real* ladies" (39).

The figurehead of such textuality, Sir Clifford, literalizes the metaphor of the price the subject pays for admission to the Symbolic register by being constructed as paralyzed from the waist down. As a generator of texts, Clifford is figured as an Arachne constructing a world of words. The stories that bring him renown seem little more than the brittle records of the smart talk circulating through the public rooms of Wragby. They are realist narratives, expressions of what Lacan, following Jakobson, would consider metonymic notations of desire,[9] woven out of "people he had known" and undoubtedly repeating what those people had said as well, making these texts merely copies of a privileged speech at Wragby. Accordingly, "Wragby" is a text, woven out of spoken discourse, as *Lady Chatterley's Lover* itself as text foregrounds, when, for example, Clifford tells his wife: "You and I are interwoven in a marriage," and she later asks herself: "Was it actually her destiny to go on weaving herself into his life all the rest of her life?" (45).

The text of Wragby is rewritten with the entry of Ivy Bolton, who functions less importantly as character than as the agent of Wragby's author-ization through her contribution to its illusion of mastery.[10] As a storyteller herself, she becomes implicated in the generation of Wragby as text, adding her Tevershall gossip to its textuality, providing it with the plethora of synecdochic details Irigaray has encouraged us to read as feminine, because, once again, metaphor is gendered masculine. The engendering of synecdochic details is foregrounded when the narrative confirms Bolton's connection with the realist tradition of "Mrs. Gaskell and George Eliot and Miss Mitford" (100). The textuality produced at Wragby with Bolton's complicity is feminine, then, in its preoccupation with detail and its lack of the power of transformation implicit in metaphoricity.

The Sounds of Silence

From the beginning the Mellors figure is the locus of silence, and eventually darkness as well, in contrast to the spoken discourse and light associated with Wragby. The silence and darkness of Wragby Park repeat the function of Sherwood Forest, evident in *Women in Love,* as a refuge from a bright world of smart talk. In fact, silence in this text clearly represents a withdrawal from intercourse with the textuality of Wragby, that bright web of words that has subverted language as a meaningful mode of expression. That world has rendered Mellors "impotent" in ways similar to those announced by his forerunner, the Tommy Dukes figure. After Mellors and Connie first make love, when he has communicated to her that he has allowed "life" to break through the defenses of his better judgment, he represents for the first time in language his sense of a denuded world, the very Sherwood Forest where Ursula and Birkin immersed themselves in the dark silence of touch, a world exposed now to light and noise. Alone and himself exposed, he metaphorizes the menace of that outside world as electric, or artificial, light. Electric light, or the energy of mind-consciousness, represents an inescapable surveillance similar to the metaphor of moonlight, a ghastly reflection of the sun. It is a force of surveillance reminiscent of Foucault's notion of the Panopticon, the oppressive, all-seeing eye. Now Mellors sees both the woman and himself, like Wragby Wood, exposed by the light that men like Clifford make in their authority over matter, their illusion of mastery. Mellors shares some of Gudrun's aversion to being looked at by the miners when she walks past their houses, for to be looked at is to be visually mastered by the looker. At the same time, it is the threat to the exposed body, the uncovered penis, metonymically associated with the phallus, that empowers signification here, makes metaphoricity possible, stirring him again sexually as well as psychically and linguistically.

It is the Mellors figure who is the agent of the exposure of the physicality of sex, for it is he, not the narrator, we need to remind ourselves, who introduces terms like *fuck* and *cunt.*[11] The exposure is, however, an unveiling of sexuality that is also a representation whose words are themselves another kind of "veiling." This is evident in the early scene in which Connie attempts her own performance of Mellors's unveiling of the physical with the signifier he uses to represent the body of desire. The scene ends with his laughter at her stumbling attempt to imitate his dialect as he is telling her that she must leave: "'Mun I?' she said. 'Maun Ah!' he corrected" (177). Her effort to use his language justifies his extending this lesson in dialectal representation of sexuality: "'Th'art good cunt, though, aren't ter?'" He explains further: "'Cunt! It's thee down theer; an' what I get when I'm i'side thee—an' what tha gets when I'm i'side thee.'" And when she confuses *cunt* with *fuck,* he corrects her one last time: "'Nay nay! Fuck's only what you do. Animals fuck. But cunt's a lot more than that. It's thee, dost see, an' th'art a lot besides an animal, aren't ter?'" (177–78).

In a sense, Lawrence is offering a paradigm of "unveiling," of the Mellors figure paradoxically exposing human sexuality as a metonym for the phallic, yet exposing it in the veiled or metaphoric form of the word. Mellors becomes the representation of the notion that the phallus is always veiled, that its power is not physical but linguistic. The explicitness of the language used by Mellors represents the inevitable movement up into the Symbolic register of the power of desire, the phallus being the metaphoric and veiled signifier for that desire. In this way the phallus is a representation of the repression of the signified beneath its bar, as well as the freedom of the signified to cross that bar, empowering a metaphoricity.

Mellors, however, must undergo a more literal exposure than this exposure of the body of love to the glaring surveillance of the electric light. In the long scene following the episode of the wheelchair in the bluebells, after Mellors has turned storyteller to relate the history of his troubles with women, Connie and he swear to "be together on oath." In the next morning's sunlight Connie insists that he must share his nakedness with her and remove his pajamas. She will brook no shyness, and although "ashamed to turn to her, because of his aroused nakedness," turn he must, despite his futile attempt to veil his "aroused nakedness" with his shirt. Through Connie's eyes, the narrative celebrates the power of this "erect phallos," this fleshly representation of the phallic power. As he suffers her gaze in silence, Mellors finally veils the phallus once again, and characteristically in language. This time the language is not metaphoric but metonymic, as Mellors displaces the phallus as signifier with the associative names of "John Thomas" and "Lady Jane," signifiers that have signification only with him as a master of tropes. The consequences of this veiling once more of the phallus in words are worth noting:

> And afterwards, when they had been quite still, the woman had to uncover the man again, to look at the mystery of the *phallos.*
>
> "And now he's tiny and soft like a little bud of life!" she said, taking the soft small *penis* in her hand." (210; emphasis added)

"Stirring, erect phallos" no more but now only a "soft small penis," the flesh that had been made word is flesh once again.

The appearance of the "phallos" signifier marks this text's attempt to trope desire as the representation of that Desire, or *jouissance,* with which Lacan figured his phallus. The quaintly antique spelling of this *phallos* with its idiosyncratic *o,* rather like Keats's antiquing of *Greek* as *Grecian,* suggests the impulse of this text to lift the vulnerable flesh of the penis into that figure of signification in the Symbolic register. As it becomes clear, this "phallos" is hardly the emblem of male domination Millett would frame it as; instead, it is Lacan's phallus, signifying the irrecoverable desire whose loss makes possible the very signification of that castration/empowerment. The phallus signifies, then, the power of metaphoricity through which the subject represents a loss of desire, never to be recuperated, except perhaps in those infrequent moments of access to the pre-Symbolic realm of the semiotic, as Kristeva (re)constructs the Lacanian Imaginary.[12]

This interrogation of the Lacanian phallus would be incomplete without paying some attention to the ongoing resistance to Lacan's choice of the phallus as a "master" signifier. Feminist theorists in particular (but not uniquely) have argued that Lacan cannot persuade them that the phallus is not the equivalent of the penis. Ragland-Sullivan defends Lacan's construction of the phallus as signifier, reminding feminists that equating the Lacanian phallus with the anatomical marker of the male is to entrap oneself in "reductionist terms of biology" (55). Similarly, Flieger points out how Lacan's construction of the "phallic signifier" represents the "antithesis of the essentialist view" of the phallus as penis (116). All the same, the metonymic associations of phallus with penis are so embedded in our language that it seems impossible to deny outright the powerful associations. Furthermore, Lacan himself could not have been unaware of the inevitable controversy when he theorized, perhaps a bit playfully, his "phallic signifier." What Barbara Johnson has to say about deconstructive practice may be helpful here. "Instead of a simple 'either/or' structure, deconstruction attempts to elaborate a discourse that says *neither* 'either/or,' *nor* 'both/and' nor even 'neither/nor,' while at the same time not totally abandoning these logics either. Deconstruction is both, it is neither, and it reveals the way in which both construction and deconstruction are themselves not what they appear to be."[13] In the same way that the phallus both "is" and "is not" the penis, Mellors in this narrative is/is not a character, for to deny that he is a character is also to become implicated in a structuralist binary of "is" *versus* "is not" in which "is not" is privileged over "is."

Exposure and Vulnerability

The narrative's exposure of Mellors to Connie's gaze opens this scene out into larger questions of the body's function in this novel, especially the nude male body. The body of Mellors is by no means the first in these texts upon which the narrative has focused its "camera eye." The "A Poem of Friendship" chapter's nude bathing scene in *The White Peacock*, for example, positions the narrator, Cyril Beardsall, as a variety of camera in order to visualize George Saxton as a male nude. The bodies of both Gerald and Birkin are also implicated in the spectacle of male exposure. Similarly, the nude body of Gilbert Noon in the Tyrol is exposed, dancing in broad daylight for the woman's desiring gaze.

The foregrounding of Mellors as male nude, however, represents an obvious and radical departure from earlier performances of self-exposure. That departure can be easily established by examining briefly a similar scene or two in an earlier text. In *The Rainbow,* for example, the narrative focuses upon the body of Skrebensky in the West End hotel room where the text positions readers as voyeurs, looking through Ursula's eyes at the beauty of his physical presence in the bath. "She watched him as he bathed . . . the electric light glinting on his wet shoulders. He stood out of the bath . . . slender and, to her, perfect, a clean, square-cut youth, without a grain of superfluous body." Then, in a gesture of what seems like transgendered sensuality, the narrative focuses Ursula's gaze upon Skrebensky as though she were a man enjoying the visual/tactile pleasure of a female other's body: "The brown hair on his body was soft and fine and adorable, he was all beautifully flushed, as he stood in the white bath-apartment" (421). This scene of Ursula's gazing at Skrebensky's naked body is not unique to *The Rainbow;* neither is it gratuitous, for Skrebensky's body is exposed once again when the lovers return to London, this time to an Italian hotel where Ursula consciously begins to confront Skrebensky's insufficiency. Ursula is again positioned by the narrative as the subject of the gaze as she watches Skrebensky bathing. His sensual beauty has not diminished: "His body was beautiful . . . she appreciated him without reserve." However, as the narrative quickly adds: "He roused no fruitful fecundity in her. He seemed added up, finished. She knew him all round, not on any side did he lead into the unknown"

(438–39). The narrative trains Ursula's gaze on Skrebensky's body, then, not to read desire but to eliminate him as a potential mate because he has failed to open a door into the unknown.

Unlike these snapshots of Skrebensky and other representations of the male nude, the portrait of Mellors offers a radical departure for so-called mainstream fiction—whatever that problematic term is meant to encompass. The graphic representation of Mellors's body offers the first extended expression of full frontal male nudity in fiction. If in depicting the nudity of other figures such as George Saxton, Skrebensky, Gerald, Birkin, and Gilbert Noon the narrative merely announces that each is unclothed, the narrative of *Lady Chatterley* more than once moves the camera in, so to speak, and stops it for a close-up of the genitals of Mellors. And, continuing the analogy of film, the narrator violates the cinematic prohibition against the representation of male desire by specifying that the reason Mellors is reluctant to turn fully toward Connie and expose himself to the gaze of a woman with whom he has already been very intimate sexually is his "aroused nakedness." This phrase *aroused nakedness* itself offers a surprisingly discreet verbal displacement for the obvious fact that Mellors has an erection in a context where there can be little question that both lovers have been aware of his arousal on previous occasions.

It should come as no surprise that the depiction of male nudity in Mellors has generally been ignored by those who have written on *Lady Chatterley's Lover.* Other than Millett, who is intent upon deflating what she reads as a celebration of the phallic grounding of patriarchy, few readers have paid much attention to the body of Mellors. In one sense it has been hedged with taboos for male readers who have been acculturated to avoid "looking" because looking has the potential to implicate the looker in the subversion of his own masculinity as well as his (hetero)sexual orientation. In any case, the narrative seems so intent upon exposing the body of Mellors (in a context that is patently heterosexual) that this dramatic gesture demands attention, especially within the framework of contemporary gender theorizing.

Roberta McGrath[14] offers what is probably the largest construct in this framework of how the masculine is represented. McGrath argues that heterosexual masculinity, like patriarchy, is typically "unseen," or "hidden from our eyes," because it is "assumed" as a given, rather than read as a cultural construction. That assumption of masculinity as an essence rather than as a social construction underlies the notion that the male body need not be shown because it is after all *known*. Because it is a given, depicting the male body seems ridiculously superfluous, to such a degree that its depiction has become a rarity. As Gill Saunders reminds us, the male nude has now become rare enough that current usage supplies the distinguishing modifier *male,* as older usage constructed sexist denotations such as *woman doctor.* She continues: "'Nude' is synonymous with 'female nude' because nakedness connotes passivity, vulnerability; it is powerless and anonymous."[15] It is the violation of the conventional boundaries between genders that the male nude enacts, for as Michael Hatt suggests, "The male nude is strangely ambivalent. It is a traditional sign of masculinity, of strength and courage. . . . Yet, at the same time, and perhaps in spite of the cultural encoding of the unclothed male body, to be nude is to be vulnerable and exposed" (27). Hatt makes clear that he is, of course, speaking of the male nude without the full frontal nudity that is almost universally eliminated in representations of the male body, regardless of how unclothed that body may be, for to expose the penis, the very symbol of masculinity, is paradoxically to put its power in jeopardy in a bizarre process of "feminizing" the phallus by exposing it as a "mere" penis. Hatt comments: "It remains true that images of the male body are relatively rare in mainstream culture and those images that do appear are almost always celebrations of physical power—the vulnerability of nudity is screened out of representations of the male (to the extent that the erect penis—unable to match up visually to its role as symbol of phallic power—is forbidden even in so-called 'soft' pornographic publications)" (27).

The trend toward reading nudity as an expression of vulnerability, or at least passivity, appears the overriding explanation for the reluctance of male artists to expose the male body. Alasdair Foster, for example, comments upon the unwillingness to provide graphic representations of the penis: "Never can that most mutable of organs measure up to the panoply of phallic aspiration behind which it lurks. Patriarchy, wary of this contradiction, reacts by making the representation of the penis in general, and the erection in particular, taboo" (46–47). And Roberta McGrath offers her own valuable speculation:

> If . . . phallic power is veiled, covert; and if it rests precisely on witholding [*sic*] the male body from scrutiny, then we have to ask

> ourselves what is at stake in exhibiting not only the naked body of the male, but particularly that visible marker of difference, the penis, on which so much power rests? For within the myth that upholds male power (and since it is a myth it must be kept secret) the anatomical penis can never live up to the great expectations of symbolic phallic power. In short, this power rests on very little. (59)

McGrath moves next toward an interesting speculation about the ambivalence in the viewer of male nudity when that viewer is neither female nor gay. She writes: "Moreover, for the heterosexual male viewer, gazing upon his like can arouse not only the fear that he is looking at another man with the repressed eye of desire but that he himself may be being looked at with that same eye. This latter aspect can arouse a fear of being objectified, of being passive, of being less than male, and consequently like a woman: powerless" (59). Appropriately enough, *Lady Chatterley's Lover* offers another scene in which the body of Mellors is in fact positioned in just such a manner, as the vulnerable object of the gaze.

The scene in which the male body is objectified by being exposed occurs as a consequence of a disagreement between the lovers. The gamekeeper has learned that he may have impregnated his lover, and he reacts against involuntarily being pressed into service as the "Chatterley stud." Because Connie is also angry, she is positioned as the conscious observer of the male body's sexual performance. As a gazing subject, the woman is empowered here, and the male body as its object performing desire is oddly feminized through the power of that gaze. Thus, it is appropriate that the narrative at this point abandons the term *phallos* to denote the focus upon a mere body part, the vulnerable *penis:*

> she lay with her hands inert on his striving body, and do what she might, her spirit seemed to look on from the top of her head, and the butting of his haunches seemed ridiculous to her, and the sort of anxiety of his penis to come to its little evacuating crisis seemed farcical. Yes, this was love, this ridiculous bouncing of the buttocks, and the wilting of the poor, insignificant, moist little penis. (171–72)

The passage is critical to the narrative's impulse to be honest, to reveal the failures or limitations of desire as well as its transformations. The text seems inclined to represent the vulnerability of men in love through the kind of Medusalike gaze of conscious observation that ends by feminizing (or castrating?) the male body.

It is finally in just such a context of the risks implicit in nakedness that the narrative may be credited with being most brave by exposing the male body. On the analogy, once again, of film, the narrative functions like a camera in its use of extended close-up. "The sun through the low window sent in a beam that lit up his thighs and slim belly, and the erect phallos rising darkish and hot-looking from the little cloud of vivid gold-red hair" opens this scene of exposure. The text focuses attention once again upon "the root of the belly, where the phallos rose thick and arching, it was gold-red, vivid in a little cloud" (210) and back twice more before Mellors is allowed to release almost instantaneously the desire of this "stirring, erect phallos" so that he may turn over to Connie his "soft small penis." Within minutes the "helpless" Mellors looks on as "the penis in slow soft undulations filled and surged and rose up, and grew hard" (211).

As Roberta McGrath has suggested, graphic representation of male sexuality positions the heterosexual male viewer—and it is impossible to avoid the term since fiction has conventionally addressed itself to a visual imagination—in a highly constricted site. Just as the male film viewer can look away, the male heterosexual reader can skip over such scenes of exposure; that is, he can refuse to allow his visual imagination to gaze at what his culture has conditioned him to identify as *the* taboo image—taboo, because to look too long is to implicate his masculinity in a gender trouble little short of self-emasculation. At the same time, John Ellis would argue that looking, like indulging in fantasy, is far less gender-distinct than we conventionally assume. Within the context of film viewing, which shares elements with fantasy, Ellis asserts that "the partial suspension of the judging function of the ego" encourages the individual to see himself or herself less as an individual than as a series of "possible positions" or "representations of figures." Ellis concludes: "They involve the dreamer or phantasiser [or *viewer,* we might add] in conceptions of self as bisexual, as occupying *both* positions with a representation of heterosexual activity, not just that of active or passive participant. Even less does it involve the dreamer or phantasiser in seeing him- or herself as exclusively 'male' or 'female' in the terms provided by our culture" (42–43).

In this way, this narrative makes an early contribution to contemporary interest in the male as the object of looking, not all of which can be easily relegated to the construction of contexts for the gay gaze. With Connie positioned in these scenes as spectator, Mellors is encouraged to overcome his resistance to the "feminizing" potential of the gaze to serve as an early expression of what Steve Neale has termed "masculinity as spectacle."[16] The body of Mellors, from one point of view, makes a spectacle of itself by allowing Connie, and by implication the reader as well, to look at its privates (to employ a quaintly appropriate term). In this regard, the body of Mellors is much more like the body of Gilbert Noon pressed into performing its nudity through the excuse of dancing for the pleasure of the female gaze. Once again, on the analogy of film, Mellors is clearly aware of his body's being-looked-at-ness, as Gerald Crich is aware, but without Gerald's relishing of the performative gestures apparent in the scene with the mare, where he is clothed, or the nude swimming scene, where he performs an exposure primarily for himself. Again on the analogy of film, this text comes very close to foregrounding consciousness of an audience looking at these spectacles of nude male bodies "reluctantly" positioned for the other's desiring gaze, whether it is the spectacle of Gilbert Noon "coerced" into exposing the vulnerability of his nude body in daylight, or Mellors in performing the display of his "*aroused* nakedness." Or, perhaps more to the point, the text is working not only to celebrate phallic power but also in exposing the penis, tumescent or detumescent, establishing the vulnerability of the penis and thereby positioning it—oh, supreme paradox!—as feminine in the fragility of its power.

The Penis as Fetish

Another interesting turn in the figuring of the phallus is offered by David Savran, who wonders at one point in his study *Taking It Like a Man* whether it is legitimate to read one function of the penis itself as a variety of fetish. Savran begins with Freud, who theorized that the fetish functions as the (male) child's substitution of an object for the maternal phallus (penis), which the child constructs to stave off castration anxiety: if mother has one, son has less worry about losing his. The function of the fetish in this Freudian context is both to affirm and to deny; in Freud's words, it is "a token of triumph over the threat of castration and a safeguard against it" ("Fetishism" 87). Freud's notion of the fetish would deny the possibility of the penis being taken as a fetish.

Savran theorizes that if the subject fashions fetishes (shoes, stockings, et al.) as substitutes for the phallus, why can't the subject's penis function as a fetish for the Lacanian phallus? In other words, if the phallus may be read as the signifier of Desire foreclosed within the Imaginary by the subject's accession to the Symbolic register, can we not legitimately see the penis standing in as a fetish for the irrecoverable Phallus? As Savran notes, Silverman explores the differences between an "imaginary" and "symbolic" phallus, the former being the one "which comes into play in the Freudian account of castration," and the latter "is the one which no subject can ever be: it signifies that which must be sacrificed to language, that which has 'faded' away."[17] In this way, we can see the Phallus in the two registers as the signifier of plenitude in the Imaginary and lack in the Symbolic. Why, then, Savran ponders (225–27), is it not possible for the penis to stand in as a fetish for that maternal phallus in the Imaginary, representing fullness of Desire or plenitude?

Lacan's text itself seems to be advancing the possibility that the penis could be a fetish. In one of his characteristically frustrating ploys of slipping in provocative insights almost as asides he knows will tantalize, if not madden, his readers because he withholds explanation, Lacan discusses how the function of the phallus relates to the "structures that will govern the relations between the sexes." He asserts: "But she finds the signifier of her own desire in the body of him to whom she addresses her demand for love. Perhaps it should not be forgotten that the organ that assumes this signifying function takes on the value of a fetish" (*Écrits* 290). Now, despite his efforts in the famous passage, cited above, where the text emphatically differentiates the phallus from "the organ, penis or clitoris, that it symbolizes," there is an inevitable muddying of the waters here, in a sense deconstructing that distinction by denoting the "organ" of the subject's male lover as having a "signifying function" with "the value of a fetish." Surely, if this is a slip of the pen, it is a Freudian slip, or one of those gaps through which (Lacan teaches us) the unconscious speaks. Most importantly, however, is the support this use of the term *organ* lends to Silverman and Savran's construction of the penis as a fetish for that imaginary or maternal phallus. To take this line of reasoning a step further, Lacan may be seen as subverting the tendency of Freud's followers to find symbols for the penis by encouraging us to see the penis itself as phallic symbol or fetish standing in for a phallus, or Desire foreclosed within the Imaginary register. That refusal to see the relationship between phallus and penis as more than simply either an equivalence or a binary opposition offers a particularly provocative entry to a literary text like *Lady Chatterley's Lover,* with its inclination to fetishize the penis as the representation of the phallus.

Reading the penis as a fetishistic replacement for the phallus goes a long way toward explaining the risks that this narrative takes in exposing the penis of Mellors and allowing John Thomas, as it/he is called, to make a spectacle of himself by being unveiled in a state of erection. The fetishistic function of the penis in the Lawrentian text helps to explain the insistent recurrence of the narrative's focus upon the male organ of Mellors. And it is not just its erect state that is represented; the text just as frequently exposes the penis in its detumescent state, although its representation as a "soft bud" is typically a prelude to its transformation into what the text persists in terming the "phallos." On this occasion, the text tracks the penis in its movement toward tumescence and away again more than once so that the camera eye of the narrative can record both its "wilting" as well as its "thrust," in a gesture that subverts the binary of "soft bud" and "thrust of a sword," for its "soft bud" state is as appealing in its feminine vulnerability as its alternative state, "the dark thrust of peace and a ponderous, primordial tenderness" (174). In this recurrent withdrawal and return of desire, the penis as fetishistic signifier of the fading of Desire parallels the signifier in Lacan's reading of Freud's "Fort/Da" in *Beyond the Pleasure Principle.* In its tumescence and detumescence the penis in this text duplicates the cast away and retrieved spool of Freud's grandson, not so much as a symbol of the absent and present mother but as a signifier of that Desire, or *jouissance,* foreclosed forever in the Imaginary.

Gender Issues

Lady Chatterley's Lover, then, offers a useful text for exploring the gender issues with which this discussion of recent psychoanalytic approaches or narratology has been involved. Because of its textuality, or self-referentiality, this narrative offers a demonstration of the reconstruction of gender in part as positionality within the text. As gender theorists have reminded us, one major consequence of patriarchy is the engendering of subject positions so that those with power are privileged as masculine, regardless of their sex or biological identity. Those who are the objects of that power are feminized across a range of social and cultural identities. One site along that spectrum is class status, with which this text is implicated. Indeed, it is quite possible to read *Lady Chatterley's Lover* as the conflict between patriarchy and phallic power, a phallic power that both authorizes and contests patriarchy.

The repository of power in this text is "author-ity." One of this text's most exciting moves is the doubling or even tripling of Clifford Chatterley's authority as its most powerful representation of patriarchy. As we have seen, Clifford is adept at negotiating the web of technological textuality; he is also an author weaving the web of his fictional textuality out of the Real of the world outside either the Imaginary or the Symbolic Orders, as Lacan denotes those two registers. It is clear that in the Clifford figure the phallus as a signifier of power cannot be equated with the flesh of the male sexual organ alone. Even though his overt impotence would logically divest him of power as a biological male, his position of authority is very near the apex of patriarchy. The force of Clifford's social or cultural authority dominates the world of this text so completely that once the lovers reveal that they have subverted that authority, there is no longer any space at Wragby for either of them, and they have no option but to flee. The lovers know full well that as long as Clifford refuses to grant Connie a divorce, he has the power of law to maintain his possession of her as his wife. More important, he is *legally* the father of Connie's child, even if she leaves him, for it is Clifford whom patriarchy has authorized as that child's father. Beyond that, perhaps, in another exciting move, this text anticipates Lacan's theorizing by constructing Clifford as an expression of the Law of the Name of the Father because it is Clifford who is the master of the Symbolic Order; it is he who controls words and other modes of representation.

It is that mastery or construction of masculinity before which Connie and even Mellors must adopt feminized subject positions. Clifford's power is nowhere more evident than in the exposure by Connie of her complicity with Mellors in an attempt to subvert not only Clifford's mastery of representation but the very power of patriarchy itself. Clifford may have been willing to conspire in Connie's subverting of conventional notions of paternity and its corollary of property rights by finding another man to father an heir for Wragby. However, Connie enrages Clifford by her treachery in deciding to rob him of *his* "child," and of any other, unless he agrees to divorce her so that he might marry another more willing co-conspirator. However, it is her choice of Mellors as co-conspirator that more truly contests Clifford's mastery, for in the text of society's fabric Mellors is of a lower class and therefore one feminized by the Chatterley ascendancy. It is not for nothing that this text positions the Chatterleys in the lower ranks of the aristocracy. As Susanne Kappeler writes in a somewhat different context: "Gender . . . lends a powerful cultural metaphor to oppression, as the working class becomes the object to the economic subject, becomes objectified, 'feminized,' animalized, commodified" (70).

Patriarchy itself is threatened by Connie's subversion of Clifford's subject position as she abandons her allegiance to his mastery in order to have relations with another who is in his own way paradoxically even more feminized than she. It is as though she has resorted to another female, or perhaps even an animal, if we follow Kappeler's line of reasoning in the passage just cited. In one sense, the Mellors figure represents femininity, or the powerless position, in his refusal to implicate himself in a structure of bourgeois "bildung," or personal development, which would normally obligate a man of his education to repress desire in order to raise himself in that social hierarchy through which patriarchy constructs masculinity, in part at least, as success.

There is unavoidable irony, then, in the old claims of Kate Millett and other second-wave feminists that this text represents masculinist preoccupation with the phallic as the instrumentation of patriarchy, for, as we have been observing, the narrative seems bent upon positioning the phallic in part as feminine in its representation of vulnerability and exposure. Not only does the text expose the penis of Mellors in a state of "aroused nakedness," but it also takes great risks in gestures that end by complicating conventional notions of gender. By allowing Mellors to be the object of Connie's gaze, Lawrence moves the representation of the phallic (in at least one sense of the term) into a potentially objectified position usually gendered as feminine. If Mellors is to be read as a masculinist who resorts on occasion to what has been construed in a contemporary context as rape, we ought not to ignore that the text also genders this masculinist in a variety of ways conventionally classified within femininity.

Indeed, the text allows Mellors himself to foreground his own femininity by revealing an awareness from the beginning of his relationship with Connie that desire has a potentially feminizing agency. The narrative cross-genders conventional expectations as it empowers the woman to approach the man and the man to express disappointment at having fallen back into desire again. Furthermore, the narrative has established that it was a variety of *agape* that energized *eros,* for it was the man's empathy with the woman's sadness at being excluded from the rhythms of life implicated in the young chick she holds: "compassion flamed in his bowels for her," and then, "At the back of his loins the fire suddenly darted stronger" (115). At the same time it is a desire "he had hoped was quiescent forever" (115), and when they part he expresses sadness that "life" has penetrated his refuge of numbness, reminding him of his vulnerability in a metaphor suggesting sexual violation: "I've got to be broken open again" (118). Paradoxically, once again, to desire another is to be feminized, or moved into a vulnerable subject position, "to be broken open again" by desire.

Finally, the pursuit of heterosexual desire in Mellors, representing a variety of "unmanning" because it is intended to subvert patriarchy, is further complicated by his revelation of homoerotic desire in his relationship with his "men," as well as with that officer under whom he served and with whom he seems to have developed an intimacy straining at the limits of the conventional male bonding one expects in homosocial activities such as soldiering. The text allows Mellors to foreground his own sense of his femininity in more conventional terms in his memory of military life. "They used to say I had too much of the woman in me—" (276), he confesses, and goes on to explain that what sets his own construction of masculinity off from the socially approved construction is his inability to abide "the twaddling, bossy impudence of the people who run this world" (276). What he (along with countless women) finds wanting in patriarchy is that "tenderness" that he is certified to possess moments later in this scene, as though that tenderness were a kind of stigma of femininity because it could not be comfortably revealed to those committed to the maintenance of patriarchy. The story of soldiering told by Mellors has at its center that colonel whom he served as lieutenant, a man he freely admits he "loved" in India. Tellingly, Mellors indicates that desire in that relationship positioned him as desirer in a subordinate role conventionally reserved for the woman; he himself implies such an awareness as the text moves toward a gesture of confession: "I lived under his spell, while I was with him. I sort of let him run my life" (216). And when the colonel died, he almost followed him.[18] As Judith Butler has suggested, the construction of heterosexual masculinity is grounded in a melancholy produced by the grieving at the loss of a same-sex love, never gratified but abandoned in order to achieve heterosexual masculinity.[19] In one sense—a Lacanian sense—this lost, unrealized desire for his colonel replicates the abandonment of Desire in the accession to the Symbolic order and representation, and once again, then, desire is a metonym for that Desire from which the subject is forever bereft. Or, to return to an earlier approach, the center of this text is elegy, a mourning for lost Desire, more specifically, to follow Butler, the desire for one's own sex, foreclosed as the price paid for male or female identity.

Mellors as Writer

In the end, this narrative implicates even Mellors in writing. Wragby is merely one locus in a world of words, and with separation he must join the others in letter writing. The concluding chapters of this narrative are, in fact, dominated by letters and the foregrounding of the postman.[20] Even the cottage in Wragby Wood, which has served as the site of lovemaking, proves not to be beyond the bounds of the English rural mail delivery, for a registered letter from British Columbia arrives, opening up western Canada as a potential site of refuge for the fugitive lovers. Although, as Lacan generalizes, the "letter" always reaches its destination, in one sense by creating its own destination or reader, there is something slightly uncanny about the breakfast after the "night of sensual passion" being interrupted by the tinkling of the postman's bell as he bicycles up the path with the letter from the other side of the world, opening the door to their future.

In a text dominated by the "writing"—both storytelling and technology—through which Wragby consolidates author-ity, the gamekeeper's hut has been up to this point a site of silence, broken by metaphorical expressions of phallic desire crossing the bar of representation as spoken language. The text of Mellors's unexpectedly long letter to Connie at the end is privileged over anything in Wragby's textual production by virtue of its offering this narrative whatever fragile closure it may have. Within the constraints of the text, this letter functions as its last will and testament, so to speak. There is an appropriateness in this text ending in a letter, for this narrative has been throughout a web of words, a concatenation of spoken discourse as well as a collection of "stories" and letters.[21]

The letter begins in Wragby's metonymic world of realist narrative and synecdochic detail, the kind of gossip one would expect of a letter to an absent loved one. It ends, however, in romantic poetry as Mellors, the writing subject, rhapsodizes lyrically on the power of desire represented in the veiled phallus. Or once again, in Lacanian terms, the language that this letter is generating as text is the veiling of the phallus, that master signifier of desire forever abandoned, or cut off, in the Imaginary register. Perhaps in response to an awareness of the vulnerability, or femininity, of the phallus as signifier of Desire, the text shifts from metonymic prose narrative to metaphoric poetry as it focuses upon the coming child, the ripening seed of that desire and the metaphor of its vulnerable tenderness. Mellors, as writing subject, turns away from the menace thus: "But never mind. All the bad times that ever have been, haven't been able to blow the crocus out: nor even the love of women. So they won't be able to blow out my wanting you, nor the little glow there is between you and me. . . . You can't insure against the future, except by really believing in the best bit of you, and in the power beyond it. So I believe in the little flame between us. For me now, it's the only thing in the world" (300). It is that strange figure, "blow the crocus out," to which we need to attend as we move toward closure.

The poetry of this passage is a complex concatenation of metaphor and metonymy, and in that regard it deconstructs the reductive binaries in which structuralist renditions of these two central tropes have often found themselves trapped. On the one hand, the phallic in this text is a metonymic part-for-the-whole of a life force, which moves through crocuses and rainbows. On the other hand, the phallic is metaphorically represented by the signifier "flame," over which the signifier "crocus" has metonymically slid to produce the statement that nothing can "blow the crocus out." Finally, as the text makes eminently clear, all these words are a replacement for the ultimate signifier, the veiled phallus, which implicates the subject in words and makes signification possible.

In the end, then, this text collapses the distance between Wragby as manor house and the gamekeeper's hut, the locus of silence in juxtaposition to the authority of Wragby's wordy web. The Mellors figure has been literally and figuratively expelled from a world of darkness and silence for the practice of writing with which the veiling of the phallus is identical. The Lacanian "Symbolic" is not to be reductively equated with mere "mind-consciousness," or the prison house of the "mental-lifer." As Stuart Schneiderman asserts: "The concept of the real implies the annihilation of the subject. When the Greeks named the wind or the sea after a god, they recognized that it is only through the structure of the symbolic order that things become real, not through perception or consciousness, not through the agency of a subject. A subject can only make the real into objects; consciousness can only make it into phenomena" (76–77). In its way, this text deconstructs the binary of phallus/penis, as well as binaries such as metonymy/metaphor and masculine/feminine, in the manner suggested by Barbara Johnson in her rendition of how deconstruction works. It demonstrates that these binaries are not mutually exclusive, at the same time that the practice of deconstruction refuses to deny that denial.

If the postmodern/post-structuralist approach to texts has met resistance among traditionalists, it is not difficult to discover why texts such as those examined here continue to exist outside the revolution in critical theorizing that erupted a generation ago. Unlike most authors of the past century, "Lawrence," or the totality of his textual productivity, has been marginalized by a preoccupation with "Lawrence the thinker," or the exponent of a dogma of psychic regeneration. While the texts of modernists such as Joyce have lent themselves to the postmodern/post-structuralist inclinations of contemporary scholarship, "Lawrence" has been something of a rallying point for humanists, unwilling to abandon the binaries of author and work, or psychoanalysis and literature, or form and meaning. No single project can counter that resistance; my aim has been to begin an effort toward moving these texts in that direction.

Notes

Preface

1. See Joyce Wexler's "D. H. Lawrence through a Postmodernist Lens."

Chapter 1. Reading Lawrence's Texts with Lacan's Readers

1. See Joseph Valente's *James Joyce and the Problem of Justice: Negotiating Sexual and Colonial Difference,* R. B. Kershner's *Joyce, Bakhtin, and Popular Literature: Chronicles of Disorder,* and Valente's *Quare Joyce,* for example.

2. Indeed, the critical production of Joycean Sheldon Brivic, author of *Joyce between Freud and Jung,* and most recently *The Veil of Signs: Joyce, Lacan, and Perception,* recapitulates psychoanalytic approaches to Joyce.

3. In her foundational text *The Revolution in Poetic Language*, Julia Kristeva reserves membership in one select group of modern writers: "only certain literary texts of the avant-garde (Mallarmé and Joyce) manage to cover the infinity of the process, that is, reach the semiotic *chora,* which modifies linguistic structures" (122). Hélène Cixous wrote *The Exile of James Joyce.*

4. In a 1999 article in the *New York Times Book Review,* Brenda Maddox speaks of Richard Ellmann's "great biography of Joyce," which left her unsatisfied about the life of Joyce's wife, Nora, whose biography Maddox wrote. In contrast, she says little about her interest in Frieda, which stimulated her to write a portrait of the Lawrence marriage. Her "idea of biography as journalism may be deeply disappointing to those who prefer to see it as a literary genre," she acknowledges, but she is an unembarrassed journalist. She adds: "Every biographer of D. H. Lawrence has to deal with the ugly incident of his kicking his dog." Maddox motivates many of us to unmoor discussions of literary texts from reference to their authors.

5. Joyce and Lawrence have been examined in tandem by James C. Cowan, "Lawrence, Joyce, and the Epiphanies of *Lady Chatterley's Lover,*" Zack Bowen, "*Lady Chatterley's Lover* and *Ulysses,*" Monroe Engel, "Contrived Lives: Joyce and Lawrence," and Paul Delany, "'A Would-Be-Dirty Mind': D. H. Lawrence as an Enemy of Joyce."

6. In a similar vein, Pamela Caughie has published *Virginia Woolf and Postmodernism.*

7. The first Lacanian study of Lawrence to appear in print was Roger Ebbatson's application of Lacan to the opening of *The Rainbow.* Other applications of Lacan to Lawrence also began as presentations at the 1985 centenary celebration of Lawrence's birth at Tufts University. These include: Ed Jewinski's effort to connect Lawrence's psychology with Lacan's; Jane A. Nelson's Lacanian reading of *The Fox;* and John N. Swift's brief use of Lacan in what is otherwise a Freudian reading of *Women in Love.*

In addition, it would be difficult to ignore the major contribution made by James M. Mellard, especially in his work of a decade ago, *Doing Tropology: Analysis of Narrative Discourse.* Mellard's introduction, "Tropology and Phenomenology of Language," offers valuable background in the functions of tropes, either dyadic, growing out of the thinking of Jakobson and Lacan or tetradic, theorized recently by Hayden White. Mellard "applies" Lacanian insights concerning metonymy and metaphor to Joseph Heller's *Something Happened.* However, he favors tetradic over dyadic tropologies.

8. Peter Brooks, *Psychoanalysis and Storytelling* 22.

9. Felman has a penchant for italics to indicate emphasis; all emphasis in the citations from her work is hers, unless otherwise noted.

10. Currie writes: "It was a key characteristic of poststructuralist narratology that it sought to sustain contradictory aspects of narrative, preserving their complexity and refusing the impulse to reduce the narrative to a stable meaning or coherent project" (3).

11. Lest the reader be confused by the reference to page 848 for the introduction to Davis's book, let me add that the Davis collection was originally an issue of *MLN,* whose plates were used for the book without changing the pagination.

12. The title of Holland's essay in Ihab Hassan and Sally Hassan's *Innovation/Renovation.* Lawrence himself, of course, was eventually to publish two studies on the subject—*Psychoanalysis and the Unconscious* (1921) and *Fantasia of the Unconscious* (1922). Students of Lawrence's fiction have paid relatively little attention to these two works and generally resisted the temptation to apply a "Lawrentian" psychoanalysis to his fictional work, perhaps with an awareness of the role of psychoanalysis in these two Lawrence books as similar to W. B. Yeats's system as outlined in *A Vision;* namely, a working out of a writer's thinking for the writer's own benefit rather than as a key to the writer's fiction and poetry.

13. Lacan reads Freud's dream images and figures in terms of a system of

notation borrowed from the structuralist Ferdinand de Saussure. Starting with Saussure's notation $\frac{S}{s}$, where S represents the signifier and s represents the signified beneath the bar, Lacan constructs an algorithm for metaphoric representation, or "identification and symbolism." On the principle of $\frac{S}{s}$, Lacan constructs $\frac{S'}{S}$, where S' displaces S as a signifier for s, or its signified. In each case the bar, or line separating the signifier from the signified beneath it, represents repression. Anthony Wilden, "Lacan and the Discourse of the Other," in his *Speech and Language in Psychoanalysis* 238–43.

See also Robert Con Davis's *Lacan and Narration: The Psychoanalytic Difference in Narrative Theory* 991.

As Davis explains: "In Lacan's notation, the unconscious chain can be designated as ($\frac{S}{S}$)—the merely metonymic relationship of a signifier to another signifier." Thus, Lacan's algorithm may be expressed as follows:

$$\frac{S'}{\ } \cdot \frac{S}{s} = \frac{S'}{\frac{s}{\frac{S}{S}}}.$$

Thus, S' represents the conscious or manifest system; s, the preconscious with its potential to become conscious; and $\frac{S}{S}$, the unconscious.

This is a very different notion of metaphor from other critics' use of the trope, ranging from Patricia Hagen's more conventionally literary approach in her book *Metaphor's Way of Knowing: The Poetry of D. H. Lawrence and the Church of Mechanism,* to James M. Mellard's more sophisticated approach to the four tropes of metaphor, metonymy, synecdoche, and irony in his book *Doing Tropology: Analysis of Narrative Discourse.*

14. Wilden draws into this discussion other binary oppositions he associates with the dichotomy of metaphor and metonymy: "The 'vertical' *paradigmatic* mode of language and the 'linear' (horizontal) *syntagmatic* mode, which is another way of stating the opposition of synchrony ('the axis of simultaneities') to diachrony ('the axis of successivities')" (246).

15. In "Two Aspects of Language and Two Types of Aphasic Disturbances," Jakobson writes: "The primacy of the metaphoric process in the literary schools of romanticism and symbolism has been repeatedly acknowledged, but it is still insufficiently realized that it is the predominance of metonymy which underlies and actually predetermines the so-called 'realistic' trend, which belongs to an intermediary stage between the decline of romanticism and the rise of symbolism and is opposed to both. Following the path of contiguous relationships, the realist author metonymically digresses from the plot to the atmosphere and from the characters to the setting in space and time. He is fond of synecdochic details" (255).

16. In *Écrits,* Lacan writes that "all 'realism' in creative work takes its virtue from metonymy" (166). Elsewhere he writes: "In a general manner, metonymy

animates this style of creation which we call, in opposition to symbolic style and poetic language, the so-called 'realist style'" (266).

17. It might be noted that as a poet/fiction writer Lawrence was following in the footsteps of his literary father Thomas Hardy. Coincidentally he was writing both poetry and short fiction in exactly the same years as his very different contemporary James Joyce. This uneasiness of readers with writers who work in both poetry and fiction persists in our time. Margaret Atwood has expressed her frustration at being criticized for writing both poetry and fiction and her awareness that her fiction, especially her novels, has eclipsed her poetry (136). Even more recently, we see it happening again in the case of Atwood's fellow Canadian Michael Ondaatje, who was virtually unknown as a poet outside Canada before his novel *The English Patient* (1992) won the Booker Prize. The great success of its filmed version will undoubtedly fix his reputation as a novelist in the popular consciousness for the rest of his career.

18. See Naomi Schor's "Female Paranoia: A Case for Psychoanalytic Feminist Criticism" for a fascinating reading of synecdoche as the clitoris, marginalized by male theorists such as Jakobson and Lacan when they allow it to be subsumed into metonymy.

19. See Jack Stewart's helpful essay, "Landscape Painting and Pre-Raphaelitism in *The White Peacock.*"

20. See Barbara Johnson's "Metaphor, Metonymy, and Voice in *Their Eyes Were Watching God.*"

21. In the introduction to a chapter called "The Class of 1968—Post-Structuralism *par lui-meme,*" in their book *Literary Theory: An Anthology,* Julie Rivkin and Michael Ryan write: "In 1979, Post-Structuralism changed names, but, as any Post-Structuralist will tell you, when names changes, things change. Post-Structuralism (a term used mostly in the anglophone academy) found itself being replaced by a new word (actually an old word transplanted from America to France and back again). That word was 'Post-Modernism'" (352). Mark Currie indicates that there is no French equivalent for *post-structuralism* (49). Even the spelling of the term is contested from either side of the Atlantic since Currie writes *poststructuralism,* without the hyphen agreed upon by American academicians.

22. See Judith Butler's *Gender Trouble.*

23. In his essay on Lawrence and Forster, Frederick McDowell also notes the shared bathing scenes of *The White Peacock* and *A Room with a View,* adding that he has found no evidence of Lawrence's having read the Forster novel before he wrote *The White Peacock.* McDowell calls attention to Dixie King's provocative attempt to argue for the influence of *Maurice* upon *Lady Chatterley's Lover.* However, it is open to question whether Forster would have trusted Lawrence to read the manuscript of *Maurice,* given the dire consequences of appearing to promote same-sex relations.

24. See Valente for a brief history of the circumstances surrounding the passage of the "Labouchere amendment" (*Quare* 6–7).

25. Margaret Storch, in "The Lacerated Male: Ambivalent Images of Women in *The White Peacock*," speaks of "Cyril Beardsall, a narrator of marked passivity who typically responds to the experience of others rather than acting directly himself" (117). Ming Dong Gu, in "Lawrence's Childhood Traumas and the Problematic Form of *The White Peacock*," disagrees: "Cyril is not merely the detached narrator he is generally believed to be, but actively participates in the whole action of the novel, upon which the entire construction depends" (128).

26. See Barbara Johnson's "The Frame of Reference: Poe, Lacan, and Derrida," 123.

Chapter 2. De-Oedipalizing *Sons and Lovers*

1. See Paul Delany's "Men in Love."

2. See Judith Ruderman's *D. H. Lawrence and the Devouring Mother.*

3. I am indebted to Corinna del Greco Lobner for this term.

4. Indeed, the author conspired in the Freudianalysis with his own Oedipal (re)construction of the text when he wrote of *Sons and Lovers:*

> It follows this idea: a woman of character and refinement goes into the lower class, and has no satisfaction in her own life. She has had a passion for her husband, so the children are born of passion, and have heaps of vitality. But as her sons grow up she selects them as lovers—first the eldest, then the second. These sons are *urged* into life by their reciprocal love of their mother— urged on and on. But when they come to manhood, they can't love, because their mother is the strongest power in their lives, and holds them. . . . As soon as the young men come into contact with women, there's a split. William gives his sex to a fribble, and his mother holds his soul. But the split kills him, because he doesn't know where he is. The next son gets a woman who fights for his soul—fights his mother. The son loves the mother—all the sons hate and are jealous of the father. . . . The son decides to leave his soul in his mother's hands, and, like his elder brother, go for passion. He gets passion. Then the split begins to tell again. But, almost unconsciously, the mother realises what is the matter, and begins to die. The son casts off his mistress, attends to his mother dying. He is left in the end naked of everything, with the drift towards death. (*Letters* 1: 476–77)

5. Peter Brooks, *Reading for the Plot: Design and Intention in Narrative* xiv. This assertion by Brooks establishes the aspiration of the present study to break free from a tradition of turning literary characters into the subjects of analysis as though they were autonomous historical figures. How *does* one avoid even the conventional approach to literary texts that has encouraged readers to think of "characters" as such, even though its practice has been problematized by contemporary

theorists who remind us that fictional characters are no more than threads in the textual web which is narrative, despite how easily we are seduced into talking about them as though characters were somehow reflections of real people we can isolate for discussion? Joseph Lewandowski, in a recent essay, "Narrativizing Desire in *Sons and Lovers,*" writes that he finds it "curious" that some critics have decided *not* to "psychoanalyze" the character of Paul Morel, as he sets out to. In essence, Lewandowski asks, rhetorically: "What's wrong with analyzing characters in fiction?" To that question we might add, What is it about this narrative that makes it virtually impossible to resist being drawn into just such analysis?

6. Quoted by Brenda Maddox, *D. H. Lawrence: The Story of a Marriage* 280.

7. Quoted by Ellie Ragland-Sullivan, *Jacques Lacan and the Philosophy of Psychoanalysis* 20.

8. Jacques Derrida remarks: "And Lacan's style was constructed so as to check almost permanently any access to an isolatable content, to an unequivocal, determinable meaning beyond writing" ("The Purveyor of Truth" 176).

9. In their provocative book *Anti-Oedipus: Capitalism and Schizophrenia,* Gilles Deleuze and Félix Guattari lump Lacan in with Freud as an exponent of the Oedipus complex because Lacan theorizes that "Castration" or accession to the Symbolic register closes off Desire in the unconscious. Lacan himself asserted that he never spoke of the Oedipus complex.

10. See my essay "Virginia Woolf and D. H. Lawrence: Exploring the Dark."

11. Deleuze and Guattari quote Lacan as follows:

> Nevertheless, it is not because I preach a return to Freud that I am not able to say the *Totem and Taboo* is a twisted story. It is in fact for that reason that we must return to Freud. No one helped me to make this known: *the formations of the unconscious*. . . . I am not saying Oedipus serves no purpose, nor that it (*ça*) bears no relationship with what we do. It serves no purpose for the psychoanalysts, that is indeed true! But since psychoanalysts are assuredly not psychoanalysts, that proves nothing. . . . These are things I set forth in their appropriate time and place; that was a time when I was speaking to people who had to be dealt with tactfully—psychoanalysts. On that level, I spoke of the paternal metaphor, I have never spoken of an Oedipus complex. (Jacques Lacan in a seminar, 1970, quoted by Deleuze and Guattari 53)

12. See also Fiona Becket's discussion of this connection between Lawrence and Deleuze and Guattari in her recent book *D. H. Lawrence: The Thinker as Poet* (63–67). It is worth noting too that Deleuze and Guattari represent a rare incidence of theorists referring to Lawrence, in dramatic contrast to Joyce, who was, as suggested earlier, the subject of writings by Derrida, Lacan, Kristeva, and Cixous, to name the most prominent French theorists attracted to Joyce's texts.

13. Quoted in Fuss 48.

14. The passage Fuss cites is located in Julia Kristeva's *Black Sun: Depression and Melancholia* (12).

Chapter 3. The Sense of an Ending in *The Rainbow*

1. See Mark Kinkead-Weekes, "The Marble and the Statue" and Charles L. Ross, *The Composition of "The Rainbow" and "Women in Love": A History.*

2. Quoted by Peter Brooks, *Reading for the Plot: Design and Intention in Narrative* 95.

3. Quoted by Brooks, *Reading* 22.

4. Juliet Flower MacCannell is very helpful in pointing out this evolution of Lacan from an earlier structuralist, or more specifically Jakobsonian, mode of thinking emphasizing "meaning" (95).

5. Quoted by Brooks, *Reading* 37.

6. Brooks, *Reading* 99. We might add to this list of "mnemonic elements" a characteristic repetition of words and phrases in *The Rainbow.* The repetition of the word *fecundity* comes to mind immediately. Such repetition gives us the sense of a textual consciousness going back over the significant terms again and again.

7. Freud's *Beyond the Pleasure Principle,* like his other writing, has too often been (mis)read as a scientific text. As McCannell has argued, the later-twentieth-century view has been more intent upon reading Freud and other psychoanalysts such as Lacan as authors, rather than scientists. This framing situation of Freud's speculating in the *Beyond* is a marvelous case in point, for Freud as writer here is being very selective in his (re)construction of this narrative. He does not indicate, for example, that the toddler is his own grandson. Furthermore, Freud may well be misreading this rudimentary text, for the "oo" and "ah" he hears may not be the infant's efforts to reproduce the signifiers "Fort" and "Da."

8. Metz 203–5. Metz points out that metaphor and metonymy seldom exist separately, citing Gérard Genette, who sees metaphor's resemblance as contingent upon metonymy's proximity so that metonymy reinforces metaphor in a more symbiotic fashion than Jakobson's antithesis suggests.

Paul de Man also deconstructs the binary of metonymy (including synecdoche) and metaphor, asserting that "The synecdoche that substitutes part for whole and whole for part is in fact a metaphor, powerful enough to transform a temporal contiguity into an infinite duration." He continues:

> Classical rhetoric generally classifies synecdoche as metonymy, which leads to difficulties characteristic of all attempts at establishing a taxonomy of tropes; tropes are transformational systems rather than grids. The relationship between part and whole can be understood metaphorically, as is the case, for example, in the organic metaphors dear to Goethe. Synecdoche is one of the borderline figures that create an ambivalent zone between metaphor and metonymy and that, by its spatial nature, creates the illusion of a synthesis by totalization. (63)

Metz's and de Man's reminders of the complexities of the metaphor/metonymy relationship are useful in responding to Gerald Doherty's attempt in "The Art of

Appropriation: The Rhetoric of Sexuality in D. H. Lawrence" to connect the selection of sexual partners in *The Rainbow* with the apparently all-encompassing poles of metaphor and metonymy. Furthermore, Doherty seems intent upon exaggerating what he sees as the "appropriative" function of metaphor as a variety of "textual rape."

9. I follow the lead of Ellie Ragland-Sullivan in capitalizing Desire to denote an immensity represented through the metonym of desire.

10. In Lawrence's story "The Horse Dealer's Daughter," *Complete Short Stories.*

11. See Stewart's "Expressionism in *The Rainbow*" 74.

12. See Jacques Derrida's "Plato's Pharmacy" 429–50.

13. The narrative binds the relationship metaphorically to the first couple's relationship by the frequently noted passages of scenic echoes as well as a number of repeated metaphors. For example, Anna anticipates Will's visits from nearby Ilkeston, where he works: "In him she had escaped. In him the bounds of her experience were transgressed: he was the hole in the wall, beyond which the sunshine blazed on an outside world" (106). Similarly, when Will goes home, with the same "stars in heaven whirling fiercely about the blackness of his head" (108), he is walking on a path similar to Tom's. That his marriage with Anna is in Will's imagination and is, like Tom's, a journey toward the unknown is underscored in his description while awaiting the wedding day: "He did not count the days. But like a man who journeys in a ship, he was suspended till the coming to port" (121).

14. Teresa de Lauretis in *Alice Doesn't: Feminism, Semiotics, Cinema* points out the grounding of traditional narrative rhythm in the arc of male tumescence and detumescence.

15. John Worthen, "Introduction," *The Rainbow* 11.

16. In "The Art of Appropriation" Doherty surprisingly terms the Skrebensky figure a "potent male colonizer" (297).

17. In stark contrast, George Ford in *Double Measure* remarks, "The horse here remains a symbol of powerful masculinity" (160). Gavriel Ben-Ephraim concurs that "the horses symbolize precisely the compelling, polarizing maleness Ursula needs" (171).

18. See Gerald Doherty's useful examination of metaphor as the "leap into the unknown" in "The Art of Leaping: Metaphor Unbound in D. H. Lawrence's *Women in Love.*"

Chapter 4. Staging the Gaze in *Women in Love*

1. In *Sex in the Head: Visions of Femininity and Film in D. H. Lawrence,* Williams shares much of my interest in spectacle and the organization of looking and being looked at in this text. Apparently she was working on the manuscript of her study at about the same time I was drafting the earliest version of this present chapter, which appeared in *Studies in the Novel* the year after *Sex in the Head*

appeared. As her subtitle suggests, Williams is primarily interested in the cinematic qualities of Lawrence's prose narrative and his attitudes toward film, especially as these issues relate to his attitudes toward women.

2. In *Male Subjectivity at the Margins* Silverman writes: "The relationship between eye and gaze is analogous in certain ways to that which links penis and phallus: the former can stand in for the latter, but can never approximate it" (130).

3. Williams asserts: "The human spectacle's disavowal of himself as spectacle is crucial to the pleasurable maintenance of distance" (87). (It becomes necessary to include Professor Williams's middle name to distinguish her from the American film theorist Linda Williams.)

4. Williams writes: "The implications of this are important, not just for an understanding of gay male desire as written by one of our century's prime voices of heterosexuality, but for the ease with which women are made able to channel a desire which we can so readily call 'gay,' a desire which seems not to originate with these women. Are these fictions with which Lawrence's women 'feel' a desire for their men which is actually homoerotic? If so, this muddies the waters not only for our understanding of heterosexuality (which evidently can so easily slip into its other, a heterosexual view facilitating homoerotic images), it also questions the 'intrinsic' gender qualities of *any* desire. Perhaps Kate Millett's point, that Kate in *The Plumed Serpent* is only 'a female impersonator,' comes near to the truth, and all we are ever dealing with in Lawrence is the male desire for men, slightly varied every now and then when the wolf dons the sheep's clothing" (101).

5. See Camille Paglia, *Sexual Personae: Art and Decadence from Nefertiti to Emily Dickinson* 110–12.

6. Brooks usefully writes that the rise of the novel coincides with the growing awareness of the concept of privacy and the vulnerability of private experience to the invasive looking of others. As a form, the novel both invites readers to intrude on the privacy of others, especially as narrative mimicked the "confession" and private letters in the epistolary novel, yet also excites some awareness of the reader's own vulnerability to the looking of others.

7. In *Masked Men* Steven Cohan cites a pertinent passage from Kirk Douglas's autobiography, which Cohan frames as follows: "This disturbing implication of transgressing proper gender roles extended to Douglas's position as a rising star since the actor felt that in order to get the part in *Champion* he had to resort to behaving like a tramp himself. Douglas recalls in his autobiography that he suffered the indignity of doing just 'what the starlets do. I took off my jacket and shirt, bared my chest and flexed my muscles. . . . I was probably the only *man* in Hollywood who's had to strip to get a part.' After the film's premiere, he reports, 'The women ogled me, as if they were looking right through my clothes'" (166).

8. Grounding his discussion in Foucault's *History of Sexuality* (volume 1), Gerald Doherty examines "the pathologization of the sexual psyche" in this text, seeing Hermione in relation to "the standard external tokens of female hysteria"

("*Ars Erotica* or *Scientia Sexualis*?: Narrative Vicissitudes in D. H. Lawrence's *Women in Love*" 137–57).

9. See Davis 985–88 for a helpful examination of oscillation in the visual text.

10. In "D. H. Lawrence (in *Women in Love*) on the Desire for Difference and 'the Facism [*sic*] in Us All,'" G. Watson asserts that it is appropriate Gerald should come in on the side of Gudrun and Loerke.

11. See Doherty's interesting discussion of the connection between death and metaphor as transformation in "Death and the Rhetoric of Representation in D. H. Lawrence's *Women in Love*."

Chapter 5. *Mr Noon* as Postmodern Text

1. This sort of "romance" of the lost manuscript is central to Ibsen's *Hedda Gabler,* in which Hedda burns Lövborg's magnum opus.

2. Michael Black, "D. H. Lawrence and Gilbert Noon" [essay review of *Mr Noon*] 10.

3. William Golding's novel *The Paper Men* (1984) also "stops" instead of ending. Indeed, its first-person narrator's last words represent his puzzled question concerning his killer: "How the devil did Rick L. Tucker manage to get hold of a gu" (191).

4. See my essay, "Byron's *Don Juan* and the Postmodern."

5. Although she does not examine *Mr Noon,* Linda Ruth Williams ends her provocative introductory book *D. H. Lawrence* with a reminder that *Lady Chatterley's Lover* also ends in midsentence, suggesting to her "tones of absence and unfinishness [sic]." Williams's last sentence is "There is not even a final full stop" (116).

Chapter 6. Revisiting Mellors's Penis in *Lady Chatterley's Lover*

1. In particular, see "The Signification of the Phallus" and "The Subversion of the Subject and the Dialectic of Desire in the Freudian Unconscious" in *Écrits.*

2. See Kaja Silverman's "The Lacanian Phallus," especially 92–93, for her discussion of the imaginary phallus and the symbolic phallus.

3. See Derrida on the "trace" in "Differance" 403–5.

4. In *The Revolution in Poetic Language*, Kristeva argues for the synchronicity of the two modalities of the "semiotic" and the "symbolic," grounded in Lacan's Imaginary and Symbolic registers, concluding: "Because the subject is always *both* semiotic *and* symbolic, no signifying system he produces can be either 'exclusively' semiotic or 'exclusively' symbolic, and is instead necessarily marked by an indebtedness to both" (93). In general, Lacan and his followers offer a welcome alternative to the entrapment of Freud and his followers in a "developmental" scheme for psychic functioning grounded in Darwinian evolutionary thought, with its inevitable meliorism.

5. See David Savran 225–27 for an enlightening discussion of distinctions between penis and phallus.

6. In explaining Lacan's notion of the gods as "real," rather than "imaginary" or "symbolic," Stuart Schneiderman asserts: "The gods and the dead are real because the only encounter we have with the real is based on the canceling of our perceptual conscious, of our sense of being alive: the real is the real whether we experience it or not and regardless of how we experience it. The real is most real when we are not there; and when we are there, the real does not adapt itself or accommodate itself to our being there" (76).

7. As we have seen, Luce Irigaray has pointed out the tendency in psychoanalysis to gender metaphor "masculine."

8. In his essay "Metaphor and Mental Disturbance: The Case of *Lady Chatterley's Lover*," Doherty follows Jakobson's rather reductive structuralist binary of metonymy and metaphor and Lacan's association of metaphor with the "symptom" to pathologize metaphor to represent impairment and disfigurement in a more medically psychoanalytic mode. Doherty's project of scientizing Lacan's notion of the symptom in a context of "mental health" is reminiscent of the legacy of Freudian psychoanalytic criticism from which contemporary criticism has been intent upon freeing itself.

9. In an endnote Lacan says: "I pay homage here to the works of Roman Jakobson—to which I owe much of this formulation" (*Écrits* 177). Lacan's discussion of metonymy and metaphor in this chapter of *Écrits*, "The Agency of the Letter in the Unconscious or Reason since Freud," is especially important to the present project.

10. The Bolton figure is also the agency of an energizing of interest in the mines, or technology, which has been seen as a kind of textuality. I am indebted for the metaphor of technology as a text to Stephen Hill, who writes in *The Tragedy of Technology*: "Seen as a cultural text, technology is therefore metaphorically equivalent to a 'written' text, and like written literary texts, is considerably autonomous, and intractible to redefinitions" (6).

11. I am not the first, of course, to note the variations of this narrative's daring in flouting the prudery of his time. It allows Mellors and even Connie the apparently full range of the language and the apparently full range of heterosexual experience. A male writer today would think more than twice about framing such a scene to foreground male nudity since he would immediately open himself up to questions of his sexual orientation. At the same time, there are strange omissions; for example, Mellors uses the terms *fuck* and *cunt* liberally, the latter with a sexist connotation to include sexual intercourse in general; and yet the narrator *never* employs a four-letter word, and even Mellors never uses the term *cock* to identify his penis, nor other terms such as *hard-on* which are also presumably within his vocabulary. Similarly, the expressions of sexual desire between Connie and Mellors veer toward the far end of the spectrum with their apparent anal

intercourse; however, there are no clear representations of oral sex, causing some readers to wonder whether fellatio and cunnilingus are more taboo than anality.

12. In her *The Revolution in Poetic Language.*

13. See her essay "Metaphor, Metonymy, and Voice in *Their Eyes Were Watching God,*" 12–13.

14. See the essay McGrath contributed to Alasdair Foster's study *Behold the Man: The Male Nude in Photography,* 56–60.

15. Quoted by Joseph A. Kestner, *Masculinities in Victorian Painting* 235. Unfortunately, Kestner provides no identification of the Saunders text.

16. Analogies of nudity in cinematic reproductions are worth noting. Writing in 1993, Neale generalizes that representations of the male, presumably in a self-conscious manner, have been virtually the exclusive province of gays, the object of looking being a gay male. Elsewhere, representations of the male, Neale goes on to say, have been rarely discussed, even though as he and others are well aware the male body has been transformed into a spectacle in film and advertising: "It is thus very rare to find analyses that seek to specify in detail, in relation to particular films or groups of films, how heterosexual masculinity is inscribed and the mechanisms, pressures, and contradictions that inscription may involve" (9). Neale examines the representations of the male body in typically "male" genres such as Westerns, war films, and other expressions of "action" entertainment. In them, he concludes, male figures are inevitably the object of voyeuristic looking, some of which is inevitably erotic even when that is not the filmmaker's intent.

17. Silverman in "The Lacanian Phallus" points out: "The almost unsurmountable rhetorical difficulties of 'The Subversion of the Subject and the Dialectic of Desire in the Freudian Unconscious' have apparently blunted the force of its candid acknowledgement that while the phallus may not be the literal penis, there is nonetheless an intimate relationship between the two terms" (89). In *Around 1981,* Gallop writes: "For as much as orthodox Lacanians protest that the phallus is not the penis, they never succeed in disentangling that association" (18).

18. James Gardiner in *A Class Apart* and Paul Fussell in *The Great War and Modern Memory* describe the commonness of homoerotic desire in relationships between officers and enlisted men in the First World War, even though this seldom produced homosexual relationships.

19. See her essay "Melancholy Gender/Refused Identification."

20. This postman, or "letter" carrier, cannot fail to bring to mind the preoccupation of the post-structuralists with the letter, especially as a result of Lacan's reading of Poe's "The Purloined Letter" and Jacques Derrida's reading of Lacan's reading in his "Le facteur de la verité," in which *facteur* may be translated as both "factor" and "postman."

21. As Ragland-Sullivan reminds us, the French psychoanalyst Serge Leclaire considers the "erotogenic zones as 'letters' . . . of the alphabet of Desire" (206); signifiers, granted, but inescapably linked to written discourse as well.

Works Cited

Barthes, Roland. "The Death of the Author." *Image, Music, Text: Essays Selected and Translated by Stephen Heath.* New York: Hill and Wang, 1977.

Bayley, John. "Like Ink and Milk." *London Review of Books* 10 September 1992: 12–13.

Beauvoir, Simone de. *The Second Sex.* New York: Knopf, 1968.

Becket, Fiona. *D. H. Lawrence: The Thinker as Poet.* New York: St. Martin's Press, 1997.

Ben-Ephraim, Gavriel. *The Moon's Dominion: Narrative Dichotomy and Feminine Dominion in Lawrence's Earlier Novels.* Rutherford, N. J.: Fairleigh Dickinson University Press, 1981.

Black, Michael. "D. H. Lawrence and Gilbert Noon." *London Review of Books* 4–17 October 1984: 10, 12.

———. "Gilbert Noon, D. H. Lawrence, and the Gentle Reader." *The D. H. Lawrence Review* 20.2 (summer 1988): 153–78.

Blanchard, Lydia. "D. H. Lawrence and His 'Gentle Reader': The New Audience of *Mr Noon.*" *The D. H. Lawrence Review* 20.2 (summer 1988): 223–35.

———. "Review Essay [on *Mr Noon*]." *The D. H. Lawrence Review* 17.2 (summer 1984): 153–59.

Blanchot, Maurice. *The Gaze of Orpheus and Other Literary Essays.* Preface by Geoffrey Hartman. Trans. Lydia Davis. Ed. with afterword by P. Adams Sitney. Barrytown, N.Y.: Station Hill Press, 1981.

Bowen, Zack. "*Lady Chatterley's Lover* and *Ulysses.*" In *D. H. Lawrence's "Lady": A New Look at "Lady Chatterley's Lover."* Ed. Michael Squires and Dennis Jackson. Athens: University of Georgia Press, 1985. 116–35.

Brandabur, A. M. "Ritual Corn Harvest in *The Rainbow.*" *The D. H. Lawrence Review* 6 (1973): 284–302.

Brennan, Teresa, ed. *Between Feminism and Psychoanalysis.* New York: Routledge, 1989.
Brivic, Sheldon. *Joyce between Freud and Jung.* Port Washington, N.Y.: Kennikat, 1980.
———. *The Veil of Signs: Joyce, Lacan, and Perception.* Urbana: University of Illinois Press, 1991.
Bronte, Charlotte. *Jane Eyre.* New York: Doubleday, 1997.
Brooks, Peter. *Body Work: Objects of Desire in Modern Narrative.* Cambridge: Harvard University Press, 1993.
———. *Psychoanalysis and Storytelling.* Cambridge, Mass.: Blackwell, 1994.
———. *Reading for the Plot: Design and Intention in Narrative.* New York: Knopf, 1984.
Butler, Judith. *Gender Trouble.* New York: Routledge, 1993.
———. "Melancholy Gender/Refused Identification." *Constructing Masculinity.* Ed. Maurice Berger, Brian Willis, and Simon Watson. New York: Routledge, 1995. 21–36.
Byrne, Janet. *A Genius for Living: The Life of Frieda Lawrence.* New York: HarperCollins, 1995.
Byron, George Gordon, Baron. *Don Juan.* Ed. with introduction by Frank H. Ristine. New York: Macmillan, 1927.
Caughie, Pamela. *Virginia Woolf and Postmodernism.* Urbana and Chicago: University of Illinois Press, 1991.
Cixous, Hélène. *The Exile of James Joyce.* Trans. Sally A. J. Purcell. New York: David Lewis, 1972.
Cohan, Steven. *Masked Men: Masculinity and the Movies in the Fifties.* Bloomington and Indianapolis: Indiana University Press, 1997.
Cohan, Steven, and Ina Rae Hark, eds. *Screening the Male: Exploring Masculinities in Hollywood Cinema.* London: Routledge, 1993.
Cowan, James C. "Lawrence, Joyce, and the Epiphanies of *Lady Chatterley's Lover.*" *D. H. Lawrence's "Lady": A New Look at "Lady Chatterley's Lover."* Ed. Michael Squires and Dennis Jackson. Athens: University of Georgia Press, 1985. 91–115.
Currie, Mark. *Postmodern Narrative Theory.* New York: St. Martin's Press, 1998.
Cushman, Keith. "*The Virgin and the Gipsy* and the Lady and the Gamekeeper." *D. H. Lawrence's "Lady": A New Look at "Lady Chatterley's Lover."* Ed. Michael Squires and Dennis Jackson. Athens: University of Georgia Press, 1985. 154–69.
Daleski, H. M. *The Forked Flame: A Study of D. H. Lawrence.* Evanston, Ill.: Northwestern University Press, 1965.
Davis, Robert Con. Introduction and "Lacan, Poe, and Narrative Repression." *Lacan and Narration: The Psychoanalytic Difference in Narrative Theory.* Baltimore: Johns Hopkins University Press, 1983. 848–59, 983–1005.

Delany, Paul. *D. H. Lawrence's Nightmare: The Writer and His Circle in the Years of the Great War.* New York: Basic Books, 1978.
———. "Men in Love." *London Review of Books* 3 September 1987: 21–22.
———. "*Sons and Lovers:* The Morel Marriage as a War of Position." *The D. H. Lawrence Review* 21.2 (summer 1989): 153–65.
———. "'A Would-Be-Dirty Mind': D. H. Lawrence as an Enemy of Joyce." *Joyce in the Hibernian Metropolis Essays.* Ed. Morris Beja and Davis Norris. Columbus: Ohio State University Press, 1996. 76–82.
Deleuze, Gilles, and Félix Guattari. *Anti-Oedipus: Capitalism and Schizophrenia.* Trans. Robert Hurley, Mark Seem, and Helen R. Lane. New York: Viking, 1977.
De Man, Paul. *Allegories of Reading: Figural Language in Rousseau, Nietzsche, Rilke, and Proust.* New Haven: Yale University Press, 1979.
Derrida, Jacques. "Differance" and "Plato's Pharmacy." *Literary Theory: An Anthology.* Ed. Julie Rivkin and Michael Ryan. Malden, Mass.: Blackwell, 1998. 383–407, 429–50.
———. "The Purveyor of Truth." *The Purloined Poe: Lacan, Derrida, and Psychoanalytic Reading.* Ed. John P. Muller and William J. Richardson. Baltimore: Johns Hopkins University Press, 1988. 173–212.
Dickens, Charles. *Nicholas Nickleby.* New York: Dodd, Mead, 1944.
Doherty, Gerald. "*Ars Erotica* or *Scientia Sexualis?*: Narrative Vicissitudes in D. H. Lawrence's *Women in Love.*" *Journal of Narrative Technique* 26.2 (1996): 137–57.
———. "The Art of Appropriation: The Rhetoric of Sexuality in D. H. Lawrence." *Style* 30.2 (1996): 289–308.
———. "The Art of Leaping: Metaphor Unbound in D. H. Lawrence's *Women in Love.*" *Style* 26.1 (1992): 50–65.
———. "Death and the Rhetoric of Representation in D. H. Lawrence's *Women in Love.*" *Mosaic* 27.1 (Mar. 1994): 55–72.
———. "The Dialectic of Space in D. H. Lawrence's *Sons and Lovers.*" *Modern Fiction Studies* 39.2 (1993): 327–43.
———. "Metaphor and Mental Disturbance: The Case of *Lady Chatterley's Lover.*" *Style* 30.1 (1996): 113–29.
Ebbatson, Roger. "The Opening of *The Rainbow.*" *D. H. Lawrence, 1885–1930: A Celebration.* Ed. Andrew Cooper. Nottingham: D. H. Lawrence Society, 1985. 72–76.
Edelman, Lee. "Homographesis." *Literary Theory: An Anthology.* Ed. Julie Rivkin and Michael Ryan. Malden, Mass.: Blackwell, 1998. 731–44.
Ellis, John. *Visible Fictions: Cinema, Television, Video.* London: Routledge and Kegan Paul, 1982.
Ellmann, Richard. *James Joyce.* New York: Oxford University Press, 1982.
Engel, Monroe. "Contrived Lives: Joyce and Lawrence." *Modernism Reconsid-*

ered. Ed. Robert Kiely and John Hildebidle. Cambridge: Harvard University Press, 1983. 65–80.
Felman, Shoshana, ed. *Literature and Psychoanalysis: The Question of Reading: Otherwise*. Baltimore: Johns Hopkins University Press, 1982.
Ferreira, Maria Aline. "*Mr Noon*: The Reader in the Text." *The D. H. Lawrence Review* 20.2 (summer 1988): 209–21.
Flieger, Jerry Aline. *The Purloined Punch Line: Freud's Comic Theory and the Postmodern Text*. Baltimore: Johns Hopkins University Press, 1991.
Ford, George. *Double Measure: A Study of the Novels and Stories of D. H. Lawrence*. New York: Norton, 1969.
Forster, E. M. *Maurice*. New York: Norton, 1971.
———. *A Passage to India*. New York: Harcourt, Brace, 1924.
———. *A Room with a View*. New York: Vintage, 1986.
Foster, Alasdair. *Behold the Man: The Male Nude in Photography*. With an essay by Roberta McGrath. Edinburgh: Stills Gallery, 1988.
Foucault, Michel. "Discipline and Punish." *Literary Theory: An Anthology*. Ed. Julie Rivkin and Michael Ryan. Malden, Mass.: Blackwell, 1998. 464–87.
———. *The History of Sexuality*. Trans. Robert Hurley. New York: Vintage, 1980.
Fowles, John. *The French Lieutenant's Woman*. Boston: Little, Brown, 1969.
Freud, Sigmund. *Beyond the Pleasure Prinicple*. 1920. *The Standard Edition of the Complete Works of Sigmund Freud*. Vol. 18. New York: Norton, 1961. 1–64. 24 vols.
———. "Fetishism." 1927. *The Standard Edition of the Complete Works of Sigmund Freud*. Vol. 21. New York: Norton, 1961. 152–57. 24 vols.
———. "Instincts and Their Vicissitudes." 1915. *The Standard Edition of the Complete Works of Sigmund Freud*. Vol. 14. New York: Norton, 1961. 109–40. 24 vols.
———. *The Interpretation of Dreams*. 1900. *The Standard Edition of the Complete Works of Sigmund Freud*. Vols. 4 and 5. New York: Norton, 1961. 24 vols.
———. *Jokes and Their Relation to the Unconscious*. 1905. *The Standard Edition of the Complete Works of Sigmund Freud*. Vol. 8. New York: Norton, 1961. 24 vols.
———. *The Psychopathology of Everyday Life*. 1901. *The Standard Edition of the Complete Works of Sigmund Freud*. Vol. 6. New York: Norton, 1961. 24 vols.
Fuss, Diana. *Identification Papers*. New York: Routledge, 1995.
Fussell, Paul. *The Great War and Modern Memory*. New York: Oxford University Press, 1975.
Gallop, Jane. *Around 1981: Academic Feminist Literary Theory*. New York: Routledge, 1992.
———. *Reading Lacan*. Ithaca: Cornell University Press, 1985.
Gardiner, James. *A Class Apart: The Private Pictures of Montague Glover*. London: Serpent's Tail, 1992.

Goldberg, S. L. "*The Rainbow*: Fiddle-Bow and Sand." *Essays in Criticism* 11.4 (1961): 418–34.
Golding, William. *The Paper Men.* New York: Farrar, Straus, Giroux, 1984.
Gu, Ming Dong. "Lawrence's Childhood Traumas and the Problematic Form of *The White Peacock.*" *The D. H. Lawrence Review* 24.2 (summer 1992): 127–44.
Hagen, Patricia. *Metaphor's Way of Knowing: The Poetry of D. H. Lawrence and the Church of Mechanism.* New York: Peter Lang, 1995.
Hassan, Ihab, and Sally Hassan, eds. *Innovation/Renovation.* Madison: University of Wisconsin Press, 1983.
Hatt, Michael. "'Making a Man of Him': Masculinity and the Black Body in Mid-Nineteenth-Century American Sculpture." *Oxford Art Journal* 15, no. 1 (1992): 21–35.
Hill, Stephen. *The Tragedy of Technology.* London: Pluto Press, 1988.
Hirsch, Marianne. *The Mother-Daughter Plot: Narrative, Psychoanalyis, Feminism.* Bloomington: Indiana University Press, 1989.
Hoffman, Frederick J. *Freudianism and the Literary Mind.* Baton Rouge: Louisiana State University Press, 1957.
Holland, Norman. "Postmodern Psychoanalysis." *Innovation/Renovation.* Ed. Ihab Hassan and Sally Hassan. Madison: University of Wisconsin Press, 1983. 291–309.
Hyde, Virginia. *The Risen Adam: D. H. Lawrence's Revisionist Typology.* University Park: Pennsylvania State University Press, 1992.
Ibsen, Henrik. *Hedda Gabler* and *A Doll's House.* Trans. Christopher Hampton. London: Faber and Faber, 1989.
Ingersoll, Earl G. "Byron's *Don Juan* and the Postmodern." *Forum for Modern Language Studies* 33.4 (1997): 302–14.
———. "D. H. Lawrence's *Mr Noon* as a Postmodern Text." *Modern Language Review* 85.2 (April 1990): 304–9.
———. "The Failure of Bloodbrotherhood in Melville's *Moby Dick* and Lawrence's *Women in Love.*" *The Midwest Quarterly* 30.4 (summer 1989): 458–77.
———. "Gender and Language in *Sons and Lovers.*" *The Midwest Quarterly* 37.4 (1996): 35–43.
———. "*Lady Chatterley's Lover*: 'The Bastard Offspring of This Signifying Concatenation.'" *Studies in Psychoanalytic Theory* 1.1 (spring 1992): 57–68.
———. "Lawrence in the Tyrol: Psychic Geography in *Mr Noon.*" *Forum for Modern Language Studies* 26.1 (1990): 1–11.
———. "The Pursuit of 'True Marriage': *Mr Noon* and *Lady Chatterley's Lover.*" *Studies in the Humanities* 14.1 (June 1987): 32–45.
———. "Staging the Gaze in D. H. Lawrence's *Women in Love.*" *Studies in the Novel* 26.3 (fall 1994): 268–80.

———. "The Theme of Friendship and the Genesis of D. H. Lawrence's *Mr Noon*." *The Durham University Journal* 52.1 (January 1991): 69–74.
———. "Virginia Woolf and D. H. Lawrence: Exploring the Dark." *English Studies* 71.2 (April 1990): 125–32.
———, ed. *Margaret Atwood: Conversations.* Princeton, N.J.: Ontario Review Press, 1990.
Irigaray, Luce. *This Sex Which Is Not One.* Trans. Catherine Porter, with Carolyn Burke. Ithaca: Cornell University Press, 1985.
Jackson, Dennis, and Fleda Brown Jackson. *Critical Essays on D. H. Lawrence.* Boston: G. K. Hall, 1988.
Jakobson, Roman. "Two Aspects of Language and Two Types of Aphasic Disturbances." *Selected Writings.* The Hague: Mouton, 1971.
Jameson, Fredric. "Imaginary and Symbolic in Lacan: Marxism, Psychoanalytic Criticism, and the Problem of the Subject." *Literature and Psychoanalysis: The Question of Reading Otherwise.* Ed. Shoshana Felman. Baltimore: Johns Hopkins University Press, 1982. 338–95.
———. *Postmodernism, or the Cultural Logic of Late Capitalism.* Durham, N.C.: Duke University Press, 1991.
Jewinski, Ed. "The Phallus in D. H. Lawrence and Jacques Lacan." *The D. H. Lawrence Review* 21.1 (spring 1989): 7–24.
Johnson, Barbara. "The Frame of Reference: Poe, Lacan, Derrida." *The Critical Difference.* Baltimore: Johns Hopkins University Press, 1980.
———. "Metaphor, Metonymy, and Voice in *Their Eyes Were Watching God.*" *A World of Difference.* Baltimore: Johns Hopkins University Press, 1987.
Joyce, James. *Dubliners.* New York: Penguin, 1967.
———. *Finnegans Wake.* New York: Viking, 1939.
———. *A Portrait of the Artist as a Young Man.* New York: Viking, 1956.
———. *Ulysses.* Ed. Hans Walter Gabler. New York: Viking, 1986.
Kappeler, Susanne. *The Pornography of Representation.* Minneapolis: University of Minnesota Press, 1986.
Kermode, Frank. *The Sense of an Ending: Studies in the Theory of Fiction.* New York: Oxford University Press, 1967.
Kershner, R. B. *Joyce, Bakhtin, and Popular Literature: Chronicles of Disorder.* Chapel Hill: University of North Carolina Press, 1989.
Kestner, Joseph A. *Masculinities in Victorian Painting.* Brookfield, Vt.: Scolar Press, 1995.
King, Dixie. "The Influence of Forster's *Maurice* on *Lady Chatterley's Lover.*" *Contemporary Literature* 23.1 (1982): 65–82.
Kinkead-Weekes, Mark. "The Marble and the Statue." *Imagined Worlds: Essays on Some English Novels and Novelists in Honour of John Butt.* Ed. Maynard Mack and Ian Gregor. London: Methuen, 1968. 371–418.

———. "The Marriage of Opposites in *The Rainbow.*" *D. H Lawrence Centenary Essays.* Ed. Mara Kalnins. Bristol, England: Bristol Classical Press, 1986. 21–39.

Kristeva, Julia. *Black Sun: Depression and Melancholia.* New York: Columbia University Press, 1989.

———. *The Revolution in Poetic Language.* Trans. Margaret Waller. Ithaca, N.Y.: Cornell University Press, 1984.

———. "Women's Time." *The Kristeva Reader.* Ed. Toril Moi. New York: Columbia University Press, 1986. 187–213.

Lacan, Jacques. *Écrits: A Selection.* Trans. Alan Sheridan. New York: Norton, 1977.

———. *The Four Fundamental Concepts of Psycho-Analysis.* Trans. Alan Sheridan. Ed. Jacques-Alain Miller. New York: Norton, 1978.

Lauretis, Teresa de. *Alice Doesn't: Feminism, Semiotics, Cinema.* Bloomington: Indiana University Press, 1984.

Lawrence, D. H. *The Complete Short Stories.* Vol. 2. New York: Penguin, 1961.

———. *Lady Chatterley's Lover and A Propos of "Lady Chatterley's Lover."* Ed. Michael Squires. Cambridge: Cambridge University Press, 1993.

———. *The Letters of D. H. Lawrence.* Ed. James T. Boulton et al. 7 vols. 1901–1913. Cambridge: Cambridge University Press, 1979–1993.

———. *A Modern Lover.* London: Martin Secker, 1934.

———. *Mr Noon.* Ed. Lindeth Vasey. Cambridge: Cambridge University Press, 1984.

———. *Phoenix: The Posthumous Papers of D. H. Lawrence.* Ed. Edward D. McDonald. London: Heinemann, 1936.

———. *Phoenix II: Uncollected, Unpublished and Other Prose Works by D. H. Lawrence.* Ed. Warren Roberts and Harry T. Moore. London: Heinemann, 1968.

———. *The Plumed Serpent.* Ed. L. D. Clark. Cambridge: Cambridge University Press, 1987.

———. *Psychoanalysis and the Unconscious,* and *Fantasia of the Unconscious.* New York: Viking, 1960.

———. *Quetzalcoatl: The Early Version of "The Plumed Serpent."* Ed. Louis L. Martz. Redding Ridge, Conn.: Black Swan Books, 1995.

———. *The Rainbow.* Ed. Mark Kinkead-Weekes. Cambridge: Cambridge University Press, 1989.

———. *The Rainbow.* Ed. John Worthen. New York: Penguin, 1981.

———. *Sons and Lovers.* Ed. Helen Baron and Carol Baron. Cambridge: Cambridge University Press, 1992.

———. *The White Peacock.* Ed. Andrew Robertson. Cambridge: Cambridge University Press, 1983.

———. *Women in Love.* Ed. David Farmer, Lindeth Vasey, and John Worthen. Cambridge: Cambridge University Press, 1987.

———. *Women in Love.* Ed. Charles L. Ross. New York: Penguin, 1982.

Leavis, F. R. *D. H. Lawrence, Novelist.* New York: Knopf, 1956.
Lewandowski, Joseph D. "Narrativizing Desire in *Sons and Lovers.*" *Studies in Psychoanalytic Theory* 2.2 (fall 1993): 50–63.
Lobner, Corinna del Greco. "Quincunxial Sherlockholmesing in 'Grace.'" *James Joyce Quarterly* 28.2 (1991): 445–50.
Lodge, David. *Modes of Modern Writing.* Ithaca: Cornell University Press, 1977.
Maddox, Brenda. "Biography: A Love Affair or a Job?" *The New York Times Book Review* 9 May 1999: 47.
———. *D. H. Lawrence: The Story of a Marriage.* New York: Simon and Schuster, 1994.
McCannell, Juliet Flower. *Figuring Lacan: Criticism and the Cultural Unconscious.* Lincoln: University of Nebraska Press, 1986.
McDowell, Frederick P. W. "Moments of Emergence and of a New Spendour: D. H. Lawrence and E. M. Forster in Their Fiction." *D. H. Lawrence's "Lady": A New Look at "Lady Chatterley's Lover."* Ed. Michael Squires and Dennis Jackson. Athens: University of Georgia Press, 1985. 58–90.
McGrath, Roberta. "Looking Hard: The Male Body under Patriarchy." *Behold the Man: The Male Nude in Photography.* By Alasdair Foster. Edinburgh: Stills Gallery, 1988. 56–60.
Mellard, James M. *Doing Tropology: Analysis of Narrative Discourse.* Urbana and Chicago: University of Illinois Press, 1987.
Metz, Christian. *The Imaginary Signifier: Psychoanalysis and the Cinema.* Trans. Celia Britton, Annwyl Williams, Ben Brewster, and Alfred Guzzetti. Bloomington: Indiana University Press, 1982.
Millett, Kate. *Sexual Politics.* Garden City, N.Y.: Doubleday, 1970.
Mulvey, Laura. *Visual and Other Pleasures.* Bloomington: Indiana University Press, 1989.
Murry, John Middleton. *D. H. Lawrence: Son of Woman.* London: Jonathan Cape, 1954.
Neale, Steve. "Prologue: Masculinity as Spectacle." *Screening the Male: Exploring Masculinities in Hollywood Cinema.* Ed. Steven Cohan and Ina Rae Hark. New York: Routledge, 1993. 9–20.
Nelson, Jane. "The Familial Isotopy in *The Fox.*" *The Challenge of D. H. Lawrence.* Ed. Michael Squires and Keith Cushman. Madison: University of Wisconsin Press, 1990. 129–42.
Neville, George Henry. *A Memoir of D. H. Lawrence (The Betrayal).* Ed. Carl Baron. Cambridge: Cambridge University Press, 1981.
Nixon, Cornelia. *Lawrence's Leadership Politics and the Turn against Women.* Berkeley and Los Angeles: University of California Press, 1986.
———. "To Procreate Oneself: Ursula's Horses in *The Rainbow.*" *ELH* 49.1 (1982): 123–42.

Orr, Leonard, ed. *Yeats and Postmodernism.* Syracuse: Syracuse University Press, 1991.

Paglia, Camille. *Sexual Personae: Art and Decadence from Nefertiti to Emily Dickinson.* New Haven: Yale University Press, 1990.

Pons, Xavier. "'Baptism of Fire': The Oedipal Element in D. H. Lawrence's *Sons and Lovers.*" *Cahiers Victoriens et Édouardiennes* 32 (1990): 101–10.

Ragland-Sullivan, Ellie. *Jacques Lacan and the Philosophy of Psychoanalysis.* Urbana and Chicago: University of Illinois Press, 1986.

Rivkin, Julie, and Michael Ryan, eds. *Literary Theory: An Anthology.* Malden, Mass.: Blackwell, 1998.

Ross, Charles L. *The Composition of "The Rainbow" and "Women in Love": A History.* Charlottesville: University Press of Virginia, 1979.

Ruderman, Judith. *D. H. Lawrence and the Devouring Mother: The Search for a Patriarchal Ideal of Leadership.* Durham, N.C.: Duke University Press, 1984.

Sagar, Keith. "The Genesis of *The Rainbow* and *Women in Love.*" *The D. H. Lawrence Review* 1.3 (fall 1968): 179–99.

Sale, Roger. "The Narrative Technique of *The Rainbow.*" *Modern Fiction Studies* 5.1 (1959): 29–38.

Sanders, Scott. *D. H Lawrence: The World of the Five Major Novels.* New York: Viking, 1973.

Sartre, Jean-Paul. *Being and Nothingness: An Essay in Phenomenological Ontology.* Trans. with an introduction by Hazel E. Barnes. New York: Citadel, 1956.

———. *Nausea.* Trans. Lloyd Alexander. Intro. Hayden Carruth. Norfolk, Conn.: New Directions, 1964.

Savran, David. *Taking It like a Man: White Masculinity, Masochism, and Contemporary American Culture.* Princeton, N.J.: Princeton University Press, 1998.

Schneiderman, Stuart. *Jacques Lacan: The Death of an Intellectual Hero.* Cambridge: Harvard University Press, 1983.

Schor, Naomi. "Female Paranoia: The Case for Psychoanalytic Feminist Criticism." *Yale French Studies* 62 (1981): 204–19.

Sicker, Peter. "Surgery for the Novel: Lawrence's *Mr Noon* and the 'Gentle Reader.'" *The D. H. Lawrence Review* 20.2 (summer 1988): 191–207.

Silverman, Kaja. "The Lacanian Phallus." *differences* 4, 1 (1992): 84–115.

———. *Male Subjectivity at the Margins.* New York: Routledge, 1992.

———. *The Subject of Semiotics.* New York: Oxford University Press, 1983.

Simpson, Hilary. *D. H. Lawrence and Feminism.* De Kalb: Northern Illinois University Press, 1982.

Skura, Meredith Anne. *The Literary Use of the Psychoanalytic Process.* New Haven and London: Yale University Press, 1981.

Spilka, Mark. *The Love Ethic of D. H. Lawrence.* Bloomington: Indiana University Press, 1955.

Squires, Michael. *The Creation of "Lady Chatterley's Lover."* Baltimore: Johns Hopkins University Press, 1983.

Squires, Michael, and Dennis Jackson, eds. *D. H. Lawrence's "Lady": A New Look at "Lady Chatterley's Lover."* Athens: University of Georgia Press, 1985.

Sterne, Laurence. *The Life and Opinions of Tristram Shandy, a Gentleman.* London: Oxford University Press, 1947.

———. *A Sentimental Journey through France and Italy.* Intro. Virginia Woolf. London: Oxford University Press, 1928.

Stewart, Jack F. "Expressionism in *The Rainbow.*" *Critical Essays on D. H. Lawrence.* Ed. Dennis Jackson and Fleda Brown Jackson. Boston: G. K. Hall, 1988. 72–92.

———. "Landscape Painting and Pre-Raphaelitism in *The White Peacock.*" *The D. H. Lawrence Review* 27.1 (1997–1998): 3–25.

———. "The Vital Art of Lawrence and Van Gogh." *The D. H. Lawrence Review* 19.2 (summer 1987): 123–48.

Storch, Margaret. "The Lacerated Male: Ambivalent Images of Women in *The White Peacock.*" *The D. H. Lawrence Review* 21.2 (Summer 1989): 117–36.

———. *Sons and Adversaries: Women in William Blake and D. H. Lawrence.* Knoxville: University of Tennessee Press, 1990.

Swift, John N. "Repetition, Consummation, and 'This Eternal Unrelief.'" *The Challenge of D. H. Lawrence.* Ed. Michael Squires and Keith Cushman. Madison: University of Wisconsin Press, 1990. 121–28.

Trilling, Diana. "Lawrence in Love." *The New York Times Book Review* 16 Dec. 1984: 3, 24–25.

Valente, Joseph. *James Joyce and the Problem of Justice: Negotiating Sexual and Colonial Difference.* New York: Cambridge University Press, 1995.

—, ed. *Quare Joyce.* Ann Arbor: University of Michigan Press, 1998.

Watson, G. "D. H. Lawrence (in *Women in Love*) on the Desire for Difference and 'the Facism [*sic*] in Us All.'" *The Cambridge Quarterly* 26.2 (1997): 140–54.

Weiss, Daniel A. *Oedipus in Nottingham: D. H. Lawrence.* Seattle: University of Washington Press, 1962.

Wexler, Joyce. "D. H. Lawrence through a Postmodernist Lens." *The D. H. Lawrence Review* 27.1 (1997–1998): 47–64.

Wilde, Alan. *Horizons of Assent: Modernism, Postmodernism, and the Ironic Imagination.* Baltimore: Johns Hopkins University Press, 1981.

Wilden, Anthony. "Lacan and the Discourse of the Other." *Speech and Language in Psychoanalysis.* Baltimore: Johns Hopkins University Press, 1968.

Williams, Linda Ruth. *D. H. Lawrence.* Plymouth, England: Northcote House, 1997.

———. *Sex in the Head: Visions of Femininity and Film in D. H. Lawrence.* Detroit: Wayne State University Press, 1993.

Women in Love. Dir. Ken Russell. With Oliver Reed, Glenda Jackson, and Alan Bates. Brandywine Productions, 1970.

Woolf, Virginia. *To the Lighthouse*. New York: Harcourt, Brace, 1927.

Worthen, John. "Introduction." *The Rainbow*. By D. H. Lawrence. New York: Penguin, 1981.

———. "The Restoration of *Women in Love*." *D. H. Lawrence in the Modern World*. Ed. Peter Preston and Peter Hoare. Cambridge: Cambridge University Press, 1989. 7–26.

Yaeger, Patricia. *Honey-Mad Women: Emancipatory Strategies in Women's Writing*. New York: Columbia University Press, 1988.

Yeats, William Butler. *The Poems of W. B. Yeats*. Ed. Richard J. Finneran. New York: Macmillan, 1983.

Index

Earl G. Ingersoll is department chair and distinguished teaching professor of English at the State University of New York, College at Brockport. He is the author or editor of seven books in twentieth-century British and Irish studies, most recently *Engendered Trope in Joyce's "Dubliners"* and *Lawrence Durrell: Conversations.*